WORDSWORTH'S VITAL SOUL

WORDSWORTH'S VITAL SOUL

The Sacred and Profane in
Wordsworth's Poetry

J. R. Watson

'. . . that first great gift, the vital soul . . .'

Humanities Press
Atlantic Highlands, New Jersey

Copyright © J. R. Watson 1982

ISBN 0–391–02563–5

First published in 1982 in the United States of America by
HUMANITIES PRESS INC.
Atlantic Highlands
N.J. 07716

Library of Congress Cataloging in Publication Data

Watson, J. R. (John Richard), 1934–
    Wordsworth's vital soul.

    Bibliography: p.
    Includes index.
    1. Wordsworth, William, 1770–1850—Religion and
ethics. 2. Religion in literature. I. Title.
PR5892.R4W3   821'.7   81–20273
ISBN 0–391–02563–5   AACR2

Printed in Hong Kong

To Pauline

Contents

List of Abbreviations

PW   *The Poetical Works of William Wordsworth*, edited by E. de Selincourt (Oxford, 1940–5)

EL   *The Letters of William and Dorothy Wordsworth, I: The Early Years*, edited by E. de Selincourt, revised by Chester L. Shaver (Oxford, 1967)

Chronology   *Wordsworth: The Chronology of the Early Years, 1770–1799*, by Mark Reed (Cambridge, Mass., 1967)

Preface

This book is an attempt to understand certain features of the poetry of Wordsworth which seem to me to be important. It is designed to uncover the ideas and intuitions which the poet shares with those who respond to the external world in a way which may broadly be termed 'religious'; I use the word 'uncover' intentionally, because I am primarily concerned with what lies beneath the surface of Wordsworth's poetry. Indeed, I hope that what follows will help to explain some of the peculiarities which appear in Wordsworth's poetry at first sight. By the word 'religious', used here in default of a better word, I do not mean Christian, although the way to a later orthodoxy is latent in what follows: this is not an account of Wordsworth and eighteenth-century Christianity, but rather an attempt to discover structures in the poetry which are akin to fundamental and primitive patterns of belief.

I began this particular enquiry into Wordsworth's poetry when I was asked by the British Council to give some lectures in Italy in 1970. The hearers of those lectures will have some difficulty in rediscovering them, for my ideas have been modified during the last decade; parts of the original lectures will be found, chiefly in Chapter 6. I am most grateful to the British Council for the invitation, and to many people in Italy who encouraged this work, especially Morris Dodderidge, Charles Clark, Andrew McKenna and Sylvia Winsor. Chapter 9 was also given as a British Council lecture, in Malta in 1976; my thanks go to Dr Peter Vernon for his help. The same chapter was later published in *Essays in Criticism* (1977), under the title 'Lucy and the Earth Mother'; I am grateful to the editors for permission to reprint it here.

I have greatly benefited from the help of those who have read and discussed sections of this work in progress, especially three former colleagues in the University of Leicester, Miss Monica Jones, Dr Kenneth Phillipps, and Dr Stephen Reno; Mr Richard Gill, of Wyggeston School, Leicester; and Dr Derek Todd, of the University of Durham. My greatest debt, however, is to my wife, Pauline, to whom I dedicate this book in gratitude and love.

J. R. WATSON

Acknowledgements

The author and publishers wish to thank the following who have kindly given permission for the use of copyright material: Faber and Faber Ltd and Grove Press Inc., for the extract from *Waiting for Godot* by Samuel Beckett, copyright © 1954, by Grove Press Inc.; Faber and Faber Ltd and Harcourt Brace Jovanovich Inc., for the extracts from 'Little Gidding', 'East Coker' and 'The Dry Salvages' from *Four Quartets* by T. S. Eliot, copyright 1943, by T. S. Eliot, renewed 1971, by Esme Valerie Eliot; David Higham Associates Ltd and New Directions Publishing Corporation, for the extract from 'Fern Hill' from *Poems of Dylan Thomas*, copyright 1945, by the Trustees for the Copyrights of Dylan Thomas.

Introduction

I

In 1861, during the composition of *Silas Marner*, George Eliot wrote
to her publisher, John Blackwood:

> I don't wonder at your finding my story, as far as you have read it,
> rather sombre: indeed, I should not have believed that any one
> would have been interested in it but myself (since William
> Wordsworth is dead) if Mr. Lewes had not been strongly arrested
> by it.[1]

The association of Wordsworth with the novel is primarily due to its
interest in childhood as a mediator of beneficent influences. The
epigraph of the novel was taken from 'Michael':

> A child, more than all other gifts
> That earth can offer to declining man,
> Brings hope with it, and forward-looking thoughts.

In *Silas Marner* the arrival of Eppie inaugurates a process of
fundamental change in Silas's life: through her he comes to see the
world afresh, in a gradual awakening whose effect is that of a
conversion very different from the kind of conversion experience
encouraged by the Lantern Yard sect. It substitutes a new kind of
religious experience for the old model:

> In old days there were angels who came and took men by the
> hand and led them away from the city of destruction. We see no
> white-winged angels now. But yet men are led away from
> threatening destruction: a hand is put into theirs, which leads
> them forth gently towards a calm and bright land, so that they
> look no more backward; and the hand may be a little child's (ch.
> 14).

'No white-winged angels now': into that 'now' we may read not only a nineteenth-century rationalism but also the whole fine awareness of George Eliot's mind, with its antennae searching the external world of her own time. It is in such a frame of mind that she thinks of Wordsworth as a man who might have been most interested in her story. Her letter to Blackwood continues: 'But I hope you will not find it at all a sad story, as a whole, since it sets – or is intended to set –in a strong light the remedial influences of pure, natural human relations.' Eppie provides the impetus for Silas's regeneration, for she manages, as George Eliot writes, 'to link him once more with the whole world.' Her function is to allow him to see again, to become aware of the richness and beauty of the created universe. It is analogous to the intention of *Lyrical Ballads*, as described by Coleridge:

> Mr. Wordsworth . . . was to propose to himself as his object, to give the charm of novelty to things of every day, and to excite a feeling analogous to the supernatural, by awakening the mind's attention from the lethargy of custom, and directing it to the loveliness and the wonders of the world before us; an inexhaustible treasure, but for which, in consequence of the film of familiarity and selfish solicitude we have eyes, yet see not, ears that hear not, and hearts that neither feel nor understand.[2]

George Eliot's intuition that Wordsworth, had he lived, would have been the most interested reader of her novel, is thus linked with the whole interconnecting theme of 'pure, natural human relations' leading to a fresh understanding and awareness of the external world. The relationships which develop in the novel have a function that is symbolic and legendary. George Eliot recalled the origin of the story in these words:

> It came to me first of all, quite suddenly, as a sort of legendary tale, suggested by my recollection of having once, in early childhood, seen a linen-weaver with a bag on his back; but, as my mind dwelt on the subject, I became inclined to a more realistic treatment.[3]

The James-like awareness of a germ of the story, of 'a dropped grain of suggestion' is close to Wordsworth's recollections of the figures behind his poetry: 'This old man I met a few hundred yards from my cottage at Town-End, Grasmere; and the account of him is taken from his own mouth' (*PW*, II. 510, note to 'Resolution and Independence'); 'I said to myself, "Cannot I by some invention do as much to make this Thorn permanently an impressive object as the storm has made it to my eyes at this moment?"' (*PW*, II. 511, note to 'The Thorn'). In the works of both authors the remembered figure, although treated with realistic detail, preserves something of its original legendary character: in George Eliot the linen-weaver with a bag on his back is given a history of loss and regeneration, while Wordsworth's leech-gatherer becomes an emblem of fortitude. 'What is generally involved', writes Wallace Jackson in an essay on 'Wordsworth and his Predecessors', 'is the gradual translation of an object from its objective status to its symbolic status; in the process a feeling that exists *below* becomes hooked-up to the subject and is drawn out by it.'[4] We approach here Coleridge's celebrated definition of the symbol in *The Statesman's Manual*, where he opposes it to an allegory which 'is but a translation of abstract notions into a picture-language'. A symbol, on the other hand,

> is characterized by a translucence of the Special in the Individual or of the General in the Especial or of the Universal in the General. Above all by the translucence of the Eternal through and in the Temporal. It always partakes of the Reality which it renders intelligible; and while it enunciates the whole, abides itself as a living part in that Unity, of which it is the representative.[5]

The process is a kind of Incarnation, which is the religious parallel which Coleridge has in mind; and one of the great difficulties of the poetry of Wordsworth is the presence in it of certain patterns of belief and behaviour which are held in a state of unobtrusive embodiment. Kathleen Raine, discussing the criticism of William Empson, writes:

> There is one type of complexity which he fails to consider, that resonance which may be present within an image of apparent simplicity, setting into vibration planes of reality and of consciousness other than that of the sensible world: the power of the symbol and symbolic discourse.[6]

'The resonance which may be present within an image of apparent simplicity' is something which is to be found in Wordsworth's poetry, not only in single reverberant lines – 'And never lifted up a single stone' – but also in the overall resonance of his poetry, in its accumulated wisdom held within images of apparent simplicity, knitting together in layers of complex interaction to produce a poetry which concerns itself with fundamental truths of religious and human life. As in all religious writing, the incarnation or expression of the eternal is open to misreading and failure of interpretation: Wordsworth's poetry has always been vulnerable to the cheap sneer. This is sometimes his own fault, for his symbols do not always seem to hold the Eternal within the Temporal in a translucent way. Yet it is also the fault of the reader, if he does not perceive that Wordsworth's poetry, as a whole, is concerned with beliefs and values which are basic to an understanding of man's relations with man, and man's relations to God. In particular, the belief in 'Nature', by which Wordsworth is so widely known, should be related to the underlying patterns of belief to which it is connected. It is the purpose of this book to explore these.

II

Certain poems of Wordsworth are marked by a startling clarity. The stanza from 'The Tables Turned' beginning 'One impulse from a vernal wood' is an example; so too are the lines from 'The Thorn' about the little pond. Yet Wordsworth stuck to these lines with an impressive integrity: when Henry Crabb Robinson questioned them, the poet replied, 'They ought to be liked.'[7] 'Ought to be' is an astonishing way of putting it, embodying as it does a sense of vital importance and of a correct frame of mind, both of which Wordsworth was striving to inculcate in his poetry. He believed that every great poet had to create the taste by which he was to be enjoyed, and he wished to be thought of as a teacher or as nothing. He himself had been taught by Dorothy, just as Silas Marner was taught by Eppie:

> She gave me eyes she gave me ears
> And humble cares and delicate fears
> A heart the fountain of sweet tears
> And love and thought and joy.[8]

His consciousness of the importance of what he had been led to believe is one reason for the authoritarian note in Wordsworth's poetry. Having learned his own lessons, and having seen his original visions, he frequently adopts a prophetic stance, as he does at the end of *The Prelude*, or in the note to the 'Immortality Ode': 'I used to brood over the stories of Enoch and Elijah, and almost to persuade myself that, whatever might become of others, I should be translated, in something of the same way, to heaven (*PW*, IV. 463). So he describes the child as

> Mighty Prophet! Seer blest!
> On whom those truths do rest,
> Which we are toiling all our lives to find,
> In darkness lost, the darkness of the grave (115–18);

The child becomes not just a leader-out, like Eppie, but a figure of magnificence and authority (so much so that it disturbed Coleridge). The prophet-child has an insight to which Romantic poets naturally aspire, a visionary insight which transcends place and time, and which is nevertheless firmly rooted in both. 'Poets', wrote Shelley, 'according to the circumstances of the age and nation in which they appeared, were called, in the earlier epochs of the world, legislators, or prophets: a poet essentially comprises and unites both these characters.'[9] It is in this spirit that Coleridge employs the figure of Ezekiel in his description of the imaginative poetry of Holy Scripture in *The Statesman's Manual*:

> The histories and political economy of the present and preceding century partake in the general contagion of its mechanic philosophy, and are the *product* of an unenlivened generalizing Understanding. In the Scriptures they are the living *educts* of the Imagination; of that reconciling and mediatory power, which incorporating the Reason in Images of the Sense, and organizing (as it were) the flux of the Senses by the permanence and self-circling energies of the Reason, gives birth to a system of symbols, harmonious in themselves, and consubstantial with the truths, of which they are the *conductors*. These are the Wheels which Ezekiel beheld, when the hand of the Lord was upon him, and he saw visions of God as he sate among the captives by the river of Chebar. *Whithersoever the Spirit was to go, the wheels went, and thither was their spirit to go: for the spirit of the living creature was in the wheels*

also. The truths and the symbols that represent them move in
conjunction and form the living chariot that bears up (for *us*) the
throne of the Divine Humanity.[10]

Coleridge is here quoting from verses 19 and 20 of the first chapter of
Ezekiel, using the image of the wheels to indicate the way in which
imaginative poetic language should be inseparable from a reality
which it expresses. He also alludes to the first verse of the chapter:
'Now it came to pass in the thirtieth year, in the fourth month, in the
fifth day of the month, as I was among the captives by the river of
Chebar, that the heavens were opened, and I saw visions of God.' In
this verse we can observe Ezekiel as accurately mindful of time and
place, and of his situation among the captives, seeing the heavens
open, and a vision of God. He is a prototype of the poet-prophet
figure, one who looks forward to the Romantics, especially to those
Romantics whose prophetic stance involves the recognition of time
and place as important in their visions. Blake's interpretation
of Ezekiel, for instance, was different, for in his water-colour of
Ezekiel's Wheels Blake depicted the figure of Ezekiel at the bottom of
the composition, half submerged in the waters of the river Chebar –
the prophet emerging from the waters which symbolize
materialism. Blake's view of prophecy involves a freedom from time
and place, from situation, even from rational objection: in *The
Marriage of Heaven and Hell* he asks Isaiah, 'does a firm perswasion
that a thing is so, make it so?' 'He replied, All poets believe that it
does, & in ages of imagination this firm perswasion removed
mountains: but many are not capable of a firm perswasion of any
thing' (plate 12). Isaiah's agreement with Blake's question, and the
way in which the firm persuaders are separated from the others,
indicates the distance between Blake and Wordsworth, whose
awareness of the contingent world is a feature of his poetry, and
whose attachment to nature upset Blake and made him ill. Yet the
role of prophet is still of great importance to Wordsworth: it combines, as Shelley saw, the functions of teacher, legislator, and poet.

   The adoption of the prophetic role suggests a certain conception
of poetry, characterized by a feeling that it should be imaginative,
instructive and serious. Thus at the end of *The Prelude*, Wordsworth
describes himself and Coleridge as speaking to men

   A lasting inspiration, sanctified
   By reason and by truth (1805 text, XII. 443–4);

and his vision in the Preface to *The Excursion* speaks of the ancient images of paradise:

> Why should they be
> A history only of departed things,
> Or a mere fiction of what never was?
> For the discerning intellect of Man,
> When wedded to this goodly universe
> In love and holy passion, shall find these
> A simple produce of the common day (49–55).

The language of religion – love and holy passion – is used to suggest not just a great consummation of the marriage between man and nature, but a sanctified relationship. The poet-prophet becomes the bearer of a religious message, and poetry a sacred activity. Certain poets have continued to think of it in this way, such as Peter Redgrove:

> Poetry's clearly a branch of religion. For myself, all the things that official religion ought to be about is in poetry. If we had a proper religion, that is, a psychologically useful religion in this country, it would be of course highly poetic. . . . What poetry is about is what is commonly called sacred. One can use any number of terms for this sense of the sacramental in existence, that everything that one does is very very real, that either within or without one there are personages who are full of knowledge and perhaps more than what we call human, or perhaps more truly human, personages in nature who suddenly appear and disappear.[11]

Critics have identified this strain in Wordsworth, from Matthew Arnold onwards, and some of them have sought to place Wordsworth's poetry in the context of the religious ideas of his time. Thus Richard E. Brantley, in *Wordsworth's "Natural Methodism"*, has demonstrated the poet's debt to Evangelical Anglicanism, and to early Methodist structures of belief. Frank McConnell, in *The Confessional Imagination*, has studied similarities between Wordsworth's language and ideas in *The Prelude* and the literature of Protestant confession. The present study is also an investigation of Wordsworth's poetry in relation to certain kinds of religious experience, but it differs from Brantley and McConnell in that it is not historically based. It is analytical rather than historical, examining the way in which Wordsworth's poetry, and his stance as prophet, are related to areas of fundamental religious experience. It explores the way in which his poetry, in Redgrove's words, 'is about . . . what is commonly called sacred'. It is also unusual, perhaps, in that it deals very little with the poetic language and style of Wordsworth; it is concerned rather with the subject-matter of his poetry, and the poetry of his subject-matter.

III

Although the poet-prophet is a man of vision, as the writings of Blake testify, it is important to realize that the true prophet is also involved in the world around him. As E. W. Heaton has written:

> Before we can understand how the prophetic faith of Israel took shape as a hope which looked towards its fulfilment in Christ, it is necessary to grasp the fact that the Hebrews set a very high value on life in this present world. Their natural centre of gravity was the present and not the future, this world and not the world to come. The last thing of which they could be accused is pietistic escapism.[12]

Wordsworth, like the Hebrew prophets, had a strong historical awareness; as Barbara Gates has recently pointed out, he saw the French Revolution with a full sense of its significance as an historical event.[13] More importantly, he shares with the Hebrew prophets the sense of community, and his reaction to the French revolution is clearly influenced by this. In the Hebrew experience, the sense of community depended on what Heaton calls 'an *inside* knowledge of personal fellowship in the community of God':

> The meaning of this prophetic communion is no more adequately represented by 'religion-and-doctrine' and 'morality-and-ethics', in isolation the one from the other, than is a poem by two prose paraphrases. No simple addition or conflation of the two can recapture the harmony, the power, and, therefore, the meaning, of their common source. Just as you must be something of a poet to understand poetry, so you must have experience of life in a personal community, before you can begin to understand the

personal revelation of God, alike through his servants the prophets, and in Jesus, his Son.[14]

The Old Testament prophets looked back to the period in the wilderness, the time of the desert community, as their ideal. 'By the time of the prophets', Heaton writes, 'the reverence and affection of those early days had been lost in the impersonal and competitive society of Canaan.'[15] The pattern is familiar, but none the less authentic: it occurs in Wordsworth as he passes from the community of his childhood to the Cambridge and London of his maturer years. His conclusion that

> The world is too much with us; late and soon,
> Getting and spending, we lay waste and powers:
>> (Miscellaneous Sonnets, part i, xxxiii)

derives its conviction from a sense of what has been lost, of an ideal that has been disregarded. In this context, past and future are set against the present, the ideal against the actual. 'Romantic art', says W. J. T. Mitchell,

> was, among other things, an art of self-conscious historicism; its concern with contemporary issues was inextricably involved with the historical or psychological recovery of the primitive and the prophetic or utopian disclosure of the future as living influences on the present.[16]

The French revolution was the political event which underpins a great deal of this artistic activity: it strove for the recovery of the primitive sense of community, and it looked forward to the ideal future. The same pattern is found in Wordsworth's poetry: *The Prelude* begins in primitive simplicity, and ends in a prophetic vision of the mind of man

> In beauty exalted, as it is itself
> Of substance and of fabric more divine.
>> (1805, XIII. 451-2)

It is through his interest in the community, and man's individual freedom within it, that Wordsworth becomes concerned with fundamental problems of society. And just as in Old Testament times the idea of community was inextricably linked with the religion of that community, so Wordsworth's poetry also concerns itself with a kind of religious belief which is very close to patterns of religious behaviour in primitive communities. We should perhaps take literally the end of sonnet XXXIII, 'The world is too much with us'

> Great God! I'd rather be
> A Pagan suckled in a creed outworn;
> So might I, standing on this pleasant lea,
> Have glimpses that would make me less forlorn;
> Have sight of Proteus rising from the sea;
> Or hear old Triton blow his wreathèd horn.

In ancient times, ancient religions; with more of the true spirit of worship, and of a right relationship between man and nature, and man and man, than the modern times of getting and spending.

IV

In Chapter V of D. H. Lawrence's *The Rainbow*, Tom Brangwen meditates during the service as he is giving away his step daughter in marriage:

> He felt himself tiny, a little upright figure on a plain circled round with the immense, roaring sky: he and his wife, two little, upright figures walking across this plain, whilst the heavens shimmered and roared about them. When did one come to an end? In what direction was it finished? There was no end, no finish, only this roaring vast space. Did one never get old, never die? That was the clue. He exulted strangely, with torture. He would go on with his wife, he and she like two children camping in the plains. What was sure but the endless sky? But that was so sure, so boundless.

Here Tom Brangwen is thinking in images, seeing himself and his wife as children beneath an immense sky on the vast plain. At the same time various fundamental questions present themselves: 'When did one come to an end? In what direction was it finished?' These are questions which ask about the meaning and purpose of life in a particularly complex and reverberant way: 'When did one' – oneself, oneself as representative of man, oneself as unit in the great cosmic process – 'come to an end?' – die, finish the journey of life, disintegrate, become as nothing. 'In what direction was it finished?' – where shall we find death, in what state shall we be when we die, what is the direction which our lives will have taken by then?

The questions which Tom Brangwen is asking concern the meaning of life, the place and purpose of man, the function of death in giving meaning to life, the insignificance of man in relation to the world around him. The picture of himself and his wife, 'two little upright figures walking across this plain', recalls the archetypal image with which Milton concludes *Paradise Lost*:

> The World was all before them, where to choose
> Thir place of rest, and Providence thir guide:
> They hand in hand with wandring steps and slow,
> Through *Eden* took thir solitarie way.

This is man at the beginning of history. For the first time he is going out on a journey that will end in death, and enclosed within the multiple meanings of the final image are reverberations which take the reader back into the poem and also forward into his own predicament. Milton's marvellous crystallization of the human situation implies its own central questions, some of which have been so movingly discussed within the poem: how does one live in a fallen world? how do we contrast that way of living with an ideal? how do we understand the workings of a just and all-powerful God, in a world of hatred and corruption, physical pain and blindness?

Milton's final image is taken up by Wordsworth in the first paragraph of *The Prelude*: 'The earth is all before me' (line 15); and Wordsworth's portrait of the free poet implies the same far-reaching questions, although they are frequently unnoticed because of the circumstantial detail. The problem of where Wordsworth was at the time[17] has obscured the image of the liberated poet who is yet also representative of man. The poet is at a certain point on a journey, *nel mezzo del cammin di nostra vita*: he is both an individual, the child born at Cockermouth, and representative, a man on the progress through life. Similarly the poem is both a private record, the poem 'addressed to S. T. Coleridge', and a great public poem, an epic in which Wordsworth plays out the part of man in the story of paradise and its loss. He finds himself in the position of Adam, with the world before him and providence his guide. *The Prelude* is thus a poem which is both history and myth: it records events in the poet's life, but arranges and selects them in such a way that they re-enact the myth of the lost paradise. His function within the poem is not allegorical but symbolic, in Coleridge's definition: it is characterized by the translucence of the Eternal through and in the Temporal, by the presence in the poem of what Philip Wheelwright has called 'depth-meanings'. 'Man lives', he writes, 'always on the verge, always on the borderland of a something more. . . . The existential structure of human life is radically, irreducibly *liminal*.'[18] This word *liminal* I have found especially useful in the discussion of Wordsworth's poetry which follows, and in any attempt to explain the aim and purpose of this study, which is basically concerned with Wordsworth as a poet 'always on the borderland of a something more'. The religious experience which involves him in an awareness of the ideal community also manifests itself in a private apprehension of the sacred. In this Wordsworth comes close to the structure of primitive religious experience: this explains not only some of the strange, authoritarian moments of his poetry, but also the working of the poetic imagination itself. Expanding on his idea of the liminal, Wheelwright notes:

> all dogmas whether theological or scientistic in kind, represent man's usual struggle to erect mental barriers against the unsettling fact of that incurably 'not quite' condition of existence. Poetic utterance by contrast can occasionally, with luck, flash through the veil of conceptualities that shape our usual view of the world and of ourselves in it, to stir brief inconclusive hints of ultimate paradox.[19]

This may happen in Wordsworth's poetry with great force and clarity, as it does in Book VI of *The Prelude*:

> when the light of sense
> Goes out in flashes that have shewn to us
> The invisible world, doth Greatness make abode,
> There harbours whether we be young or old.
> Our destiny, our nature, and our home
> Is with infinitude, and only there;
> With hope it is, hope that can never die,
> Effort, and expectation, and desire,
> And something evermore about to be (VI. 534–42).

At other times it is less obvious, but it is the argument of this book that much of Wordsworth's imaginative activity is governed by structures which are close to those of religious experience, and that this is a major reason for Wordsworth's continued importance. In my view, it also has some relevance to what might be called the 'two voices' problem: I do not share the view that Wordsworth was a great poet who was guilty of curious lapses of poetic tact, and who wrote certain lines which cannot be taken seriously. This study attempts to see such lines as part of a greater whole, and to find a context within which they can live, and move, and have their being. This context I see as primarily and fundamentally religious: in the introduction to *The Sacred and the Profane*, to which this study is greatly indebted, Mircea Eliade writes: 'The reader will very soon realize that *sacred* and *profane* are two modes of being in the world, two existential situations assumed by man in the course of his history.'[20] The place of Wordsworth in this pattern is clearly on the side of the sacred, for he is a poet who is powerfully conscious of the sacred possibilities of the world; when he writes

> One impulse from a vernal wood
> May teach you more of man,
> Of moral evil and of good,
> Than all the sages can. . . .

his assertion gains sense and force when it is placed within the context of a belief in sacred time and sacred place. Eliade suggests that there is an 'abyss' dividing the two modes of being, and I think it possible that some of the hostile criticism of Wordsworth has been thought out on the other side of the abyss. Similarly, at the end of the savage desecration of 'Nutting', the poet is confronted by a feeling that will not be denied –

> I felt a sense of pain when I beheld
> The silent trees, and saw the intruding sky. –
> Then, dearest Maiden, move along these shades
> In gentleness of heart; with gentle hand
> Touch – for there is a spirit in the woods (52–6).

The awareness of this spirit, I have tried to suggest, is connected with the Romantic poet's conception of his role as prophet, and with Wordsworth's sense of the prophet in relation to the community. It involves also a coming to terms with the self, which in Wordsworth's case is manifested in the recurrent image of home, and of being at home. In all of these the imagination engages with the external world in what Wordsworth regarded as primary poetic activity:

> He considers man and the objects that surround him as acting and re-acting upon each other, so as to produce an infinite complexity of pain and pleasure; he considers man in his own nature and in his ordinary life as contemplating this with a certain quantity of immediate knowledge, with certain convictions, intuitions, and deductions which by habit become of the nature of intuitions; he considers him as looking upon this complex scene of ideas and sensations, and finding everywhere objects that immediately excite in him sympathies which, from the necessities of his nature, are accompanied by an overbalance of enjoyment.[21]

Much of Wordsworth's poetry is concerned with the process described here: he is interested in immediate knowledge, the apprehension of the world by the senses, and the experience of childhood in its encounter with the external world; and he is interested also in the way in which man structures his world, the way in which he acquires knowledge and understanding about it – his 'convictions, intuitions, and deductions'. The structure of his understanding is the subject of this book.

V

Tom Brangwen's interior monologue in *The Rainbow* has a remarkable similarity to a passage from Book I of *The Prelude*, in which Wordsworth describes the child bathing in the stream at Cockermouth, and standing beneath the sky. I have used this passage as a starting point for three interlocking enquiries into Wordsworth's poetry. These correspond, rather arbitrarily, to Wordsworth's own division of his subject into three – 'On Man, on Nature, and on Human Life' – and together they illuminate the work of the prophet-poet in complementary ways. In the first, there is an examination of the way in which the poet sees the world around him, and the way in which he sees man in the community. In the second, his beliefs about man and nature are examined in relation to patterns of elementary religious life; while the third section deals with the poet's understanding of himself and the relation of this to the growth of human tenderness and the places that he saw as home. The fact that these enquiries can all proceed from the same passage in *The Prelude* should serve to emphasize that they are different strands of the same imaginative activity, and that they all spring from the way in which Wordsworth perceives and interprets the world around him. I hope to show that Wordsworth's childhood vision, as described in *The Prelude*, leads to his conception of the poet as prophet, and to his understanding of the world in ways that are sacred rather than profane.

Part I

On Man

Only after a life-time have I come to understand that even a real event may be the enactment of a myth, and from that take on supernatural meaning and power. In such cases myth is the truth of the fact, not fact the truth of the myth.

Kathleen Raine, *Defending Ancient Springs*, pp. 123–4.

1 Childhood

I

The two-part *Prelude*, written in 1799, ends its first paragraph with a description of the child bathing:

> Beloved Derwent! fairest of all Streams!
> Was it for this that I, a four years' child,
> A naked Boy, among thy silent pools
> Made one long bathing of a summer's day?
> Basked in the sun, or plunged into thy streams,
> Alternate, all a summer's day, or coursed
> Over the sandy fields, and dashed the flowers
> Of yellow grunsel, or when crag and hill,
> The woods and distant Skiddaw's lofty height
> Were bronzed with a deep radiance, stood alone,
> A naked Savage in the thunder shower (i. 16–26)?[1]

At the entrance to Wordsworth's great autobiographical poem, this unforgettable picture of the child (expanded in later texts) shows him as a young savage, in a state of delightful primitive simplicity. He plays with the silent water, feels the warmth of the sun, and runs over the sandy fields with his feet brushing at the groundsel. The child has a direct relationship with his environment through his senses: the external world is apprehended as cool water, warm sun, sandy earth under the feet, the rain of the thunder shower. Much of the power of this section comes from the picture of the naked savage, which conveys the sense of a human being in an immediate, unstructured relationship with the world around him. But this is more than an image: it is the beginning of a description of childhood which presents, with remarkable intuition, a picture of how the child comes to understand the world; and by linking the child with primitive man, this understanding becomes part of a process which is fundamental and universal. The child, in the first book of *The*

Prelude, does what primitive man was concerned to do, 'applying himself to the most difficult task, that of systematizing what is immediately presented to the senses'.[2] In so doing he moves from the perception of things in the external world as *stimuli*, to use Lévi-Strauss's word (*'perçus comme des stimulants'*), to the conception of them as *signs* (*'conçus comme des signes'*).[3] An obvious example is the episode of the boat-stealing, where the huge cliff which appears to be moving after him is interpreted by the child as evidence that nature is perpetually observant and watchful, ready to admonish those who do wrong. The fact that boat-stealing is not a serious crime is immaterial; the important thing for the poet is the reminder of some powerful force at work in the universe. Book I of *The Prelude* is concerned, principally, with such signs and the poet's reading of them: gradually he assembles what for him can be the only reading from the signs. The process corresponds closely to Lévi-Strauss's metaphor for the development of mythical thought, in his famous image of *'bricolage'*. The *'bricoleur'*, or handyman, does his work with whatever materials and tools he happens to have. He collects things at random on the principle that they 'may always come in handy'. Out of them he makes new constructions, though always using the old bits and pieces which he possesses (unlike the scientist, who examines the world for what is new). Lévi-Strauss describes him at work:

> His first practical step is retrospective. He has to turn back to an already existent set made up of tools and materials, to consider or reconsider what it contains and finally, and above all, to engage in a sort of dialogue with it and, before choosing between them, to index the possible answers which the whole set can offer to his problem. He interrogates all the heterogeneous objects of which his treasury is composed to discover what each of them could 'signify' and so contribute to the definition of a set which has yet to materialize but which will ultimately differ from the instrumental set only in the internal disposition of its parts.[4]

In *The Prelude*, Wordsworth is a *'bricoleur'*. He cross-examines his resources, creating a mythology from the heterogeneous elements of his own childhood, leaving some out and elevating others to positions of importance because of their significance. His childhood experiences at Penrith, for instance, or the daily routine of school work at Hawkshead, are omitted in favour of the outdoor pursuits and the games in the cottage. These seemed to Wordsworth, when he interrogated his past, to be the experiences which 'signified'. They were a heterogeneous collection:

> Ah me! that all
> The terrors, all the early miseries
> Regrets, vexations, lassitudes, that all
> The thoughts and feelings which have been infus'd
> Into my mind, should ever have made up
> The calm existence that is mine when I
> Am worthy of myself (I. 355–61)!

Similarly, beyond his childhood, the experiences in Cambridge, London and France all had to be used to make the '*bricolage*' of the poet's myth: that he had been brought up in favoured circumstances, benevolently influenced by nature, and saved from being overwhelmed by events through the love of nature and some human help. For Wordsworth this was mythology as truth, the result (like primitive myths) of sustained observation and classification of the external world, and his relationship to it. For myths, as Lévi-Strauss has pointed out, are not the product of man's mind turning its back on reality:

> Their principal value is indeed to preserve until the present time the remains of methods of observation and reflection which were (and no doubt still are) precisely adapted to discoveries of a certain type: those which nature authorized from the starting point of a speculative organization and exploitation of the sensible world in sensible terms.[5]

Wordsworth the child, running over the sandy fields like a young savage, is to develop into Wordsworth the man, conscious of the limitations of time and place; in the process he perceives the sensible world in his own sensible terms, observing and reflecting on the events of his own life in a way which, for him, creates a myth which is inescapable and true. And by beginning with the naked child as savage, Wordsworth directs attention to the fundamental, even anthropological, nature of the poem, since it is concerned with what Lévi-Strauss called 'the central problem of anthropology, viz., the passage from nature to culture'.[6]

II

In this initial appearance, the child seems to be unaffected by anything except the primary apprehension of the external world as stimulus. In Rousseau's phrase, he 'abandons himself solely to the consciousness of his present existence'.[7] Rousseau's anticipations of structuralist anthropology are so remarkable that his theories may be useful at this point, even though his precise influence on Wordsworth may have been slight.[8] In his *Discours sur les Fondements de l'Inégalité parmi les Hommes*, Rousseau is concerned to discover, as William Boyd has written, 'not the details of life in a long-forgotten state of nature, of which he himself frankly says that it is impossible to say anything, but those ultimate facts about human nature which are the basis of society'.[9] Rousseau's ideal was not animal man, static in indolent stupidity (or what Wordsworth, in the Preface to *Lyrical Ballads*, called 'savage torpor'), but the noble savage, poised at a moment when he was able to recognize his fellow-men and their needs, yet before the development of property. The poise comes at a point which connects nature and culture, the state of nature and the state of reasoning; the moment of passage between an affective, unstructured view of the world, and an intellectual, systematizing view. This moment is the one in which man becomes conscious of himself as a species, and spontaneously feels compassion for his fellow-men (*la pitié naturelle, que les moeurs les plus dépravées ont encore peine à détruire*).[10] This, in Lévi-Strauss's words, is 'the only psychic state of which the content is indissociably both affective and intellectual, and which the act of consciousness suffices to transfer from one level to the other'.[11] A non-structuralist way of describing it is provided by Léon Emery (discussing Rousseau's reading of travel books):

> The savage, as these readings led Rousseau to see him, is indeed still a child of nature, for he is ignorant of property, politics and what we call civilization, yet he is not at one with the natural order, that is to say with the vegetable and animal realms. He has a hut, rudimentary techniques, a family, feelings and the religion of the heart. It appears that at this level we have attained the best possible balance between the conditions of our physical existence and the degree of soul and intellect that enable us to enjoy them.[12]

Wordsworth indicates a state like this in his revision of the bathing passage, when he

stood alone
Beneath the sky, as if I had been born
On Indian Plains, and from my Mother's hut
Had run abroad in wantonness, to sport,
A naked Savage, in the thunder shower (1. 300–4).

where the addition of the Indian plains and his mother's hut
suggests exactly the kind of movement from affectivity to intellectuality described by Lévi-Strauss, as the poet-child becomes
conscious of himself and his relations to others, in the first instance
his family.

Although the processes of development are analogous to those of
the savage mind, both Rousseau and Wordsworth are fully aware
that they are living in the eighteenth century and not in primitive
times. As Geoffrey Symcox has written:

> Rousseau's cry of 'back to nature' was by no means as simplistic as
> is usually assumed. He realized that civilization was here to stay.
> The question was not to destroy it – he did not want to 'go and
> live in the woods like a bear' – but to improve it by resurrecting
> certain human qualities which had been submerged in the
> onward march of intellectual and material progress.[13]

The original and crucial stage in this development was the arrival of
the idea of property. Rousseau reserves this for a dramatic
beginning to the second part of the *Discours*:

> The first person who, having enclosed a piece of land, had the
> idea of saying 'this is mine', and who found people simple enough
> to believe him, was the true founder of civilized society. What
> crimes, wars, murders, what miseries and horrors might not
> human kind have been spared by someone who, pulling up the
> stakes or filling in the ditch, might have cried to his fellows:
> 'beware of listening to this impostor; you are lost if you forget that
> fruits belong to everyone, and the land to no-one.'[14]

If a child is in a natural state, either viewing the world affectively or
balanced between affectivity and intellectuality, he is akin to the
savage before the coming of property; yet in historical time he
belongs to his own century. One of the fascinating processes of the
first books of *The Prelude* is concerned with the perception of the
world in different ways, as the natural instincts of the savage mind

which acknowledge no debts to time and place, have to come to
terms with the historical situation. Affectivity meets intellectuality
at every point, and particularly over the question of property. Thus
two of the most significant and dramatic moments in Book I are
directly concerned with the child Wordsworth's apprehension of
Rousseau's *ceci est à moi*. In the first of these, when the child steals
from others' snares

>   a strong desire
> O'erpower'd my better reason, and the bird
> Which was the captive of another's toils
> Became my prey; and, when the deed was done
> I heard among the solitary hills
> Low breathings coming after me, and sounds
> Of undistinguishable motion, steps
> Almost as silent as the turf they trod (1. 325–32).

Here the child's instincts, his intuitive desire to hunt and to survive,
conflict with an acknowledgement of what, in his time and place,
would be considered right and wrong. So although he sees himself as
a hunter ('In thought and wish . . . I was a fell destroyer') he is also
aware of a voice of reason which is conscious of property and its
demands. When reason is overcome by this natural intuition, he
hears nature as sign; the sinister breathings are an admonition, to
show him that he must accommodate himself to the world in which
he lives. In his own life Wordsworth was re-enacting the confrontation so fascinating to the eighteenth century between the savage
and the cultivated; he was seeking to accommodate the best
qualities of both, in a way normally held to be impossible. Writing of
Omai, the South Sea Islander so admired by Dr Johnson for his
natural gentility of manners, Cowper lamented that 'We found no
bait/To tempt us in thy country';[15] we have been spoiled for the
kind of disinterested goodness that is to be found there.
Wordsworth, like Rousseau, is concerned to preserve the human
qualities in the face of an advanced civilization: so he is like a
savage, yet aware of nature as sign, indicating his best path forward.

  After the initial portrayal of the child bathing, the first three
episodes of the two-part *Prelude* are all concerned with stealing.
After the plundering of snares comes the birds-nesting, followed by
the boat-stealing. Interestingly, it is the second of these which is least
accompanied by admonitory signs from nature:

> Though mean
> And though inglorious were my views, the end
> Was not ignoble. Oh, when I have hung
> Above the raven's nest, by knots of grass
> Or half-inch fissures in the slippery rock
> But ill sustained, and almost, as it seemed,
> Suspended by the blast which blew amain,
> Shouldering the naked crag, oh, at that time,
> While on the perilous ridge I hung alone,
> With what strange utterance did the loud dry wind
> Blow through my ears; the sky seemed not a sky
> Of earth, and with what motion moved the clouds (i. 55–66)!

The child seems assisted by nature here, hanging by knots of grass and small hand-holds, and even, it would seem, held up by the wind; and although the wind and the sky and the clouds seem wonderfully strange and unearthly, they are not menacing. Nature, it appears, sees the robbing of nests as natural, and as a practice which calls for no admonition; whereas, in the boat-stealing episode which follows, there is the most memorable of all instances in Wordsworth of 'nature as sign'. Paradoxically, it seems as if nature is being associated with civil law.

In the two-part *Prelude* the influences on the favoured child are described as 'spirits' and 'quiet powers', while there are also 'Severer interventions, ministry/More palpable' (i. 79–80). It is these interventions which lead the child to the shepherd's boat, and encourage him to take it. As he moves into the middle of the lake

> the huge cliff
> Rose up between me and the stars, and still
> With measured motion, like a living thing
> Strode after me (i. 111–14).

This phenomenon can be accounted for by simple trigonometry, and yet Wordsworth never attempts to explain it in this or any other way. It remains, plainly and obviously, as an example of nature conceived as a sign. Thus the transition from nature as stimulus to nature as sign is accompanied by an increased awareness of property and civil law, as the child-savage seeks to accommodate himself to the time and place in which he lives. Rousseau would have recognized the fundamental importance of the process: 'Émile', he

wrote, 'is not a savage to be banished to a desert, but a savage made
to inhabit cities.'[16]

III

Wordsworth describes himself as a 'four years' child' bathing in the
stream (in the two-part *Prelude* of 1799; later it becomes 'a five years'
Child'). The age, whether four or five, corresponds in activity,
freedom and energy with the second stage in *Emile*, in which
Rousseau treats of the child from the age of five to twelve. The first
thing which he emphasizes is freedom, the freedom to learn by
hurting himself or getting into danger –

> Instead of letting him stifle in the used-up air of a room, let him be
> taken daily into the open air. There let him run about, let him
> play, let him fall over a hundred times a day, so much the better:
> he will learn more quickly to pick himself up again. The blessings
> of freedom will compensate for many bruises.[17]

He goes on to argue that, since many children die before
adolescence, it is wrong to lead them 'with chains of every sort', to
prepare them for a life which they may never come to enjoy:

> Fathers, do you know the moment when death awaits your
> children? Do not prepare remorse for yourselves by taking away
> from them the few moments that Nature has given them. As soon
> as they can feel the delight of existing, let them enjoy it; and make
> sure that at whatever hour God may summon them, they will not
> die without having tasted life.[18]

Wordsworth's corresponding example of this is the boy hooting to
the owls, who is allowed the happiness of a natural freedom before
his early death. He reminds us of the ever-present danger of
mortality, and the importance of full life in nature during whatever
life we have; and if he remains in *The Prelude* partly as a warning, we
can see the implications of his life in the behaviour of the other boys.
Rousseau's recommendations resemble Wordsworth's celebration
of sheer physical vitality, the 'round of tumult'(ii. 7) and the
'boisterous race'(ii. 46) of his early years. Children, said Rousseau,
must be allowed to 'jump, and run, and shout, whenever they wish

to do so. All their movements are the needs of their constitution, which is seeking to strengthen itself.'[19] Wordsworth describes the changing seasons which provide their different amusements –

> every change
> Of exercise and sport, to which the year
> Did summon us in its delightful round (i. 199–201).

Children should not be pampered, and one way of making them miserable is to accustom them to obtain whatever they want; and Wordsworth often comes very close to the spartan strain which is found in Rousseau:

> No delicate viands sapped our bodily strength:
> More than we wished we knew the blessing then
> Of vigorous hunger, for our daily meals
> Were frugal, Sabine fare – and then, exclude
> A little weekly stipend, and we lived
> Through three divisions of the quartered year
> In pennyless poverty (ii. 78–84).

Naturally Rousseau recommends a diet of 'common and simple dishes', though it is difficult to imagine Ann Tyson leaving the cupboard and the fruit room always open, as Rousseau suggests.[20] As the child develops, however, the most important educator is seen by both writers as experience. Practical lessons, in *Emile*, demonstrate that a pail of oak chips is lighter than a pail of water, and it is by getting lost and hungry that Emile learns the value of astronomy. One special coincidence is Rousseau's idea that children 'should have many sports by night', so that they may be freed from a fear of the dark.[21] Above all, however, there is Rousseau's insight that

> Nature wishes that children should be children before being men. If we wish to upset this process, we will produce too-early fruit, which will have neither ripeness nor taste, and which will quickly go rotten: we shall have young doctors and old children. Childhood has ways of seeing, of thinking, of feeling, which are right for it; nothing is less sensible than to wish to substitute our own. . . . [22]

which returns our attention, not only to the active, boisterous
existence of children, but also to their way of seeing the world
around them. Wordsworth portrays this, as we have seen, as nature
as stimulus giving way to nature as sign; but more important than
either is his perception of these ways of seeing as interactive and
simultaneous. The child's developing mind

> Even as an agent of the one great mind,
> Creates, creator and receiver both,
> Working but in alliance with the works
> Which it beholds. Such, verily, is the first
> Poetic spirit of our human life –
> By uniform controul of after years
> In most abated and suppressed, in some
> Through every change of growth or of decay
> Preeminent till death (ii. 303–10).

As creator and receiver, the child discovers mythological patterns
by combining sign and stimulus; the idea unites the two ways of
perceiving relationships set forth by Lévi-Strauss in his opposition of
'conçu' and 'vécu'. Discussing certain phenomena of ethno-
zoology, he writes:

> it is clear that relationships such as we have just mentioned by
> way of example are *conceived*, not *experienced*. In formulating them,
> the mind allows itself to be guided by a theoretical rather than by
> a practical aim.[23]

Roger C. Poole comments:

> This distinction conçu/vécu suggests to us a fascinating
> conception of a dual creativity behind symbolic patterns, a
> creativity which would result either from having 'lived' some-
> thing and drawn the consequences from that experience, or a
> creativity which would *project* its 'conceptual' patterns *into* its
> materials as a result of intellectual desires and aims of its own,
> even if these were unconscious.[24]

It is this dual creativity which is present in so much of Wordsworth's
poetry of childhood, and which leads to his discovery, not only of the
vivid external world, but also of the meanings of that world for man.

It is this relationship between man and nature which is the fundamental concern of his poetry.

IV

Martin Buber once described education 'of men by men' as

> the selection of the effective world by a person and in him. The educator gathers in the constructive forces of the world. He distinguishes, rejects, and confirms in himself, in his self which is filled with the world. The constructive forces are eternally the same: they are the world bound up in community, turned to God.[25]

Wordsworth anticipates Buber in seeing education as a constructive process which involves a relationship with the outside world. The main subject of *The Prelude*, in its broadest sense of 'subject', is education: through school, Cambridge, and later experience, to a stable and hopeful understanding of the human mind and its relationship to the external world, in particular to 'the world bound up in community, turned to God'. This is not a matter of ignoring evil, but of distinguishing, rejecting the bad, and confirming in himself the world which is constructive and good. In *The Prelude* the emphasis during the school years is on natural education: neither the two-part *Prelude* nor the 1805 text stresses school work. Instead, the process of education through beauty and through fear is shown in the boat-stealing and birds-nesting, the skating and card playing. In each case the developing mind comes to see nature as a sign: the emotions aroused by the first two are awe, by the second two tenderness and love. Yet the external world also continues to exist as stimulus, and the dual process is creatively at work in the vivid apprehension of the natural scene, and the understanding of it. The process is continued in part two of the two-part *Prelude*, with the visits to Furness Abbey and to the inn on the eastern shore of Windermere, after which the boy minstrel blew his flute upon the rock. The whole scene is portrayed – the children playing, strawberries and cream for tea, and then the return over the darkening lake – but then, with the beautiful 'oh', the tone changes: the 'oh' carries the reader effortlessly into a deeper dimension, one in which the scene becomes active. In subdued sexual metaphors, in which the mind and heart are lain upon, sunk into, and held, the relationship is consummated:

> But ere the fall
> Of night, when in our pinnace we returned
> Over the dusky lake, and to the beach
> Of some small island steered our course, with one –
> The minstrel of our troop – and left him there,
> And rowed off gently, while he blew his flute
> Alone upon the rock, oh, then the calm
> And dead still water lay upon my mind
> Even with a weight of pleasure, and the sky,
> Never before so beautiful, sank down
> Into my heart and held me like a dream (ii. 205–14).

In this the child is receiver, acknowledging the sheer beauty of the moment; nature is perceived as stimulus, and there is hardly any conception of sign, unless the recognition of such beauty constitutes it. Yet with the 'oh', the mind does move into a creative recognition of beauty, as though it is understanding the signs which are being made. This is a process of creative reception, and quite distinct from any intellectual understanding, as the passage which follows makes clear:

> already I began
> To love the sun, a boy I loved the sun
> Not as I since have loved him – as a pledge
> And surety of my earthly life, a light
> Which while I view I feel I am alive –
> But for this cause, that I had seen him lay
> His beauty on the morning hills, had seen
> The western mountain touch his setting orb
> In many a thoughtless hour, when, from excess
> Of happiness, my blood appeared to flow
> With its own pleasure, and I breathed with joy (ii. 217–27).

Here the poet distinguishes between a conscious, mature love of the sun as evidence of his own life and existence – I see the sun, therefore I am – and a more sensuous love of sunrise and sunset which makes him feel physically more alive. This is a non-intellectual process, a deepening of intensity which is primarily receptive yet also creative.

What Wordsworth is doing in these passages is establishing the order of ways in which the world can be perceived: besides nature as stimulus and nature as sign, there is a third category, nature as scientifically or intellectually apprehended. This is the uncreative relationship between the mind and the external world, what Buber called the *I–It*, 'that wisdom which perceives a closed compartment in things, reserved for the initiate and manipulated only with the key'.[26] The other, whether sign or stimulus (and sometimes both) is 'the world of relation', Buber's *I–Thou*, described by Wordsworth in the Preface to *The Excursion*:

> How exquisitely the individual Mind
> (And the progressive powers perhaps no less
> Of the whole species) to the external World
> Is fitted: – and how exquisitely, too –
> Theme this but little heard of among men –
> The external World is fitted to the Mind (63–8);

In a memorable passage in *I and Thou*, Buber considers various ways of perceiving a tree: as picture, as movement, as species, as scientific object in number, space and time. But

> It can, however, also come about, if I have both will and grace, that in considering the tree I become bound up in relation to it. The tree is now no longer *It*. . . . To effect this it is not necessary for me to give up any of the ways in which I consider the tree. There is nothing from which I would have to turn my eyes away in order to see, and no knowledge that I would have to forget. Rather is everything, picture and movement, species and type, law and number, indivisibly united in this event.[27]

The perception is inclusive and unifying, Coleridgean in its apprehension of the 'One Life', and acknowledged by Wordsworth in his tribute to Coleridge:

> Thou, my friend, art one
> More deeply read in thy own thoughts, no slave
> Of that false secondary power by which
> In weakness we create distinctions, then
> Believe our puny boundaries are things
> Which we perceive, and not which we have made (ii. 249–54).

The categorizing mind separates man from nature by failing to relate to the total individuality, the 'this-ness' of the object. Thus the true stepping into relationship is opposed to science ('We murder to dissect') just as it is opposed to mysticism. Continuing his celebration of Coleridge, Wordsworth writes:

> To thee, unblinded by these outward shews,
> The unity of all has been revealed;
> And thou wilt doubt with me, less aptly skilled
> Than many are to class the cabinet
> Of their sensations, and in voluble phrase
> Run through the history and birth of each
> As of a single independent thing.
> Hard task to analyse a soul, in which
> Not only general habits and desires,
> But each most obvious and particular thought –
> Not in a mystical and idle sense,
> But in the words of reason deeply weighed –
> Hath no beginning (ii. 255–67).

It certainly is a hard task to analyse such a soul, but Wordsworth consistently endeavours to express the quintessential relationship between man and the external world in his poetry; to do so he distinguishes it from science, and yet the external world is present in all its material properties. When Wordsworth says 'And lovely is the rose' in the Immortality Ode, the rose exists in all its magnificence and its loveliness; there is no mysticism. Buber, coincidentally, writes of Goethe and the rose:

> How lovely and how legitimate the sound of the full *I* of Goethe! It is the *I* of pure intercourse with nature; nature gives herself to it and speaks unceasingly with it, revealing her mysteries to it but not betraying her mystery. It believes in her, and says to the rose, 'Then thou art it' – then it takes its stand with it in a single reality.[28]

In this condition there is a full awareness of the self, and a full apprehension of the external world, the two relating to each other and enhancing each other through love. Both Buber and Wordsworth associate this with the life of the child and the life of the primitive. The chief concern of primitive man, writes Buber, is not with the products of analysis and reflection, 'but with the true original unity, the lived relation'.[29] The development of civilization and the growth of the child to adulthood have the same effects:

> The history of the individual and that of the human race, in whatever they may continually part company, agree at least in this one respect, that they indicate a progressive augmentation of the world of *It*.[30]

It is by studying the child that we are given the fullest insight into the *I–Thou*, the primary relationship which arises out of natural combination. Buber begins with the ante-natal life of the child, which is 'purely natural combination, bodily interaction and flowing from the one to the other'. He quotes an old Jewish saying that 'in the mother's body man knows the universe, in birth he forgets it', which, he says, 'reads like the imperfect decipherment of an inscription from earliest times'.[31] But to replace this natural connection comes relation:

> time is granted to the child to exchange a spiritual connexion, that is, *relation*, for the natural connexion with the world that he gradually loses. He has stepped out of the glowing darkness of chaos into the cool light of creation. But he does not possess it yet; he must first draw it truly out, he must make it into a reality for himself, he must find for himself his own world by seeing and hearing and touching and shaping it. . . . Like primitive man the child lives between sleep and sleep (a great part of his waking hours is also sleep) in the flash and counter-flash of meeting.[32]

In the same way Wordsworth's infant babe has his primary relationship with the universe, as (in Buber's words) creation 'rises up to meet the grasping senses':

> No outcast he, bewildered and depressed;
> Along his infant veins are interfused
> The gravitation and the filial bond
> Of Nature that connect him with the world.
> Emphatically such a being lives
> An inmate of this *active* universe (ii. 291–6).

So Buber describes a tiny child exploring the world around him:

Before anything isolated can be perceived, timid glances move out into indistinct space, towards something indefinite; and in times when there seems to be no desire for nourishment, hands sketch delicately and dimly in the empty air, apparently aimlessly seeking and reaching out to meet something indefinite. You may, if you wish, call this an animal action, but it is not thereby comprehended. For these very glances will after protracted attempts settle on the red carpet-pattern and not be moved till the soul of the red has opened itself to them; and this very movement of the hands will win from a woolly Teddy-bear its precise form, apparent to the senses, and become lovingly and unforgettably aware of a complete body.[33]

Wordsworth is more explicit in associating this with love, though both writers would see the child's affective mode of perceiving, his 'apprehensive habitude' as something which exalts both the perceiver and the perceived. In Wordsworth the child exists in his mother's love, and 'Doth gather passion from his mother's eye' (ii. 273); so his mind struggles to combine rather than separate, and his creative and receptive power 'irradiates and exalts':

> his mind spreads,
> Tenacious of the forms which it receives.
> In one beloved presence – nay and more,
> In that most apprehensive habitude
> And those sensations which have been derived
> From this beloved presence – there exists
> A virtue which irradiates and exalts
> All objects through all intercourse of sense (ii. 283–90).

So that the life of the self, and the life of nature, are in this ideal state truly interactive, and mutually enriching.

V

We have seen that Wordsworth's conception of the ideal childhood, beginning with his portrayal of the child as savage, is not just a state of happiness; it involves other complex concerns, and in particular it addresses itself to ways in which man relates to the world around him. In childhood certain imaginative faculties are powerfully active: notably the capacity for myth-making, and the sense of relation. We may observe, finally, how close these faculties are to the central features of Wordsworth's poetry: the creative imagination, and the central self.[34]

The child is a creator and a perceiver, his mind working in alliance with the external world which it beholds, and Wordsworth designates this as 'the first/Poetic spirit of our human life':

> Such, verily, is the first
> Poetic spirit of our human life –
> By uniform controul of after years
> In most abated and suppressed, in some
> Through every change of growth or of decay
> Preeminent till death (ii. 306–10).

This is paralleled by Blake, who (according to Henry Crabb Robinson) spoke of the faculty of vision 'as one he had had from early infancy. He thinks all men partake of it, but it is lost by not being cultivated'.[35] In both poets, there is an association of 'the first Poetic spirit' with childhood, and in Wordsworth the word 'first' is invested with more than one meaning. When he writes, 'Such, verily, is the first/Poetic spirit of our human life', the word 'first' means not only the first as opposed to the second or later poetic spirit (whatever that may be: a poetic spirit that depends on more mature knowledge, of other poets or of the pain of life, perhaps) but also the 'first' in the sense of 'primary' and thus 'fundamental', or even 'best'. The 'verily' adds a remarkable seriousness and weight to this assertion ('Verily, verily I say unto you . . . ') which compels the reader to take it very seriously as an expression of the poet's views of the imagination. At this stage the imagination is the creative and receptive power: the power to absorb nature through the senses, and to enter into a creative understanding of it, an *I–Thou* relationship. It is Coleridge's secondary imagination, which when it cannot dissolve, diffuse or dissipate, 'struggles to idealize and to unify'.[36] In the same spirit Buber writes that 'the first myths were hymns of praise'.[37] It is the relationship which Wordsworth celebrates in the first books of *The Prelude*: indeed, this is the importance of the two-part *Prelude*, that it shows Wordsworth enjoying this first poetic spirit without any of the later modifications which come from his experiences in Cambridge, London, and France. In the later books there is a profound awareness of the loss of the original *I–Thou* relation, but also of its replacement by a maturer, more human knowledge of suffering and mortality. The process is briefly, and magisterially, demonstrated in the Immortality Ode, and alluded to in 'Tintern Abbey': in both poems there is a compensation for the original loss, as well as an awareness of what the primary poetic relationship was. And in acquainting ourselves with Wordsworth's poetry, this primary poetic spirit should be seen as a point of departure and return.

The central self of Wordsworth's poetry is connected with this, for it is through the experiencing imagination that the *I–Thou* relation exists, at least in any conscious way. Buber acknowledges a preconscious relation in the spiritual history of primitive man: 'Already in the original relational event he speaks the primary word *I–Thou* in a natural way that precedes what may be termed visualisation of forms – that is, before he has recognised himself as *I*.'[38] This is followed by the event of separation, the consciousness of the self as *I* and the external world as *It*, and then by the spirit, which unites the *I* to the *Thou* in relationship. As we have seen, the process exalts and irradiates both the external world and the self: which perhaps should cause us to modify the customary view of Wordsworth as 'the egotistical sublime', or to see that brilliant phrase as indicating a process of creative interaction rather than of dominating self-hood. There is, to be sure, a great deal of preoccupation with himself in Wordsworth: but this is the necessary part of the relation which is at the centre of his poetry, between a living consciousness and the world which surrounds it.

2 Community

I

The two-part *Prelude*, as we have seen, is Wordsworth's childhood seen as myth: the '*bricoleur*' interprets the signs to make what seems to him a sensible reading of the sensible universe, and in Wordsworth's case the myth is one of childhood happiness, which permits a growth of imagination and a relationship with the external world. Permitting this free development, and surrounding or complementing it, is another mythical deduction, the myth of the good community. As with the patterns of childhood, the word 'myth' here implies, not untruth or wishful thinking, but a system derived from observation: in this case, the schoolboy pleasures of Hawkshead, perhaps contrasted with the family bereavements and the uncongenial relations at Penrith. The experiences which are remembered as significant may be private and mysterious, but they take place within the context of a loving and caring community, and the word 'home' has a special importance. After the boat-stealing and the vision of the pursuing crag, the poet notes

> I left my bark
> And through the meadows homeward went with grave
> And serious thoughts (i. 117–19);

In the two-part *Prelude* there is no indication that this happened at Patterdale, and that the house to which the poet returned was the village inn; yet whether inn or cottage, the return to normal society is an important part of the whole experience, placing the astonishing epiphany within the context of normality. Loneliness and home are counterbalanced again a few lines later:

> In November days,
> When vapours rolling down the valleys made
> A lonely scene more lonesome, among woods

37

At noon, and 'mid the calm of summer nights
When by the margin of the trembling lake
Beneath the gloomy hills I homeward went
In solitude, such intercourse was mine (i. 143–9).

Similarly, in the skating episode which follows, the poet is 'like an untired horse/That cares not for its home' (i. 155–6), an image which fulfils a double function, stressing not only the young man's animal energy but also the fact that eventually he has a home to go to. During the skating episode, the poet has moments of individual exultation and vision, yet it seems as if these moments of insight would not have arisen without the joyous sense of communal delight. The pronouns change from 'we' to 'I' and back to 'we' again, as the child slips away and then rejoins his friends.

Although this appears in Part i of the two-part *Prelude*, it is in Part ii that the individual is securely placed within the community. Part ii begins with games, going on even after the old people and the workmen have gone to bed, which suggests not only the vitality of youth, but also the tolerant presence of young and old together in the village. With these evenings spent out of doors, and the rowing races, Part ii provides a strong flavour of shared experience; the description of the return from the inn on the eastern side of Windermere is especially rich in this respect, for it suggests an almost primitive ritual. There seems to be a conscious collective decision to set down the boy minstrel on the rock, and then to row off and listen to him. When the poet is deeply affected by the beauty of the scene, his individual moment of awareness is enveloped and shared by the communal experience. In the same way, the other pleasures of Part ii are shared ones – meals bought with pocket money after the half-yearly holidays, the ride to Furness Abbey, and the visit to Coniston Hall. In each case the poet takes his place as one of a group, and shares their normal delights and pleasures: this, of course, gives more credibility to his moments of individual insight. Even in the 'spots of time' passages, which are found in Part i of the two-part *Prelude*, the unusual is embedded in the ordinary. The child sees the gibbet on an excursion with 'honest James', and the girl whom he sees carrying a pitcher is a sign that he is not alone; the peculiar insight of the passage is that the first human life he meets after getting lost is so strange and yet also so ordinary – a girl carrying a pitcher through the wind. Similarly the second moment, waiting for the horses, is something which is ordinary and very natural: it happens while the child is looking forward to being at home in the holidays.

The two-part *Prelude*, as we have seen, is a poem of celebration: we must look to the later books for the process of deeper understanding through loss and gain, and this is true of Wordsworth's sense of community just as much as his sense of the child and his vision. The account of the Cambridge years, in particular, is valuable in its confirmation of the poet's attitude towards the community he had known in his early years. At Cambridge he had many friends, and yet he gives the impression of a man turning in towards himself and detached from the others, perhaps because of his recognition of his developing powers. Although he had 'invitations, suppers, wine, and fruit' (III. 41), he nevertheless found himself listening for some inner, authentic voice:

> I look'd for universal things; perused
> The common countenance of earth and heaven;
> And, turning the mind in upon itself,
> Pored, watch'd expected, listen'd (III. 110–13);

He contrasts this inner solitude with the multitudes around him, balancing the words 'solitude' and 'multitude' in plain antithesis:

> So was it with me in my solitude;
> So often among multitudes of men.
> Unknown, unthought of, yet I was most rich,
> I had a world about me; 'twas my own,
> I made it; for it only liv'd to me,
> And to the God who look'd into my mind (III. 139–44).

From this state he gradually awakens, to become sociable and gay; and yet at Cambridge this is not a natural and organic community, built on love, but rather an indiscriminate enjoyment, or casual association. Sometimes the enjoyments were strikingly similar to those which he had left behind – riding, sailing on the water under the stars – but they gave rise to no similar depth of feeling:

> We saunter'd, play'd, we rioted, we talk'd
> Unprofitable talk at morning hours,
> Drifted about along the streets and walks,
> Read lazily in lazy books, went forth

> To gallop through the country in blind zeal
> Of senseless horsemanship, or on the breast
> Of Cam sail'd boisterously; and let the stars
> Come out, perhaps without one quiet thought (III. 251–8).

The difference between this accidental conjunction of under-graduates and the true life of a working community is seen very clearly in the contrast between Book III and Book IV. Book IV is notable for its marvellous reconstruction of a homecoming, and the sense of belonging to a community informs the whole book, from the moment when the poet bounds down the hill shouting for the ferryman to the final episode of the discharged soldier. There is throughout a delightful sense of familiarity: the ferryman is 'the old Ferryman' and the boat is 'the well-known Boat'; after an hour's walk the poet sees the church, unchanged, and is reunited with his 'old Dame'. No doubt both the ferryman and Ann Tyson were aged, but the 'old' is equally a sign of familiarity. Immediately the poet greets everything, inanimate as well as animate, rooms, court, garden, stream; he meets his friends and shouts greetings across fields, takes his place at 'our domestic Table' (the 'our' suggesting the poet's feeling of being part of the house, almost part-owner) and sleeps in his old bed. Perhaps by contrast with the life at Cambridge, he discovers a new quality in the lives of those whom he loved:

> A freshness also found I at this time
> In human Life, the life I mean of those
> Whose occupations really I lov'd.
> The prospect often touch'd me with surprize,
> Crowded and full, and chang'd as seem'd to me,
> Even as a garden in the heat of Spring,
> After an eight-days' absence (III. 181–7).

Looking at the woodmen and shepherds, he regarded their lives 'in a sense/Of love and knowledge' (204–5); he discovered within himself a new tenderness and love as he watched Ann Tyson fall asleep over her Bible. During this long vacation there is, for Wordsworth, a very active and wide-ranging emotional life: in his walks round Esthwaite Water he rediscovers moments of intense natural power, and less deeply, he finds himself engaged once again in all sorts of amusements and youthful pastimes:

                                  gawds,
And feast, and dance, and public revelry,
And sports and games (less pleasing in themselves,
Than as they were a badge glossy and fresh
Of manliness and freedom) (IV. 273–7)

and in the state of mind in which his changing emotions moved so
quickly – the 'party-colour'd show of grave and gay' (347) – one
such occasion gives way to the moment of unconscious
commitment, on the way home after the dance. Once again the
singular experience has the community enjoyment as its frame and
origin: having spent a night of harmless enjoyment, the poet is
aware, as he walks home, not only of the beauty of the scene around
him but also of the life going on in its daily round:

                                              all
The solid Mountains were as bright as clouds,
Grain-tinctured, drench'd in empyrean light;
And, in the meadows and the lower grounds,
Was all the sweetness of a common dawn,
Dews, vapours, and the melody of birds,
And Labourers going forth into the fields (IV. 333–9).

The last line is simple and brilliant; it acknowledges (as the opening
of Book II does) that there are men going to work while the revellers
make for bed, that there is a rhythm of waking, sleeping and work in
the community against which the life of the returned undergraduate
is seen.
    Finally in Book IV the sense of belonging to a community is
powerfully concluded by the memorable episode of the discharged
soldier. The soldier is a strange and rather terrifying figure. He is
quite alone, with no dog or attendant; he seems to want nothing, for
he makes no attempt to move from the milestone to the nearby
village. When the young undergraduate plucks up courage and
addresses him, he answers sensibly, but in a curiously indifferent
way, as if somehow uninvolved with his own plight. Yet the
important feature of the episode is not the soldier's predicament but
the fact that the poet knows exactly where to go and what to do. He
knows which labourer will not mind being woken up, and takes the
soldier to him, 'Then sought with quiet heart my distant home'

(504). Here the word 'home' is an appropriate final word for Book IV, since 'home' is the theme of it. The poet can return to his bed in the familiar cottage with a clear conscience, because he knows that he has done what he could for the soldier, and in so doing he has shown himself to be a member of a loving and caring community. He is one of the inhabitants of the area through which the soldier is passing, and his reaction to the soldier's plight emphasizes that he still (in spite of all the Cambridge influence) belongs there.

II

Wordsworth's sense of community is seen very clearly in the first four books of *The Prelude*, and it can be further defined by its opposite in the description of London in Book VII. Here the contrast between a loved community and a collection of people thrown together, found in the Cambridge section, is developed and amplified. London, to Wordsworth, was a place of wonder from childhood, which he longed to explore more fully. He had heard one thing, in particular, which seemed astonishing to a child brought up in a rural community:

> Above all, one thought
> Baffled my understanding, how men lived
> Even next-door neighbours, as we say, yet still
> Strangers, and knowing not each other's names (VII. 117–20).

Astonishment is the keynote of the London book: such multitudes of people, such a variety of shops and trades, and such a labyrinth of streets. The mind is distracted by a succession of occupations: exhibitions, theatres, law courts, the churches. But at the centre of the whole experience there is an absence of any spirit of organic community. The poet cannot know people, and so he is prevented from loving them. He lives in a house, not a home (76–7), and finds himself unable to relate to others:

> How often in the overflowing Streets,
> Have I gone forward with the Crowd, and said
> Unto myself, the face of every one
> That passes by me is a mystery.
> Thus have I look'd, nor ceas'd to look, oppress'd

By thoughts of what, and whither, when and how,
Until the shapes before my eyes became
A second-sight procession, such as glides
Over still mountains, or appears in dreams;
And all the ballast of familiar life,
The present, and the past; hope, fear; all stays,
All laws of acting, thinking, speaking man
Went from me, neither knowing me, nor known (VII. 594–606).

So that when he sees the blind beggar, with his brief story written on
a paper pinned to his chest, the poet realizes how little he can know
of his fellow-man: in this case the basic facts, in others nothing.

The climax of this inability to know or connect, or even to act
meaningfully, is found in the Hieronymus Bosch-like description of
St Bartholomew's fair. In this the bewildering, monstrous activity,
with its freaks of nature and perverted things, with the tents and
booths 'vomiting, receiving' (693), is seen by the poet as an epitome
of the true nature of the city itself:

An undistinguishable world to men,
The slaves unrespited of low pursuits,
Living amid the same perpetual flow
Of trivial objects, melted and reduced
To one identity, by differences
That have no law, no meaning, and no end (VII. 699–704);

The opposite of this is shown immediately afterwards, as the poet
returns to the organic community with the undramatic Helvellyn
fair at the beginning of Book VIII. In this, the participants are 'a little
Family of Men' (7), having their quietly delightful day. Farmers
buy and sell cows and sheep, and a farmer's daughter, 'Some sweet
Lass of the Valley', sells the produce of her father's orchard: beneath
the shadow of the great mountain, and protected by its embrace, the
folk seem little, yet in spirit great because of their living relationship
to the world about them:

They move about upon the soft green field:
How little They, they and their doings seem,
Their herds and flocks about them, they themselves,
And all that they can further or obstruct!
Through utter weakness pitiably dear

As tender Infants are: and yet how great!
For all things serve them; them the Morning light
Loves as it glistens on the silent rocks,
And them the silent Rocks, which now from high
Look down upon them; the reposing Clouds,
The lurking Brooks from their invisible haunts,
And Old Helvellyn, conscious of the stir
And the blue Sky that roofs their calm abode (VIII. 49–61).

Here the gentle wave-like rhythms ('They, they . . . ', 'them;
them . . . ' blend with the images of vulnerability ('soft', 'little',
'utter weakness', 'tender Infants') and the suggestions of light,
silence and calm, to produce a convincing picture of a community
contented and involved with the world that surrounds them, and
happy with each other. It is easy to suggest that the poet is
prejudiced in his account of these two fairs, and obviously he views
one with a kind of fascinated horror, and the other with a deep
affection and tenderness. But he is not, of course, presenting an
objective sociological account: he is using the two fairs to make a
point about organic and non-organic communities and their ways of
life. The ideal community is one in which a natural gaiety prevails,
as opposed to the violent thirst for the sensational, freakish or
monstrous. The people of the Helvellyn fair have come together for
a day to enjoy a very precious kind of happiness, based on mutual
love and a shared experience. It is an annual event, one which they
welcome as a respite from the ordinary routine of work.

Although this is an annual ritual, it has no religious or sacred
connotations: but in its status, its relationship to the customary daily
practice of the society, it corresponds to the liminal phase of Arnold
van Gennep's *rites de passage*.[1] This phase (from the Latin *limen*, or
'threshold') stands between the first phase of separation and the
final one of aggregation, in which the subject is re-integrated into
society. In this case the participants in the country fair have
deliberately separated themselves from the rest of the world: they
have taken their own private holiday, and even, in one case,
exchanged roles for something humbler:

But One is here, the loveliest of them all,
Some sweet Lass of the Valley, looking out
For gains, and who that sees her would not buy?
Fruits of her Father's Orchard, apples, pears,

(On that day only to such office stooping)
She carries in her Basket, and walks round
Among the crowd, half pleas'd with, half ashamed
Of her new calling, blushing restlessly (VIII. 36–43).

The emphasis on the new calling is strange, until it is realized that a feature of liminal states is the assumption of a humble position by those who are customarily high or secure. The sweet lass is one part of this 'little Family of Men' that has set itself apart on this day and entered a liminal phase, as described by Victor W. Turner:

> We are presented, in such rites, with a 'moment in and out of time', and in and out of secular social structure, which reveals, however fleetingly, some recognition (in symbol if not always in language) of a generalized social bond that has ceased to be and has simultaneously yet to be fragmented into a multiplicity of social ties. These are the ties organized in terms either of caste, class, or rank hierarchies or of segmentary oppositions in the stateless societies beloved of political anthropologists. It is as though there are here two major 'models' for human interrelatedness, juxtaposed and alternating. The first is of society as a structured, differentiated, and often hierarchical system of politico-legal-economic positions with many types of evaluation, separating men in terms of 'more' or 'less'. The second, which emerges recognizably in the liminal period, is of society as an unstructured or rudimentarily structured and relatively undifferentiated *comitatus*, community, or even communion of equal individuals who submit together to the general authority of the ritual elders.[2]

Turner's summary is of great significance for Wordsworth, not only because of the Helvellyn fair passage, but because so much of his poetry is concerned with the meeting of Turner's two 'models'. Although the second emerges recognizably in the liminal period, and is patently present in the Helvellyn fair, it exists as an ideal throughout Wordsworth's poetry, where it is associated with the community, the relatively unstructured society that he knew as a child. In this society men are equal and free, and are to a large extent untroubled by distinctions of caste, class or rank; if there is a structure to the society, it is rudimentary, and less important than the sense of community which emerges, as it were, between the structural lines. This alternative model is called by Turner *'communitas'*, which, he observes, is similar to Buber's term 'community':

> Community is the being no longer side by side (and, one might add, above and below) but *with* one another of a multitude of persons. And this multitude, though it moves towards one goal, yet experiences everywhere a turning to, a dynamic facing of, the others, a flowing from *I* to *Thou*. Community is where community happens.[3]

Turner comments:

> Buber lays his finger on the spontaneous, immediate, concrete nature of communitas, as opposed to the norm-governed, institutionalized, abstract nature of social structure. Yet communitas is made evident or accessible, so to speak, only through its juxtaposition to, or hybridization with, aspects of social structure.[4]

In the society which Wordsworth describes in the early books of *The Prelude* (and throughout the two-part *Prelude*) it is not that distinctions of structure are absent; they just do not matter. The schoolboy exists in a society in which status is forgotten in the 'flowing from *I* to *Thou*' which occurs, not only among the boys themselves, but in such encounters as the joyful return meeting with the ferryman, with his old friends, and with Ann Tyson. The spontaneous *communitas* which survives here is pointed up sharply by the Cambridge episode of the party in Milton's old room, and the late arrival in chapel:

> Upshouldering in a dislocated lump,
> With shallow ostentatious carelessness,
> My Surplice, gloried in, and yet despised,
> I clove in pride through the inferior throng
> Of the plain Burghers, who in audience stood
> On the last skirts of their permitted ground,
> Beneath the pealing Organ. Empty thoughts!
> I am ashamed of them (III. 316–23);

Here is a prime example of structure, of a rank and caste hierarchy which is fundamentally inimical to the *communitas* experienced at school and during the long vacation, the state in which man could meet man without intervenient structural differences.

III

The Helvellyn fair episode shows a spontaneous *communitas* becoming recognizable on a fair-day, a recurring festival in which a community is in a liminal state. I have argued that *communitas* existed in the society of Wordsworth's childhood, because the absence of structural hierarchies permitted it, and perhaps because it was, in relation to other societies, marginal – remote and undeveloped. When, in 1799, the poet retired 'to his native mountains, with the hope of being enabled to construct a literary Work that might live', this may not have been unconnected with a memory of a community, as well as with the local scene. Certainly 'Home at Grasmere', some of which was written shortly after the return,[5] is concerned with the people as well as with the place:

From crowded streets remote,
Far from the living and dead wilderness
Of the thronged World, Society is here
A true Community, a genuine frame
Of many into one incorporate (612–16).

The loss of integration into such a community is profoundly sad. It reaches its most moving expression in Wordsworth in 'The Brothers', also written not long after the return. The poem has its origins in an incident in which a young man walked in his sleep and fell from Pillar Crag; yet it shifts the interest to the unfortunate man's brother, Leonard, who had left his native country to go to sea. After twenty years he returns, resolved to settle down again among his native hills. When he hears from the priest of the death of his brother, Leonard finds himself unable to continue with his plans; he leaves the priest (who does not know him) and meditates on all that he has learnt:

his early years
Were with him: – his long absence, cherished hopes,
And thoughts which had been his an hour before,
All pressed on him with such a weight, that now,
This vale, where he had been so happy, seemed

A place in which he could not bear to live:
So he relinquished all his purposes.
He travelled back to Egremont: and thence,
That night, he wrote a letter to the Priest,
Reminding him of what had passed between them;
And adding, with a hope to be forgiven,
That it was from the weakness of his heart
He had not dared to tell him what he was.
This done, he went on shipboard, and is now
A seaman, a grey-headed Mariner (421–35).

In its understatement this picture of the grey-haired mariner is as
moving as the last sight of the better-known ancient mariner; in
both cases they lose contact with the community in which they once
lived, and remain exiles, growing older and condemned to a life of
perpetual movement. The ancient mariner passes 'like night, from
land to land'; and Leonard's life as an old seaman is contrasted with
the life he has left behind in Ennerdale, a life which knows change,
but change tempered with stability. Indeed, when changes occur,
they are recorded and become a part of local knowledge, thus
helping to bind the inhabitants still more closely together:

                              a sharp May-storm
Will come with loads of January snow,
And in one night send twenty score of sheep
To feed the ravens; or a shepherd dies
By some untoward death among the rocks:
The ice breaks up and sweeps away a bridge;
A wood is felled: – and then for our own homes!
A child is born or christened, a field ploughed,
A daughter sent to service, a web spun,
The old house-clock is decked with a new face;
And hence, so far from wanting facts or dates
To chronicle the time, we all have here
A pair of diaries, – one serving, Sir,
For the whole dale, and one for each fire-side – (150–64)

The priest, who speaks these lines, shows how individual and
collective memories blend to make a community. It is the
community, too, which sanctions the brotherly love between
Leonard and James, and supports it:

Leonard.   It seems, these Brothers have not lived to be
             A comfort to each other –
Priest.   That they might
             Live to such end is what both old and young
             In this our valley all of us have wished,
             And what, for my part, I have often prayed (285–9):

When Leonard goes to sea, the more delicate James is looked after by them all:

He was the child of all the dale – he lived
Three months with one, and six months with another;
And wanted neither food, nor clothes, nor love:
And many, many happy days were his (343–6).

Such mutual support and communal love is what Leonard loses, and in the end finds himself unable to regain. He cannot bring himself to unfold his story, nor can he become reintegrated into the community.

The idea of the community continues in Wordsworth's poetry as a powerful and valuable force. In *The Excursion*, the Pastor stands in opposition to the Solitary, whose disappointment and disillusion have cut him off from mankind; and in 'Michael', Luke is supported by the good wishes and prayers of all the neighbours. In his suffering, too, Michael has the pity of them all:

                'Tis not forgotten yet
The pity which was then in every heart
For the Old Man – and 'tis believed by all
That many and many a day he thither went,
And never lifted up a single stone (462–6).

So that it is the community which turns his misery into tragedy, because it is by the community that he is recognized and pitied.

IV

The myth of the ideal community, therefore, is something which begins in social observation, is developed in the Cambridge and London years, and continues to inform the poetry written after the

return to Grasmere in December 1799. In the poems discussed
above, it is an explicitly significant force; but it is also implicit, in
various ways, in the early poems and in the *Lyrical Ballads*. For
instance, *An Evening Walk*, written during Wordsworth's first two
college vacations and incorporating parts of the earlier 'The Vale of
Esthwaite', is a poem which depends very much on contemporary
influences such as the picturesque. Yet at the centre of the poem, not
apparently concerned with this, is the harrowing description of the
soldier's widow. Her husband has been killed in the American War
of Independence (an unjust colonialist war) and the widow is left
houseless and unsupported, alone with her two children. The
seasons go by: she is faint with the summer heat, beaten by rain and
wind, and finally frozen to death with her children. As a portrait of a
suffering family, it is a powerful and prescient one: an episode in
1792, when a poor woman was found dead on Stainmoor with two
children, is a testimony of its lack of exaggeration. It has something
in common with the middle scenes of *King Lear*: denied a roof, the
woman 'wilders o'er the lightless heath' (285) and shrieks at the
storm ' "Now ruthless Tempest launch thy deadliest dart!" ' (291).[6]
As a spectacle of suffering, this jars with the rest of the poem's benign
description, what Geoffrey Hartman has called its 'incredible visual
appetite';[7] yet its stark portrayal of unhappiness is perhaps
intentional, for it demonstrates bitterly that the picturesque
landscape is not enough, and that it needs to be associated with a
loving and caring community. Nature itself is indifferent to the poor
woman, who needs the protection of others to live, and the love of
others to become fully human.

The primary focus of *An Evening Walk* would seem to be on the
landscape, seen in all its variety at different times of the day and
under different lights. Yet it is also possible to focus on a certain
quality of dissatisfaction in the poem, a note of persistent
melancholy. The portrayal of the picturesque scenes is described at
the beginning of the poem as a curiously artificial exercise, a kind of
cheering up:

> Fair scenes! with other eyes, than once, I gaze,
> The ever-varying charm your round displays,
> Than when, erewhile, I taught, 'a happy child,'
> The echoes of your rocks my carols wild:
> Then did no ebb of chearfulness demand
> Sad tides of joy from Melancholy's hand;

In youth's wild eye the livelong day was bright,
The sun at morning, and the stars of night,
Alike, when first the vales' the bittern fills
Or the first woodcocks roam'd the moonlight hills (17–26).

The recurring notes of melancholy are too insistent to be dismissed
as traditional. They appear, for instance, with a disquieting
modulation from the conventional to the macabre:

– No purple prospects now the mind employ
Glowing in golden sunset tints of joy,
But o'er the sooth'd accordant heart we feel
A sympathetic twilight slowly steal,
And ever, as we fondly muse, we find
The soft gloom deep'ning on the tranquil mind.
Stay! pensive, sadly-pleasing visions, stay!
Ah no! as fades the vale, they fade away.
Yet still the tender, vacant gloom remains,
Still the cold cheek its shuddering tear retains (379–88).

Here there is a disturbing transition from 'tender' to 'vacant', which
suggests that as the landscape fades the pleasing melancholy turns
once again to fundamental unhappiness. The image of the ebb,
from the early section quoted above, corresponds to the fading
landscape of the second: in both the poet is left with a permanent
unhappiness. The landscape may be a consolation, but the sadness is
persistent beneath.

The sadness is connected with the development of an adult
consciousness, and the awareness that life is not as simple as it was
when he was a happy child; it also acknowledges the pain of
separation from a loved one, in the first line, and the 'memory of
departed pleasures' (16). That separation and loss is a theme of the
poem is confirmed by the section near the end in which darkness
(which leaves the poet only with sadness) may be succeeded by the
dawn of hope, and a new happiness. There is a glimpse, far on in the
future, of a restored happiness, of an idyllic life together in a little
cottage: hope, though now 'striving in vain',

decks for me a distant scene,
(For dark and broad the gulph of time between)
Gilding that cottage with her fondest ray,

(Sole bourn, sole wish, sole object of my way;
How fair its lawn and silvery woods appear!
How sweet its streamlet murmurs in mine ear!)
Where we, my friend, to golden days shall rise . . . (413–19).

The vision is wistful, and the prospect is far away. In the foreground is the landscape in all its beauty, but also the pain of human living: the separation from loved ones, and, at the centre of the poem, the uncared-for soldier's widow. She and her children are bereaved by the war, and acknowledged as no one's responsibility; they die, not only because they are cast off by the army and the state, but also because they have no loving and caring community which – as Wordsworth's other poems show – might have prevented their deaths.

V

Cambridge and London, in their different ways, had sharpened Wordsworth's insight into the nature of an ideal community, and his awareness of the happiness of his childhood; *An Evening Walk* is an uncomfortable witness to the feeling for the beauty of his childhood landscape coupled with a poignant sense of unregarded and undeserved suffering. That such pain and such beauty exist side by side is the unresolved difficulty of the poem. The visit to France which follows marks a further stage in the encounter with the problems of man in society, the community and its relation to the individual.

In 1790, Wordsworth and Robert Jones had walked through France on their way to the Alps, and had found the country 'standing on the top of golden hours', in a state of what is recognizably spontaneous *communitas*. They saw

How bright a face is worn when joy of one
Is joy of tens of millions (VI. 359–60).

On his return in 1791, unsettled and uncommitted, this first impression was given substance and strength by the teaching of Beaupuy, who instructed Wordsworth in the political thought of the revolution. Wordsworth later rationalized his previous neglect of these things, suggesting that his uninformed political mind was due to the fact that he had been born into a society where class distinction was almost unknown:

> It was my fortune scarcely to have seen
> Through the whole tenor of my school-day time
> The face of one, who, whether boy or man,
> Was vested with attention or respect
> Through claims of wealth or blood (IX. 221–5);

and he now came to see the revolution as the construction, through political means, of the same kind of society. In the light of the turbulent years of 1791 and 1792, the walking tour through Switzerland assumes (in *Descriptive Sketches*) a new shape: the excitement of the scenery gives way to an awareness of the state of a nation. As in *An Evening Walk*, the poem juxtaposes natural beauty and human unhappiness; now the poet's concern is with a community rather than with individual misery. There are several portraits of unhappy or unfortunate individuals, such as the chamois hunter, or the Grison gipsy, but these become a part of a more comprehensive scene in which many Swiss are in exile, the traveller is appalled by the sight of begging children, and the shrine of Einsiedlen shows the crippled in mind and body looking for cures. Beyond all this are the Alps, which

> ascending white in air,
> Toy with the Sun, and glitter from afar (51–2, 1793 text).

In the light of this contrast between the sufferings of man and the beauties of Alpine scenery, it is possible that the poet's pose of melancholy in *Descriptive Sketches* is not entirely manufactured. *The Prelude* certainly suggests a disillusion at some time during the years which followed, chiefly on account of the declaration of war with France in 1793; the subsequent course of the revolution, and the conduct of the British government, may have been reasons for the bitter power of the 'Letter to the Bishop of Llandaff' and the poems of the years which follow.

VI

The transition between the Wordsworth of 1788, returning from Cambridge to spend his long vacation at Hawkshead, and the

Wordsworth of 1793, living in London and writing the 'Letter', is not just a transition of time and place, or even of experience; it is a transition from one kind of society to another. By the accidents of birth and upbringing, Wordsworth had found himself in a society that was rural, simple, egalitarian; it was small and uncomplicated, and encouraged local loyalties and a sense of solidarity. His subsequent experience in London, Cambridge and France was accompanied by an immersion into an entirely different kind of society: in five years he had made the personal transition from a pre-modern, small-scale environment, to a modern industrialized and urbanized society. He was experiencing, with great immediacy and rapidity, a profound long-term historical and sociological change. He had entered, abruptly and shockingly, what is sometimes known as the 'mass society':

> a territorially extensive society, with a large population, highly urbanized and industrialized. Power is concentrated in this society and much of the power takes the form of manipulation of the mass through the media of mass communication. Civic spirit is poor, local loyalties are few, primordial solidarity is virtually nonexistent. There is no individuality, only a restless and frustrated egoism. It is like the state of nature described by Thomas Hobbes, except that public disorder is restrained through the manipulation of the elite and the apathetic idiocy of the mass. The latter is broken only when, in a state of crisis, the masses rally round some demagogue.[8]

This description, a modern one, summarizes a widely-held nineteenth-century view which arose at least partly as a reaction to the French Revolution. Its resemblance to the deductions which Wordsworth made from his own experience is clear: it emphasizes the loss of local loyalties, of true individuality, and of civic spirit. It sees the mob as vulnerable to the persuasion of a demagogue, as Wordsworth saw Paris falling under the sway of Robespierre; and it emphasizes the manipulative power of mass communications. At first sight this last element seems too modern for the age of Wordsworth, until it is remembered how much emphasis he placed on the poet as 'a man speaking to men', as a teacher, and as travelling before men as well as at their side. It is this view of mass society which informs the final paragraph of *The Prelude*:

Then, though, too weak to tread the ways of truth,
This Age fall back to old idolatry,
Though men return to servitude as fast
As the tide ebbs, to ignominy and shame
By Nations sink together, we shall still
Find solace in the knowledge which we have,
Bless'd with true happiness if we may be
United helpers forward of a day
Of firmer trust, joint-labourers in a work
(Should Providence such grace to us vouchsafe)
Of their redemption, surely yet to come (XIII. 431–41).

Here the poet sees his role (and that of Coleridge) quite clearly: he is
to act, in his own way, as a reformer, an agent against corruption of
the individual and society, and as an upholder of the values which
he remembers as good from the society of his childhood and youth.
In the face of the modern mass society, the poet is to assert the values
of an earlier age: and this is the spirit which invests the poetry of the
next few years with its uncompromising strength and austere
power.[9]

3 Man in Society – the Poetry of Reform .

Wordsworth's concern with man in society is continued in the poems of social protest written from 1795 to 1797, particularly the female vagrant's story in the Salisbury Plain poems, and the 'Imitation of Juvenal', with its attack on the rottenness and corruption of public life. But before considering the Salisbury Plain poems in detail, it is necessary to look at the remarkable circumstances of their composition. The story is well known: how Wordsworth set out with William Calvert, and was then left alone on Salisbury Plain; and how he then walked alone over the Plain, across and up to the Wye Valley, and thence to North Wales. It was perhaps the most memorable of all Wordsworth's journeys: 'my rambles over many parts of Salisbury Plain', he told Isabella Fenwick in 1843, 'left on my mind imaginative impressions the force of which I have felt to this day.'[1] The period of solitude probably lasted for two or three weeks: during it the poet had visions of the ancient Britons, of human sacrifices, and of Druids; he took in sights and sounds which, as Mary Moorman points out, are brought 'before the eye and ear with a curious melancholy vividness'.[2] He also met the little girl of 'We are Seven', and the tinker who later became Peter Bell: by this time Wordsworth (who had probably been sleeping rough) was looking so unkempt and farouche that the tinker thought he might be a murderer, so that both poet and tinker were afraid of each other.[3] The whole process of this journey, from the separation from 'normal' society to the return, has a striking resemblance to the primitive rituals first described by Arnold van Gennep in *The Rites of Passage*. They are of three different kinds: rites of separation, of transition, and of incorporation. The second of these, sometimes known as the 'liminal' phase, has already been described in relation to the Helvellyn fair; it must now be related to the other two, in a structure which has been conveniently summarized by Victor Turner:

> Van Gennep has shown that all rites of passage or 'transition' are marked by three phases: separation, margin (or *limen*, signifying 'threshold' in Latin), and aggregation. The first phase (of separation) comprises symbolic behaviour signifying the detachment of the individual or group either from an earlier fixed point in the social structure, from a set of cultural conditions (a 'state'), or from both. During the intervening 'liminal' period, the characteristics of the ritual subject (the 'passenger') are ambiguous; he passes through a cultural realm that has few or none of the attributes of the past or coming state. In the third phase (reaggregation or reincorporation), the passage is consummated. The ritual subject, individual or corporate, is in a relatively stable state once more and, by virtue of this, has rights and obligations *vis-à-vis* others of a clearly defined and 'structural' type; he is expected to behave in accordance with certain customary norms and ethical standards binding on incumbents of social position in a system of such positions.[4]

Although Wordsworth was not involved in any ritual processes as such, his state, particularly in the 'liminal' period, corresponds closely to the condition of a man during the *rites de passage*. Liminal positions exist between two states, and they involve a complete loss of normal structured or sociological identity within the system: 'they have no status, property, insignia, secular clothing indicating rank or role, position in a kinship system'.[5] As we have seen, the liminal period is one in which the normal structured society is reversed or abandoned (kings before crowning, for example), and it is associated (as in the Helvellyn fair episode) with *communitas*. *Communitas* is opposed to structure: it involves also a heightening of awareness, a quickening of human interrelatedness. Turner provides another useful summary:

> *Communitas* breaks in through the interstices of structure in liminality; at the edges of structure, in marginality; and from beneath structure, in inferiority. It is almost everywhere held to be sacred or 'holy', possibly because it transgresses or dissolves the norms that govern structured and institutionalized relationships and is accompanied by experiences of unprecedented potency.[6]

When Wordsworth's circumstances during the Salisbury Plain
journey are considered, together with the importance he attached to
it and the unexpected potency of his experiences, it would seem that
(although he would not have had the theoretical knowledge to
recognize it as such) he was in a 'liminal' state. In *The Prelude* he
describes the influence upon him of casual acquaintances on the
high road:

> When I began to inquire,
> To watch and question those I met, and held
> Familiar talk with them, the lonely roads
> Were schools to me in which I daily read
> With most delight the passions of mankind,
> There saw into the depth of human souls,
> Souls that appear to have no depth at all
> To vulgar eyes (xii. 161–7).

These people from whom the poet learns are most frequently the
'marginal men', on the edge of society, lowly and obscure (xii. 182);
and as travellers on a road, they are withdrawn, at least for the time
of their journey, from their place in the structured society. As one of
them, Wordsworth has a powerful imaginative experience in the
communitas of his liminal state:

> There on the pastoral Downs without a track
> To guide me, or along the bare white roads
> Lengthening in solitude their dreary line,
> While through those vestiges of ancient times
> I ranged, and by the solitude overcome,
> I had a reverie and saw the past,
> Saw multitudes of men, and here and there,
> A single Briton in his wolf-skin vest
> With shield and stone-axe, stride across the Wold;
> The voice of spears was heard, the rattling spear
> Shaken by arms of mighty bone, in strength
> Long moulder'd of barbaric majesty.
> I called upon the darkness; and it took,
> A midnight darkness seem'd to come and take
> All objects from my sight; and lo! again
> The desart visible by dismal flames (xii. 315–30)!

In this and the vision of human sacrifice which follows, and the later vision of the Druids, the poet is conscious of an insight which could not be achieved under normal conditions. Coleridge picked up the unusual intensity of the whole episode, according to Wordsworth: he told Wordsworth

> That also then I must have exercised
> Upon the vulgar forms of present things
> And actual world of our familiar days,
> A higher power, have caught from them a tone,
> An image, and a character, by books
> Not hitherto reflected (xii. 360–5).

which suggests that this may have been the origin of the distinction between fancy and imagination, rather than the reading of *Descriptive Sketches* described in *Biographia Literaria*. More important than this, however, is the way in which the powerful imaginative experience of the liminal man is linked to an *I–Thou* moment of *communitas*:

> and I remember well
> That in life's every-day appearances
> I seem'd about this period to have sight
> Of a new world, a world, too, that was fit
> To be transmitted and made visible
> To other eyes, as having for its base
> That whence our dignity originates,
> That which both gives it being and maintains
> A balance, an ennobling interchange
> Of action from within and from without,
> The excellence, pure spirit, and best power
> Both of the object seen, and eye that sees (xii. 368–79).

In *The Prelude* this discussion of the full possibilities of human life, the balanced interaction between the internal and external, is followed immediately by the 'climbing of Snowdon' passage. But between this great possibility, this mountain experience in which man's potential is fully realized in his perception of magnificent nature, and the Wordsworth of 1793 on Salisbury Plain, there is a great gulf: it is the gulf which is occupied by human cruelty and misery, by war, poverty and neglect. So, fresh from his liminal experience, Wordsworth turns back to society to write the Salisbury Plain poems.

II

Even before the journey across Salisbury Plain his mind was running on matters of war and poverty; during a month spent in the Isle of Wight he watched the fleet at Spithead preparing for war, contrasting the beauty of the summer evening with the noise of gunfire and all that it implied:

> But hark from yon proud fleet in peal profound
> Thunders the sunset cannon; at the sound
> The star of life appears to set in blood,
> And ocean shudders in offended mood,
> Deepening with moral gloom his angry flood.[7]

'I left the place', Wordsworth later recorded in his Advertisement to 'Guilt and Sorrow', 'with melancholy forebodings. The American war was still fresh in memory. The struggle which was beginning, and which many thought would be brought to a speedy close by the irresistible arms of Great Britain being added to those of the Allies, I was assured in my own mind would be of long continuance, and productive of distress and misery beyond all possible calculation.'[8] The contrast between peace and war, happiness and misery, security and destitution, is a major feature of the Salisbury plain poems. Stephen Gill has given these the titles 'Salisbury Plain' (1793–95) and 'Adventures on Salisbury Plain' (1795–99).[9] The first of these opens with the savage, who is content with his hard lot because he has never known anything better:

> Hard is the life when naked and unhouzed
> And wasted by the long day's fruitless pains,
> The hungry savage, 'mid deep forests, rouzed
> By storms, lies down at night on unknown plains
> And lifts his head in fear, while famished trains
> Of boars along the crashing forests prowl,
> And heard in darkness, as the rushing rains
> Put out his watch-fire, bears contending growl

And round his fenceless bed gaunt wolves in armies howl.

Yet is he strong to suffer, and his mind
Encounters all his evils unsubdued;
For happier days since at the breast he pined
He never knew, and when by foes pursued
With life he scarce has reached the fortress rude,
While with the war-song's peal the valleys shake,
What in those wild assemblies has he viewed
But men who all of his hard lot partake,
Repose in the same fear, to the same toil awake (1–18)?

His position is perilous and unpleasant: there are wars, he is
houseless, and the prey of wild beasts. While these are repeated in
the poem, civilized man is made more unhappy because he is
conscious of his position. He is aware of previous pleasure and of the
injustices of society:

The thoughts which bow the kindly spirits down,
And break the springs of joy, their deadly weight
Derive from memory of pleasures flown,
Which haunts us in some sad reverse of fate,
Or from reflection on the state
Of those who on the couch of Affluence rest,
By laughing Fortune's sparkling cup elate,
While we of comfort reft, by pain depressed,
No other pillow know than Penury's iron breast (19–27).

In the narrative which follows, the traveller crosses the plain under
an angry red evening sky. The storm approaches, and he can find
nowhere to shelter until he sees what appears to be an ancient castle.
A voice urges him to flee, because the castle belongs 'to hell's most
cursed sprites'. So he flees through the wet and moonless night,
until, exhausted, he finds an old ruin. It had been built by a
religious foundation as a shelter for travellers, but for some
unspecified reason 'there no human being could remain/ And now
the walls are named the dead house of the plain' (125–6). Entering,
the traveller is terrified by another voice, which turns out to be that
of a woman crying in her sleep; he wakes her, and she thinks initially
that he is a ghost. When she discovers that he is not, the two talk to
each other with relief, taking comfort in their common humanity,
and discussing the visions which each has seen on the plain.

Wordsworth seems unsure about the woman: she is a Lake
Country girl whose former beauty is seen in delicate yet erotic
natural imagery:

> Like swans, twin swans, that when on the sweet brink
> Of Derwent's stream the south winds hardly blow,
> 'Mid Derwent's water lillies swell and sink
> In union, rose her sister breasts of snow,
> (Fair emblem of two lovers' hearts that know
> No separate impulse) or like infants played,
> Like infants strangers yet to pain and woe.
> Unwearied Hope to tend their motions made
> Long Vigils, and Delight her cheek between them laid (208–16).

But he blurs this effect of the girl who was 'once the prime of
Keswick's plain' by making this not simply a description of her
downfall, but a grandiose comment on the transience of youthful
happiness. It is followed, however, by the extended story of her life,
published in the 1798 *Lyrical Ballads* as 'The Female Vagrant'. It
begins in typical Wordsworthian idyllic conditions: the girl lives
with her father by the side of Derwentwater, existing by means of
fishing and caring for a small flock of sheep. She remembers the
simple pleasures of gardening, gathering cowslips, the sound of
church bells, the pattern of rural domesticity and innocence. Then
comes the cruel change: not only are they driven out of their home,
but they lose the connection with the place they have loved and the
dead mother and wife who is buried there:

> 'At last by cruel chance and wilful wrong
> My father's substance fell into decay.
> Oppression trampled on his tresses grey:
> His little range of water was denied;
> Even to the bed where his old body lay
> His all was seized; and weeping side by side
> Turned out on the cold winds, alone we wandered wide.

> 'Can I forget that miserable hour
> When from the last hill-top my sire surveyed,
> Peering above the trees, the steeple-tower
> That on his marriage-day sweet music made?
> There at my birth my mother's bones were laid
> And there, till then, he hoped his own might rest.

Bidding me trust in God he stood and prayed:
I could not pray, by human grief oppressed,
Viewing our glimmering cot through tears that never ceased
(255–70).

The situation has affinities with the expulsion from paradise in
Paradise Lost, when Adam and Eve look back at their old home and
shed natural tears. But the world which is all before this father and
daughter is cruel and unstable. They make their way to the home of
the girl's betrothed, and live happily for a short while: she has three
children, and her father dies in peace. But the war brings with it an
economic depression; the husband, unable to beg, joins the army for
the sake of his hungry children, and his wife and the children go
with him to America. There, within a year, the husband and
children die, leaving the woman alone and destitute. She is shipped
back to England, where she becomes a wanderer.

The morning after the storm seems more comforting; the dawn is
beautiful, and it is succeeded by a fine morning as the traveller and
the woman make their way to the nearest village, where they will
receive a simple kindness. The poet intervenes to tell them so:

Enter that lowly cot and ye shall share
Comforts by prouder mansions unbestowed.
For you yon milkmaid bears her brimming load,
For you the board is piled with homely bread (417–20).

But they are reminded that this is a brief oasis in the desert of misery:

And think that life is like this desart broad,
Where all the happiest find is but a shed
And a green spot 'mid wastes interminably spread (421–3).

This version of the poem concludes with an angry commentary on
the injustices and miseries of society:

Not only is the walk of private life
Unblessed by Justice and the kindly train
Of Peace and Truth, while Injury and Strife,
Outrage and deadly Hate usurp their reign;
From the pale line to either frozen main
The Nations, though at home in bonds they drink

The dregs of wretchedness, for empire strain,
And crushed by their own fetters helpless sink,
Move their galled limbs in fear and eye each link (442–50).

Imperialism is here the object of another Blakean image, though the poem goes on in the manner of Shelley:

Say, rulers of the nations, from the sword
Can ought but murder, pain and tears proceed?
Oh! what can war but endless war still breed (507–9)?

                            Must law with iron scourge
Still torture crimes that grew a monstrous band
Formed by his care, and still his victims urge,
With voice that breathes despair, to death's tremendous verge
                                                    (519–22)?

and it ends with a violent, direct, revolutionary call:

Heroes of Truth pursue your march, uptear
Th'Oppressor's dungeon from its deepest base;
High o'er the towers of Pride undaunted rear
Resistless in your might the herculean mace
Of Reason; let foul Error's monster race
Dragged from their dens start at the light with pain
And die; pursue your toils, till not a trace
Be left on earth of Superstition's reign,
Save that eternal pile which frowns on Sarum's plain (541–9).

III

The direct intervention of the poet's speaking voice is part of the general crudeness and unevenness of 'Salisbury Plain'. At its centre there is the forceful portrayal of the oppressed and uprooted family, but this is blurred by Spenserian and Gothic elements, and by the moralizing on youth and time. Stephen Gill's edition of the Salisbury Plain poems enables us to follow the transformation of this into the much finer 'Adventures on Salisbury Plain' (1795–*c*.1799). In this version the traveller meets an aged soldier, badly shod, with swollen legs, and 'propp'd on a trembling staff', a figure who anticipates the leech gatherer in some respects, for when the traveller offers to help him, a certain light flashes from his eyes, a 'wintry lustre'. Yet there are others who are more miserable than he, for he has a house, and is going to meet a daughter in distress:

> his heart was riven
> At the bare thought: the creature that had need
> Of any aid from him most wretched was indeed (25–7).

The reversal of the *King Lear* situation gives more point to the next stage of the poem, in which the traveller finds himself alone at night on the plain, without even Lear's hovel for shelter. At this point Wordsworth begins to build up the traveller's identity, using the account of a murder committed in 1786 (as Stephen Gill points out,[10] he may have seen the mouldering body hanging in chains at Alconbury on his way to Cambridge in 1787). He is a sailor who returns after two years at sea, only to be press-ganged into the navy; after years of fighting, he is released but denied any prize money, which he had hoped to take to his wife as a reward for her lonely years. Angry and frustrated, he journeys home, and within sight of his own house he meets a traveller, robs him and kills him. It is notable that in the account which follows Wordsworth does not emphasize the supernatural (as his probable source does) except for the account of stones rolling over on their own; he seems more concerned to portray the natural than to introduce any Gothic elements. On Salisbury Plain (Wordsworth keeps the location of his original) he sees a body hanging in irons on a gibbet, but no voices issue from the ruined castle. Instead the poet comments on the ruin, seeing it as a witness of barbaric cruelty in former times and of human misery in this:

> Thou hoary Pile! thou child of darkness deep
> And unknown days, that lovest to stand and hear
> The desart sounding to the whirlwind's sweep,
> Inmate of lonesome Nature's endless year;
> Ever since thou sawest the giant Wicker rear
> Its dismal chambers hung with living men,
> Before thy face did ever wretch appear,
> Who in his heart had groan'd with deadlier pain
> Than he who travels now along thy bleak domain (154–62)?

He wanders on until, as in the earlier version, he reaches 'the dead house of the Plain'. Here he meets the female vagrant, who is no longer described as 'the prime of Keswick's plain' and is no longer the occasion of a meditation on transient happiness. But the process by which her initial security is destroyed is made much more explicit. Instead of the vague

> At last by cruel chance and wilful wrong
> My father's substance fell into decay.
> Oppression trampled on his tresses grey:
> His little range of water was denied;
>
> ('Salisbury Plain', 255–8)

there is now a fully described process of social change and upheaval, as a new landowner destroys the old independent peasantry:

> Then rose a mansion proud our woods among,
> And cottage after cottage owned its sway,
> No joy to see a neighbouring house, or stray
> Through pastures not his own, the master took;
> My Father dared his greedy wish gainsay;
> He loved his old hereditary nook,
> And ill could I the thought of such sad parting brook.
>
> But, when he had refused the proffered gold,
> To cruel injuries he became a prey,
> Sore traversed in whate'er he bought and sold:
> His troubles grew upon him day by day,
> Till all his substance fell into decay (300–11).

The process is one which is liable to destroy not only the individual, but also the organic community. It can be seen at work in an entry by Dorothy Wordsworth in the Grasmere journal for 18 May 1800: 'John Fisher overtook me on the other side of Rydale. He talked much about the alteration in the times, and observed that in a short time there would be only two ranks of people, the very rich and the very poor, "for those who have small estates", says he, "are forced to sell, and all the land goes into one hand".'[11] Thus this version of the poem gives more precise examples of man's cruelty to man. In the same way, the female vagrant's account of her husband's war service is more circumstantial. The first version moves quickly through the period of economic depression, the recruiting campaign, and the husband's enlistment, which is immediately followed by the landing of the whole family in America. The second gives a terrible picture of an army waiting to set sail:

> There foul neglect for months and months we bore,
> Nor yet the crowded fleet its anchor stirred.
> Green fields before us and our native shore,
> By fever, from polluted air incurred,
> Ravage was made, for which no knell was heard.
> Fondly we wished, and wished away, nor knew,
> 'Mid that long sickness, and those hopes deferr'd,
> That happier days we never more must view:
> The parting signal streamed, at last the land withdrew.
>
> (361–9)

Which is followed by another new stanza, describing the fleet battling its way through the autumn storms across the Atlantic.

In both versions there is a pause at the point when the woman, having lost her husband and three children, finds herself back on an English ship bound for home. The first version then concludes with a brief account of her return to her native land but to no home, for she has nowhere to go to. It is in this second part of the vagrant's story that the additions are most interesting, for they continue to expand the original in ways which show an emergence of some Wordsworthian (and perhaps Coleridgean) preoccupations. It begins by expanding the original stanza XLI, which is concerned with the horrors of war, deepening and extending its account of a siege:

> The mine's dire earthquake, and the pallid host
> Driven by the bomb's incessant thunder-stroke
> To loathsome vaults, where heart-sick anguish toss'd,
> Hope died, and fear itself in agony was lost!
> Yet does that burst of woe congeal my frame,
> When the dark streets appeared to heave and gape,
> While like a sea the storming army came,
> And Fire from Hell reared his gigantic shape,
> And Murder, by the ghastly gleam, and Rape
> Seized their joint prey, the mother and the child! (438–47).

Not only are the horrors of war shown more vividly; the woman's

fate on her return is shown in much more detail. In the first version
she is 'three years a wanderer'; the second shows her cast adrift,
sleeping in an outhouse, starving, and after three days taken to
hospital. Now Wordsworth introduces the contrast between those
who suffer and those who do not:

> I heard my neighbours, in their beds, complain
> Of many things which never troubled me;
> Of feet still bustling round with busy glee,
> Of looks where common kindness had no part,
> Of service done with careless cruelty,
> Fretting the fever round the languid heart,
> And groans, which, as they said, would make a dead man start.
>
> (489–95)

The contrast is obvious, and looks forward to the final episodes of
the poem as well as back to the soldier at the beginning, whose
daughter is even more miserable and dependent than he is.
Wordsworth not only provides different layers of suffering, but
shows the ease with which those who are not suffering become
discontented. Meanwhile it is the outsiders, the gipsies, who give the
woman help on her discharge from hospital; she is befriended by
them, but is unable to countenance their life which includes
robbery, and so she becomes a vagrant, with nowhere to go. It
seems, as she concludes her tale, as if her only meaningful action is
the retelling of her story:

> She ceased, and weeping turned away,
> As if because her tale was at an end
> She wept; – because she had no more to say
> Of that perpetual weight which on her spirit lay (555–8).

The vagrant is like the ancient mariner: the retelling of her story
seems to be the single, necessary course of action left to her, the one
thing that gives meaning to her life. The events which lead up to this
state are, of course, very different from those which occur in
Coleridge's poem; indeed the printing of the woman's story in the
1798 *Lyrical Ballads* under the title of 'The Female Vagrant' makes a
neat contrast with 'The Ancient Mariner', and shows very clearly
the working out of the plans described by Coleridge in *Biographia
Literaria*. According to Coleridge, *Lyrical Ballads* was to be a series of

poems of two sorts: in one, 'the incidents and agents were to be, in part at least, supernatural'; in the other 'subjects were to be chosen from ordinary life'. While it is not sensible to claim for 'The Female Vagrant' the same kind of imaginative impact as 'The Ancient Mariner', the fact remains that they deal with a similar pattern of experience, a transition from normal happiness to a state of mind which is severely disturbed and which only finds relief in describing its suffering. In Wordsworth's poem the woman dwells on the past, telling the sailor when she resumes that ''twill ease my burden'd mind' (423). In her case the misery is brought about by a series of personal calamities: the initial destruction of the home by the landowner, the economic depression which subsequently destroys her life with her husband, the war which carries off her husband and children, and finally her loneliness and destitution, so that

> homeless near a thousand homes I stood,
> And near a thousand tables pined, and wanted food (467–8).

The stages of her downfall are a paradigm of Wordsworth's obsessions at this time, and make a fascinating contrast to the mysterious action of 'The Ancient Mariner', with its patterns of guilt and expiation. In 'Salisbury Plain' this contrasting similarity is blurred, since the vagrant's story is only one part of the complex action. When she has finished, she and the sailor, who is beset by guilty thoughts, travel on towards the nearest dwelling. On the way they meet a family, which, in contrast to their own, is still united: but the father is beating the child cruelly for some trivial offence, and the spectacle forms a pathetic contrast to the loneliness of the two wanderers, and to their characters – for the sailor, although a murderer, is mild and kind, and the woman is a victim of undeserved suffering. Now the father, who has his family, is unnecessarily enraged (as the people in the hospital complain of things which never trouble the female vagrant); and when the sailor intervenes the father heaps abuse on him, abuse which is horribly prophetic –

> Calling him vagabond, and knave, and mad,
> And ask'd what plunder he was hunting now;
> The gallows would one day of him be glad (635–7).

We are reminded of how true this is when the sailor comforts the

child, and finds blood streaming from his head at the same spot as
the blood came from the man whom he murdered. Yet it is the
sailor, the murderer, who addresses them when they become calm:

> 'Tis a bad world, and hard is the world's law;
> Each prowls to strip his brother of his fleece;
> Much need have ye that time more closely draw
> The bond of nature, all unkindness cease,
> And that among so few there still be peace (658–62):

After this episode, the vagrant and the sailor continue, through a
scene of idyllic pastoral happiness, where a babbling brook winds
through a pleasant valley and a cottage chimney smokes between
the trees. Like the valley of the great dairies in *Tess of the
D'Urbervilles*, the place resounds with the noise of cheerful labour
and the signs of fertility:

> The dripping groves resound with cheerful lays,
> And melancholy lowings intervene
> Of scatter'd herds, that in the meadows graze,
> While through the furrow'd grass the merry milk-maid strays.
> (672–5)

At the cottage the travellers receive 'Comfort by prouder mansions
unbestowed', a good breakfast, and part company, the woman
leaving first; but she is soon back, bringing with her the dying wife of
the sailor (who is also, presumably, the daughter the old soldier was
going to meet at the beginning of the poem). The wife tells her story
briefly: how she was driven from her home and separated from her
two children, because of the suspicion that her husband had done
the murder. When the sailor reveals himself as her lost husband, she
dies of sudden joy; but although her dying looks seem to bless him,
he has little comfort from them, and wishes himself dead. At this
point, after they have kindly seen to the funeral, the cottage folk
realize the truth:

> recollection ran
> Through each occurrence and the links combin'd,
> And while his silence, looks, and voice they scan,
> And trembling hands, they cried, 'He is the man!'
> Nought did those looks of silent woe avail.

'Though we deplore it much as any can,
The law,' they cried, 'must weigh him in her scale;
Most fit it is that we unfold this woful tale' (803–10).

Their decision is a simple and understandable reaction: justice is a necessary matter. In a case like this, however, the law cannot take account of the circumstances, and there is an illuminating difference between what the cottagers, and later the law, see to be the case, and what the reader, who has a knowledge of the sailor's state of mind, feels. The sailor is one of the many unfortunates in the poem, who is enraged by the injustice and frustration which he suffers, and who commits, like Tess Durbeyfield, a single violent act of rebellion against his fate, against the accumulated injustice and ill-fortune of his life. For this he is duly hanged, and hung in irons.

I have already suggested two parallels between 'Adventures on Salisbury Plain' and *Tess of the d' Urbervilles*; a possible third comes in the penultimate stanza of Wordsworth's poem, which antici-pates both Tess's 'I am ready' and Hardy's bitter ' "Justice" was done':

Confirm'd of purpose, fearless and prepared,
Not without pleasure, to the city strait
He went and all which he had done declar'd:
'And from your hands,' he added, 'now I wait,
Nor let them linger long, the murderer's fate.'
Nor ineffectual was that piteous claim.
Blest be for once the stroke which ends, tho' late,
The pangs which from thy halls of terror came,
Thou who of Justice bear'st the violated name!

The final stanza, however, is very different from the figures of Angel Clare and Liza-Lu bent to the earth at the execution of Tess. For suddenly we find Wordsworth anticipating not Hardy but Camus:

They left him hung on high in iron case,
And dissolute men, unthinking and untaught,
Planted their festive booths beneath his face;
And to that spot, which idle thousands sought,
Women and children were by fathers brought;
And now some kindred sufferer driven, perchance,
That way when into storm the sky is wrought,

Upon his swinging corpse his eye may glance
And drop, as he once dropp'd, in miserable trance (820–8).

Here the sailor's isolation and the destruction of his family are bitterly contrasted with the fathers' enjoyment as they bring their wives and children on a family outing. When they do so they become like the dissolute hawkers, unthinking and untaught. The reader, for his part, has been forcibly made to think, and forcibly taught: he can see that the sailor is mild and good, that his single act of murder was totally uncharacteristic, and indeed that there is more than one kind of murder. There is the murder of war, in which soldiers are 'the brood/That lap (their very nourishment!) their brother's blood' (386–7); and there is the murder which is destruction – the destruction of a man, his wife, and the orphaning of his children, or (in the case of the female vagrant, who is not as irrelevant as might be supposed) the ruin of a happy life and marriage.

The end of the poem is thus a powerful statement of an over-simplification. To call the sailor a murderer, and to hang him up as a public spectacle, is inadequate to the case as we know it. It is like the trial of Meursault in *L'Étranger*, which in the pursuit of justice traces Meursault's actions at the home, the funeral, with his girl friend, and on the beach. The conclusion is that he is a murderer without a spark of human feeling; but the reader is aware that this is not the whole story, and that Meursault is a normal, if selfish, young man, who momentarily reacts violently to a certain set of circumstances. When the trial is nearly over the judge intimates –

he would be glad to hear, before my counsel addressed the court, what were the motives of my crime. So far, he must admit, he hadn't fully understood the grounds of my defence.

I tried to explain that it was because of the sun, but I spoke too quickly and ran my words into each other. I was only too conscious that it sounded nonsensical, and, in fact, I heard people tittering (p. 103).

The spectators who titter at Meursault are the descendants of those who brought their children to gaze on the sailor hanging in irons. In both cases the contrast lies between the guilty sufferer and the unguilty and unsuffering, who thoughtlessly regard the whole thing as a spectacle. The final image, however, is of a fellow-sufferer, driven by the storm, dropping in a trance like the sailor himself, which suggests a continuity of misery.

IV

'Adventures on Salisbury Plain' is a sustained study in marginal figures, isolated from the remainder of society, and assisted by other marginal men, such as the gipsies. The community between the sailor and the soldier's widow is the result of this: in their liminality (attended, as it should be, by poverty and destitution) they encounter each other in a spontaneous *I–Thou* meeting. The sailor's decision to give himself up marks the end of the liminal phase, the re-integration into society, which proceeds to punish him. In spite of his summary trial and execution, there is a certain grim satisfaction for the sailor in returning to society:

> Confirm'd of purpose, fearless and prepared,
> Not without pleasure, to the city strait
> He went and all which he had done declar'd (811–13):

Re-integration and death are better than perpetual isolation: and one nightmare which Wordsworth and Coleridge explore in some other poems of these years is the terror of perpetual isolation. In both *The Borderers* and 'The Ancient Mariner', for example, the protagonists are stuck in a liminal phase, unable to return to normality. In *The Borderers*, Rivers-Oswald is destroyed by power (which also destroyed the French politicians); instead of returning to society, as the sailor does after his crime, Rivers prefers to exercise power with a freedom that comes from having no human ties. He approaches his situation rationally, turning it to his best advantage, and his motives are to be found in the constitution of his character:

> in his pride which borders even upon madness, in his restless disposition, in his disturbed mind, in his superstition, in irresistible propensities to embody in practical experiments his worst & most extravagant speculations, in his thoughts & in his feelings, in his general habits & his particular impulses, in his perverted reason justifying his perverted instincts. The general moral intended to be impressed by the delineation of such a character is obvious: it is to shew the dangerous use which may be made of reason when a man has committed a great crime.[12]

The last sentence, which has been seen as evidence of a reaction against Godwin, emphasizes the dangers of isolation, of an isolation which is a perverted liminality. It is a liminality which is manipulative, not submissive; powerful, not poor; lacking in *communitas* (the 'fellowship' which Rivers envisages with Mortimer is a ghastly parody of *communitas*) and without hope of re-integration.

The Borderers sharpens our understanding of the individual and his relation to the community by demonstrating an arrested process: as a trauma arrests the normal psychological development, so Rivers's crime places him in an arrested ritual state. In his separation from the community he is characteristic of Wordsworth's poetry in this period; Wordsworth is investigating various kinds of separation and re-integration in the poems of individual experience and social reform which are his particular concern in the years leading up to 1798.

4 Man in Society: Creative and Uncreative Separation

Wordsworth, in his early poetry, was concerned with two things: the good community, with its possibilities for an independent, free and creative experience; and the individual's responsible use of that freedom, in his relation with the society in which he lives. When that society is in need of reform, the individual is seen as struggling to maintain the integrity of his beliefs and behaviour in the face of inimical conditions. The state of late eighteenth-century society (outside the relatively primitive society of Wordsworth's childhood) was such that the good man was compelled to become marginal. So we have the poet himself in London; Beaupuy among his fellow officers in France; and figures such as the soldier's widow and the sailor, who are neglected and destroyed by society. How man reacts to such a falling-short of the ideal community is part of Wordsworth's chief concern: the sailor becomes a criminal and a fugitive, though retaining his essential benevolence; Rivers and Mortimer become outlaws, one for the best of motives, the other using his separation from society malevolently.

The central poem which deals with the integrity of the individual, his unswerving adherence to the myth which he knows to be truth, is *The Prelude*. It is also the concern of *The Ruined Cottage*, which focuses the attention more immediately on the victims of an inadequate society, and then suggests a meaningful relationship between such a tragedy and the understanding gained from a life whose liminality permits a degree of spontaneous *communitas*, that of the pedlar.

At the centre of *The Ruined Cottage* is the ruin itself, the walls open to the sky and the garden overgrown with weeds. It provides a meeting place of past and present, and a symbol of a family destroyed; it remains, like a stage set, after the actors have moved away. The departure of the poet and his friend, the old pedlar Armytage, like that at the end of *Descriptive Sketches*, is reminiscent of

Lycidas (as Jonathan Wordsworth has pointed out);[1] it also has a
brief allusion, in the 'farewell look', to the end of *Paradise Lost*:

> The old man rose and hoisted up his load.
> Together casting then a farewell look
> Upon those silent walls, we left the shade;
> And, ere the stars were visible, attained
> A rustic inn, our evening resting-place (534–8).

As Adam and Eve look back at the ruined paradise, so the poet and
pedlar take a last look at a cottage which had once seen a simple
rural happiness; and as *Descriptive Sketches* is concerned with a
painful contemporary reality seen against a background of a lost
golden age, so *The Ruined Cottage* demonstrates the power of famine,
disease and war to destroy an innocent family.

The family's happiness is founded on the father's industry and the
mother's love. When the father falls ill at a time of hardship caused
by bad harvests and war, the family's savings are consumed, and
unemployment is high. The enforced idleness has an immediate
effect on the stability of the family, as Robert becomes depressed
and irritable:

> One while he would speak lightly of his babes
> And with a cruel tongue, at other times
> He played with them wild freaks of merriment,
> And 'twas a piteous thing to see the looks
> Of the poor innocent children (179–83).

In this poem the children are used as powerful indicators of the
progressive downfall of the family. They begin as pretty babes,
become frightened and insecure infants, and finally end up as dead
or in the care of the parish. One of the fragments of 'Incipient
Madness' identified by Jonathan Wordsworth as an origin of *The
Ruined Cottage*,[2] shows Wordsworth using the children as Blake
might have done: they are the victims of poverty and inequality,
whose innocence contrasts powerfully with the corruption of adult
society. The episode shows a tantalizing moment:

> I have seen the Baker's horse
> As he had been accustomed at your door
> Stop with the loaded wain, when o'er his head

Smack went the whip, and you were left, as if
You were not born to live, or there had been
No bread in all the land. Five little ones,
They at the rumbling of the distant wheels
Had all come forth, and, ere the grove of birch
Concealed the wain, into their wretched hut
They all return'd (*The Music of Humanity*, pp. 5–6).

Here the lines 'as if/You were not born to live, or there had been/No bread in all the land', recall 'Holy Thursday' from Blake's *Songs of Experience*, with its thesis that if children are hungry and poor 'It is a land of poverty!':

And their sun does never shine,
And their fields are bleak and bare,
And their ways are filled with thorns:
It is eternal winter there.

In Wordsworth's poem the moment is caught with authentic detail and understatement, when the mother appears:

She said – that wagon does not care for us –
The words were simple, but her look and voice
Made up their meaning (*The Music of Humanity*, p. 6).

In *The Ruined Cottage* the looks of Margaret, as the pedlar perceives them, are an important indication of her state of mind. Even after her death the pedlar sees her in his mind's eye:

        So familiarly
Do I perceive her manner and her look
And presence, and so deeply so I feel
Her goodness, that not seldom in my walks
A momentary trance comes over me (365–9).

In his trance he imagines Margaret asleep, waiting like a figure in a fairy tale to re-awaken to a new life with the returned Robert; but this is wishful thinking, and the reality is Margaret's inexorable decline.

The sufferings of the family are seen against a background of the passing seasons, as the pedlar visits the cottage, usually in spring and autumn. The first lines, however, present a contrast:

'Twas Summer and the sun was mounted high.
Along the south the uplands feebly glared
Through a pale steam, (1–3).

On such a day the poet envisages an ideal way of passing the time:

Pleasant to him who on the soft cool moss
Extends his careless limbs beside the root
Of some huge oak whose aged branches make
A twilight of their own, a dewy shade
Where the wren warbles while the dreaming man,
Half-conscious of that soothing melody,
With side-long eye looks out upon the scene,
By those impending branches made more soft,
More soft and distant (10–18).

'more soft/More soft'; the ideal here certainly seems too luxurious, a
self-indulgent picture of a dreamy contemplation which is altogether unsuited to the strenuous happenings which follow. Perhaps
because of this picture of himself enjoying the beauties of nature, the
poet's description of himself toiling across the common is querulous
and grumbling. It is very hot, the insects are a nuisance, and even
the bursting of the gorse seeds gets on his nerves:

Across a bare wide Common I had toiled
With languid feet which by the slipp'ry ground
Were baffled still, and when I stretched myself
On the brown earth my limbs from very heat
Could find no rest, nor my weak arm disperse
The insect host which gathered round my face
And joined their murmurs to the tedious noise
Of seeds of bursting gorse that crackled round (19–26).

As a foil to what follows, this needs no explaining. The poet begins in
a mood of discontent brought about by refinement; by the end of the
poem he is sadder and wiser, like the wedding guest. At the
beginning he finds the overgrown garden a 'cheerless spot', when he
slakes his thirst from the well; and the old man's first words are

    I see around me here
Things which you cannot see. We die, my Friend,

Nor we alone, but that which each man loved
And prized in his peculiar nook of earth
Dies with him, or is changed, and very soon
Even of the good is no memorial left (67–72).

'And some there be, which have no memorial; who are perished, as
though they had never been; and are become as though they had
never been born; and their children after them.' The echo of
Ecclesiasticus, xliv is clear, but even without it we should not be able
to mistake the pedlar's solemnity, the sudden lofty utterance and the
measured grandeur of the rhythm. The pedlar's task is to make the
poet 'see': to show the reality behind the cheerless ruin. The old man
goes on to relate (contrasting it with the way in which poets call on
hills and streams to mourn) that

Sympathies there are
More tranquil, yet perhaps of kindred birth,
That steal upon the meditative mind
And grow with thought (79–82).

This is the aim of many of the *Lyrical Ballads*, to provide an occasion
for sympathy to 'grow with thought'. 'Simon Lee', for instance, is
'no tale', 'but, should you think,/Perhaps a tale you'll make it.' In
The Ruined Cottage we may begin the process by observing how
Ecclesiasticus, xliv continues:

But these were merciful men, whose righteousness hath not been
forgotten.

With their seed shall continually remain a good inheritance, and
their children are within the covenant.

Their seed standeth fast, and their children for their sakes.

Their seed shall remain for ever, and their glory shall not be
blotted out.

Their bodies are buried in peace; but their name liveth for
evermore.

The people will tell of their wisdom, and the congregation will
shew forth their praise.

Margaret is certainly one of the merciful, and her righteousness has
not been forgotten, by the pedlar at least:

> Many a passenger
> Has blessed poor Margaret for her gentle looks
> When she upheld the cool refreshment drawn
> From that forsaken spring, and no one came
> But he was welcome, no one went away
> But that it seemed she loved him (98–103).

But the remainder of the passage exists only as a terrible irony. The
family is destroyed: with her seed there remains no good
inheritance, for there is only a dead baby and a parish orphan
remaining. Their bodies are not buried in peace, and their name
does not live for evermore; instead of people and congregations
telling of their wisdom and showing forth their praise there is only
the pedlar to keep alive their memory. Everything else has been
destroyed by the wicked and inhuman system which forces men into
the army and leaves their wives and children destitute.

Margaret's death is, like the ending, reminiscent of *Lycidas*,
because it poses the same question: why do the good die, while the
wicked live and prosper? In *The Ruined Cottage* this state of affairs is
accepted as inevitable and treated with the muted indignation
which is part of the pedlar's natural seriousness:

> Oh Sir, the good die first,
> And they whose hearts are dry as summer dust
> Burn to the socket (96–8).

Margaret was not only charitable, but charitable with kindness. She
is also, at the beginning of the poem, a type of natural and contented
motherhood, with an industrious husband who works with the
rhythm of the seasons, using the long daylight hours of spring and
summer:

> I have heard her say
> That he was up and busy at his loom
> In summer ere the mower's scythe had swept
> The dewy grass, and in the early spring
> Ere the last star had vanished (121–5).

The seasons provide a background for the destruction of the family. It is the failure of two harvests, followed by the war, which begins the period of trouble, particularly in winter. In the second autumn the husband falls ill, and on his recovery the link between work and season is lost: he

> idly sought about through every nook
> Of house or garden any casual task
> Of use or ornament, and with a strange
> Amusing but uneasy novelty
> He blended where he might the various tasks
> Of summer, autumn, winter, and of spring (166–71).

The pedlar's first visit after Robert's disappearance is in early spring, when Margaret is still hopeful and busy in the garden; but he comes back in late summer to find the promise of a good crop unfulfilled. The garden is overgrown and untidy, and the pedlar fails to awaken much hope in her. When he returns in the following spring, he finds the ground unprepared for sowing, which is an indication of her further stage of misery, though she still keeps Robert's clothes, loom and staff ready. That autumn he finds that the little babe is dead; though Margaret still walks along the way with him, begging him to enquire after Robert.

Spring, autumn, spring, autumn; the years are marked by the seasons of seed-time and harvest, which emphasize the hopeless negligence of Margaret's life. In the five years which follow we have to imagine the continuing pattern of decline; the pedlar goes elsewhere, and only hears of the last years and her death. She hopes to the end, with a compulsive affection for the place where she has been happy:

> Yet still
> She loved this wretched spot, nor would for worlds
> Have parted hence; and still that length of road,
> And this rude bench, one torturing hope endeared,
> Fast rooted at her heart. And here, my friend,
> In sickness she remained; and here she died,
> Last human tenant of these ruined walls (486–92).

The narrative ends, as it began, with the ruin; but now we, and the poet, share the pedlar's ability to see more than meets the eye in it.

The ruin, at this point, takes on a double character: it is a wretched spot (487), echoing the 'cheerless spot' (60) which the poet first finds it to be; yet it also becomes beautiful in its desolation, as the pedlar observes:

> I well remember that those very plumes,
> Those weeds, and the high spear-grass on that wall,
> By mist and silent rain-drops silvered o'er,
> As once I passed, did to my mind convey
> So still an image of tranquility,
> So calm and still, and looked so beautiful
> Amid the uneasy thoughts which filled my mind,
> That what we feel of sorrow and despair
> From ruin and from change, and all the grief
> The passing shews of being leave behind,
> Appeared an idle dream that could not live
> Where meditation was. I turned away,
> And walked along my road in happiness (513–25).

The transition from wretchedness to beauty, tranquillity and happiness is the central mystery of Wordsworth's poetry. There are several possible explanations of the process, but none is entirely satisfactory. It could be said, for instance, that the poet, like Chaucer's Troilus, becomes aware of human life as essentially transitory, the 'passing shews of being' (522). Or it could be inspired by the contemplation of human endurance, of man's capacity to continue hoping when all seems lost; to this might be added the satisfaction at getting things into perspective, the feeling that the poet has progressed from this grumbling discontent at the beginning to a perception of what others have to suffer. In perceiving this, too, the poem ends in compassion and in brotherly love:

> I stood, and leaning o'er the garden gate
> Reviewed that Woman's suff'rings; and it seemed
> To comfort me while with a brother's love
> I blessed her in the impotence of grief (497–500).

The sufferings of the family inspire a deeper humanity; yet still there is, I think, a mystery about the transition from such a story of unrelieved wretchedness to the pedlar's meditation, and his turning away in happiness. Wordsworth's exploration of the mystery is found in the character of the pedlar.

II

The fragment describing the pedlar was written between January and March 1798. Sections and lines of it were later incorporated into *The Prelude* and *The Excursion*, for it contains many of his central ideas. 'Never again', writes Jonathan Wordsworth, 'did Wordsworth state so confidently the beliefs that underlie his greatest poetry.'[3] He sees the unifying force of 'The Pedlar' as the perception, through natural beauty, of the One Life; this suggests that the fragment has a good deal in common with Coleridge's thought at this time, but also with the idea of nature found in 'Tintern Abbey' and the credal lyrics.

Like *The Ruined Cottage* (and *The Prelude*) the fragment begins with weather – 'In storm and tempest and beneath the beam/Of quiet moons' – though the first influence is of sound, 'by form/Or image unprofaned'. The phrase 'power in sound' (line 3) echoes Coleridge's marvellous synthesis in 'The Eolian Harp', 'A light in sound, a sound-like power in light', in his description of the One Life; but while Coleridge finds the apprehension of the One Life in the joyous rhythms of the created world, Wordsworth's pedlar listens to sounds which have their origin much further away, in time and space:

> sounds that are
> The ghostly language of the ancient earth,
> Or make their dim abode in distant winds (6–8).

As in *The Prelude* 'the common range of visible things' grew dear to the poet, so the pedlar's obscure intimations of sublimity are given form and substance:

> To his mind
> The mountain's outline and its steady form
> Gave simple grandeur, and its presence shaped
> The measure and the prospect of his soul
> To majesty; such virtue had the forms
> Perennial of the ancient hills; nor less
> The changeful language of their countenance
> Gave movement to his thoughts, and multitude,
> With order and relation (23–31).

The pedlar's childhood is then discussed: he was born in a poor home in Cumberland, and learned to read the Bible in a lonely school; returning home, he

> saw the hills
> Grow larger in the darkness, all alone
> Beheld the stars come out above his head,
> And travelled through the wood, no comrade near,
> To whom he might confess the things he saw (21–5).

The insistent emphasis on solitude contrasts with *The Prelude*'s more realistic description of the child Wordsworth as one of a race of boys; here the attention is focused sharply on to the single child. In the account of his involvement with nature, images and ideas occur which are later to be fully explored in *The Prelude*. His communion with nature is 'not from terror free' (27), and

> deep feelings had impressed
> Great objects on his mind with portraiture
> And colour so distinct that on his mind
> They lay like substances, and almost seemed
> To haunt the bodily sense (30–4).

When he becomes a shepherd in later childhood and youth, he relates his early reading of the Bible and Foxe's *Book of Martyrs* to his experience among the mountains. It is a movement from an initial apprehension which is so purely that of natural religion that it seems incompatible with prayer or praise:

> In such access of mind, in such high hour
> Of visitation from the living God,
> He did not feel the God, he felt his works.
> Thought was not: in enjoyment it expired.
> Such hour by prayer or praise was unprofaned;
> He neither prayed, nor offered thanks or praise;
> His mind was a thanksgiving to the power
> That made him. It was blessedness and love (107–14).

It was in the mountains that he really *felt* his faith (Wordsworth gives capitals to FEEL, for emphasis), and he communicates with powers which are beyond the usual experience of man:

> All things there
> Breathed immortality, revolving life,
> And greatness still revolving, infinite.
> There littleness was not, the least of things
> Seemed infinite, and there his spirit shaped
> Her prospects, nor did he *believe* – he saw (123–8).

It is not a matter of faith but of immediate apprehension of an infinite power; and everything which distracted the mind from it, such as the books which the schoolmaster supplied, was counted as loss:

> What could he do?
> Nature was at his heart, and he perceived,
> Though yet he knew not how, a wasting power
> In all things which from her sweet influence
> Might tend to wean him (157–61).

There are two kinds of knowledge: a simple, natural knowledge in which the fundamental laws of science have their demonstration in the world around:

> While yet he lingered in the elements
> Of science, and among her simplest laws,
> His triangles they were the stars of heaven,
> The silent stars; his altitudes the crag
> Which is the eagle's birth-place, or some peak . . . (164–8).

and another kind,

> the lifelessness
> Of truth by oversubtlety dislodged
> From grandeur and from love (177–9).

and he reverences a high truth, which is 'A holy spirit and a breathing soul' (181). Thus he observes Newton's rainbow and the laws of the *Optics* in the waterfalls:

> I have heard him say
> That at this time he scanned the laws of light
> Amid the roar of torrents, where they send

From hollow clefts up to the clearer air
A cloud of mist, which in the shining sun
Varies its rainbow hues (196–201).

Yet this is an uneasy accommodation between nature and the
rational intellect: at this stage in his development the pedlar is
'o'erpowered/ By nature' (187–8) and longs for nature to assert itself
in storms and tempests, because

>   From his intellect,
> And from the stillness of abstracted thought,
> He sought repose in vain (194–6).

His only moments of complete content are when he feels the great
activity of nature, in an apprehension which is beyond the reach of
the intellect:

>   He was only then
> Contented when with bliss ineffable
> He felt the sentiment of being spread
> O'er all that moves, and all that seemeth still,
> O'er all which, lost beyond the reach of thought
> And human knowledge, to the human eye
> Invisible, yet liveth to the heart;
> O'er all that leaps, and runs, and shouts, and sings,
> Or beats the gladsome air; o'er all that glides
> Beneath the wave, yea, in the wave itself,
> And mighty depth of waters (206–16).

The whole passage has affinities with Psalm 104, the great hymn of
praise to God the Creator:

> O Lord, how manifold are thy works! in wisdom hast thou made
> them all: the earth is full of thy riches.

> So is this great and wide sea, wherein are things creeping
> innumerable, both small and great beasts.

although, as Jonathan Wordsworth has pointed out, the belief in the
One Life which follows is not necessarily Christian and biblical; it is
the spontaneous reaction of a man who has known a unity with
created things, and can recapture this in moments of transport:

                    for in all things
He saw one life, and felt that it was joy.
One song they sang, and it was audible,
More audible than when the fleshly ear,
O'ercome by grosser prelude of that strain,
Forgot its functions, and slept undisturbed (217–22).

As at other times the eye is made quiet in order to allow a release of
vision, so here the ear is subordinated to a higher kind of hearing;
usually it is so overwhelmed by the sounds of nature that it closes
itself to their inner meaning and their combined beauty. Now, in a
shamanic vision, it finds a unity with, and hears a voice from 'all
that leaps, and runs, and shouts, and sings,/ Or beats the gladsome
air'. It is this kind of experience which unfits the pedlar for the
profession of teaching, so that he resigns his post and becomes a
pedlar. In so doing he acknowledges that he possesses many of the
characteristics described by Max Weber in his concept of *charisma*: it
is 'a certain quality of an individual personality by virtue of which
he is set apart from ordinary men and treated as endowed with
supernatural, superhuman, or at least specifically exceptional
qualities'.[4] He achieves this through his unusual awareness of
nature, and confirms it by his separation from the ordinary routines
of mankind. In particular charisma, says Weber ('and this is
decisive'), 'always rejects as undignified any pecuniary gain that is
methodical and rational. In general, charisma rejects all rational
economic conduct'.[5] His job as a teacher is recommended to him by
his father (227–30), and when he gives it up

                    The old man
Blessed him and prayed for him, yet with a heart
Foreboding evil (236–8).

As Weber notes, ' "Pure" charisma is contrary to all patriarchal
domination. . . . It is the opposite of all ordered economy. It is the
very force that disregards economy.'[6] So in the pedlar's wandering
and unsettled life there is a disregard of routine, and independence
and originality that is close to the prophetic:

Charismatic authority is thus specifically outside the realm of
every-day routine and the profane sphere. In this respect it is
sharply opposed both to rational, and particularly bureaucratic,

authority, and to traditional authority, whether in its patriarchal, patrimonial, or any other form. Both rational and traditional authority are specifically forms of everyday routine control of action; while the charismatic type is the direct antithesis of this.[7]

This is evidently close to the liminality which we have seen to be a feature of Wordsworth's early poems: here, though, it becomes something else, for the pedlar has a power which is denied to the others. He has an unusual relationship with the rest of society. He moves unharmed 'Among the impure haunts of vulgar men' (250), and evil only serves to bring him closer to others:

> Every shew of vice to him
> Was a remembrancer of what he knew,
> Or a fresh seed of wisdom, or produced
> That tender interest which the virtuous feel
> Among the wicked, which when truly felt
> May bring the bad man nearer to the good,
> But, innocent of evil, cannot
> Sink the good man to the bad (253–60).

Since he walks from place to place he spends much time in company with nature, which keeps his mind 'in a just equipoise of love' (268). Thus he is able to sympathize with all that was enjoyed, and all that was endured:

> He could afford to suffer
> With those whom he saw suffer. Hence it was
> That in our best experience he was rich,
> And in the wisdom of our daily life.
> For hence, minutely, in his various rounds
> He had observed the progress and decay
> Of many minds, of minds and bodies too;
> The history of many families,
> And how they prospered, how they were o'erthrown
> By passion or mischance, or such misrule
> Among the unthinking masters of the earth
> As makes the nations groan (283–94).

The charismatic qualities of the pedlar have given him an unusual capacity for entering into the suffering of others without being overcome. This is because 'He was a chosen son' (326) who was able to hear the voice of nature in wind, mountain and stream. He perceives the active universe in all its forms:

> To every natural form, rock, fruit, and flower,
> Even the loose stones that cover the highway,
> He gave a moral life; he saw them feel,
> Or linked them to some feeling. In all shapes
> He found a secret and mysterious soul,
> A fragrance and a Spirit of strange meaning (332–7).

This is a power which can transform the visible world: with his charisma the pedlar can see further, and see more clearly, a plenitude of being, a world in which he is aware of forces and powers which are denied to ordinary men:

> He had a world about him – 'twas his own,
> He made it – for it only lived to him,
> And to the God who looked into his mind (339–41).

This is a clear statement of his exceptional power, which sets him apart from other men:

> Such sympathies would often bear him far
> In outward gesture, and in visible look,
> Beyond the common seeming of mankind (342–4).

It is important to realize, however, that in this process the kind of suffering which Margaret and her family undergo is not ignored: the poem itself, with its meticulous chronicle of details and its dignified sympathy, is evidence of the pedlar's full awareness of misery. What, in his liminality, he can do, is to comfort, and even suffer with those who are suffering, without being overcome by a sense of the pointless misery of the whole human process. In this context Jeffrey's mockery of the pedlar seems monstrously inappropriate:

> Did Mr Wordsworth really imagine, that his favourite doctrines were likely to gain anything in point of effect or authority by being put into the mouth of a person accustomed to higgle about tape, or brass sleeve-buttons? . . . A man who went about selling

flannel and pocket-handkerchiefs in this lofty diction, would soon frighten away all his customers.[8]

Jeffrey has, not unnaturally, failed to perceive the pedlar's status in relation to the community: a status which exists, not on the socio-economic level that he would have comprehended, but on a much more obscure, and more important level. In his own liminality the pedlar is the preserver of the spontaneous *communitas* which is lost by the structured, or bureaucratic society; and for him the world, with its happiness and its sorrow, is transformed, so that it contains a beauty and a meaning which are unattainable by most men. It is this beauty and meaning which Wordsworth comes to regard as the poet's fundamental duty to observe and record.[9]

5 *Lyrical Ballads*: Preface and Preparation

The concluding lines of *The Prelude* present a picture of Wordsworth and Coleridge as joint-labourers in the service of mankind, looking forward to a better world:

> Prophets of Nature, we to them will speak
> A lasting inspiration, sanctified
> By reason and by truth; what we have loved,
> Others will love; and we may teach them how;
> Instruct them how the mind of man becomes
> A thousand times more beautiful than the earth
> On which he dwells, . . (xiii. 442–8).

In using the word 'prophet', and by laying claim to this elevated role of inspired teacher in such lofty language, Wordsworth is deliberately defining himself and Coleridge as possessors of charismatic power. By a coincidence, 'prophet' is also Weber's word for 'a purely individual bearer of charisma, who by virtue of his mission proclaims a religious doctrine or divine commandment'.[1] The prophet is distinguished from the priest by virtue of his personal call, and bases his claim to authority on personal revelation and charisma. His prophecy is unremunerated: 'The typical prophet propagates ideas for their own sake and not for fees, at least in any obvious or regulated form.'[2]

Sometimes the prophets become, in Weber's term, 'legislators'. This happens most frequently at a time of social tension, when the legislator, notably the Greek *aisymnete*, would resolve conflicts between classes and produce new and sacred laws. Although the prophet's fundamental concern is religion and revelation, he is also, in transitional phases, linked to the teacher of ethics; but he is distinguished from the ordinary teacher of ethics by his vital emotional preaching and his consciousness of a directly revealed religious mission.[3] A moment of such revelation comes to Wordsworth during his first long vacation, as described in Book IV of *The Prelude*:

> I made no vows, but vows
> Were then made for me; bond unknown to me
> Was given, that I should be, else sinning greatly,
> A dedicated Spirit. On I walk'd
> In blessedness, which even yet remains (IV. 341–5).

Although the poet is not conscious of the vows at the moment of their making, he is later able to look back and see the moment as one of dedication. The prophetic sense of mission and dedication informs the opening passage of *The Prelude*: caressed by the breeze, the 'sweet breath of Heaven', the poet feels within

> A corresponding mild creative breeze,
> A vital breeze which travell'd gently on
> O'er things which it had made, and is become
> A tempest, a redundant energy
> Vexing its own creation (I. 44–7).

The breeze is not just 'creative' in the sense of being poetic, but it is actually seen as the power which makes things and later travels over them; it is the power of spring after winter, of thaw after frost,

> the hope
> Of active days, of dignity and thought,
> Of prowess in an honorable field,
> Pure passions, virtue, knowledge, and delight,
> The holy life of music and of verse (I. 50–4).

The inspired nature of the experience, and the holiness of the role, are reiterated in the next paragraph, which anticipates the conclusion of the whole poem in its use of 'prophecy':

> to the open fields I told
> A prophecy: poetic numbers came
> Spontaneously, and cloth'd in priestly robe
> My spirit, thus singled out, as it might seem,
> For holy services: great hopes were mine;

My own voice chear'd me, and, far more, the mind's
Internal echo of the imperfect sound;
To both I listen'd, drawing from them both
A chearful confidence in things to come (i. 59–67).

Throughout this early part of Book i, the poet is conscious of an inadequacy before the revealed vision, and a fitfulness which is unworthy of the promise. Prophets (Isaiah, for instance) have always doubted their fitness, and in Wordsworth's case it takes the form of unhappiness about the impediments that seem to have interrupted his great work: procrastination, selfishness, and a false activity. He has a mind

            that every hour
Turns recreant to her task, takes heart again,
Then feels immediately some hollow thought
Hang like an interdict upon her hopes.
This is my lot; for either still I find
Some imperfection in the chosen theme,
Or see of absolute accomplishment
Much wanting, so much wanting in myself,
That I recoil and droop, and seek repose
In listlessness from vain perplexity,
Unprofitably travelling towards the grave,
Like a false steward who hath much received
And renders nothing back (i. 259–71).

In spite of this, the poet proclaims his underlying fitness for the prophetic role. In his self-enquiry, he discovers that he possesses the first and greatest necessary gift, 'the vital soul' (161). The theme which above all he wishes to express in his preaching is 'some philosophic Song/Of Truth that cherishes our daily life' (231–2). This may seem different from the revelation of divine mystery or message which is the function of the central prophet-types; but Wordsworth's awesome sense of the poet and his task means that this is not the case. In Book i he addresses a governing, creative power:

Wisdom and Spirit of the universe!
Thou Soul that art the eternity of thought!
That giv'st to forms and images a breath
And everlasting motion! not in vain,

> By day or star-light thus from my first dawn
> Of Childhood didst Thou intertwine for me
> The passions that build up our human Soul,
> Not with the mean and vulgar works of Man,
> But with high objects, with enduring things,
> With life and nature, purifying thus
> The elements of feeling and of thought,
> And sanctifying, by such discipline,
> Both pain and fear, until we recognize
> A grandeur in the beatings of the heart (i. 428–41).

It is perhaps significant that this comes immediately after the boat-stealing episode, with its quality of revelation; so too, after the skating scene, the poet again celebrates the power behind such manifestations:

> Ye Presences of Nature, in the sky
> And on the earth! Ye Visions of the hills!
> And Souls of lonely places! can I think
> A vulgar hope was yours when Ye employ'd
> Such ministry, when Ye through many a year
> Haunting me thus among my boyish sports,
> On caves and trees, upon the woods and hills,
> Impress'd upon all forms the characters
> Of danger or desire, and thus did make
> The surface of the universal earth
> With triumph, and delight, and hope, and fear,
> Work like a sea (i. 490–501)?

In these instances, the poet not only provides memorable experiences, or spots of time, but he also relates them to a deeper area of significance. They become a revelation of some power in the universe, and the poet becomes the prophet of that power.

II

In the celebrated letter to John Wilson, written in June 1802, Wordsworth described the poet's function as follows:

> You have given me praise for having reflected faithfully in my

Poems the feelings of human nature. I would fain hope that I have done so. But a great Poet ought to do more than this: he ought, to a certain degree, to rectify men's feelings, to give them new compositions of feeling, to render their feelings more sane, pure, and permanent, in short, more consonant to nature, that is, to eternal nature, and the great moving spirit of things.[4]

The final phrase is the mainspring, to which all the other parts of the paragraph are bound. The feelings are consonant to nature, and by nature is not meant physical nature, but eternal nature and the spirit which invests all things. Wilson's eighteenth-century notion of the poet as a reflector of human nature is seen as only a beginning: it is superseded by the assumption of a moral purpose and power which first corrects evil (rectifying men's feelings) and then encourages positive goodness (rendering their feelings more sane, pure, and permanent), while at the same time putting men in contact with an eternal reality. The role of the poet as described here is very close to that of the prophet as outlined by Weber, from his consciousness of his special powers, to his exertion of that power by his personal gifts, to his 'seizing' of power (rather than receiving it from any human agency) to his transitional function as a teacher of ethics. All of these are found in Wordsworth's discussion of the poet and his role in the Preface to *Lyrical Ballads*.

The object proposed in *Lyrical Ballads* was 'to make the incidents of common life interesting by tracing in them, truly though not ostentatiously, the primary laws of our nature: Chiefly as far as regards the manner in which we associate ideas in a state of excitement.'[5] The association of ideas in a state of excitement is fundamental, as we shall see, to the development of language, and especially to metaphor; but leaving that aside for the moment, we may concentrate on 'the primary laws of our nature' as the area of concern, the interest in what Wordsworth later calls 'elementary feelings'. The true poet, who is attempting to express such feelings, is

a man speaking to men: a man, it is true, endued with more lively sensibility, more enthusiasm and tenderness, who has a greater knowledge of human nature, and a more comprehensive soul, than are supposed to be common among mankind; a man pleased with his own passions and volitions, and who rejoices more than other men in the spirit of life that is in him; delighting to contemplate similar volitions and passions as manifested in the goings-on of the Universe, and habitually impelled to create them where he does not find them.[6]

Here the poet is first and foremost a man, able to communicate with other men and sharing with them human feelings and sorrows. But he is a very special kind of man, who is possessed of special powers, including a more 'comprehensive soul' and a capacity for rejoicing in his own powers, an awareness of his own nature and office. Shaman-like, he also has 'a disposition to be affected more than other men by absent things as if they were present; an ability of conjuring up in himself passions . . . '.[7] He also wishes 'to bring his feelings near to those of the persons whose feelings he describes, nay, for short spaces of time perhaps, to let himself slip into an entire delusion, and even confound and identify his own feelings with theirs'.[8] The loss of self, and the sense of freedom to travel between himself and others, is the mark of the shaman and the ecstatic in all civilizations. It is a state which transcends the limiting constrictions of the human condition, the limits of time, place, and corporeal reality. It is connected with the 'waking dream', with the fact that, as Eliade puts it, 'the dynamisms of the unconscious are not governed by the categories of Space and Time as we know them in conscious experience'.[9] Because of this, the only restriction on the poet is, as Wordsworth recognizes, the need to give pleasure; and this pleasure is a fundamental acknowledgment of the processes of living, moving and having our being – 'it is a homage paid to the native and naked dignity of man, to the grand elementary principle of pleasure, by which he knows, and feels, and lives, and moves'.[10] In consequence the poet is concerned with the primary interaction between man and the external world:

He considers man and the objects that surround him as acting and re-acting upon each other, so as to produce an infinite complexity of pain and pleasure; he considers man in his own nature and in his ordinary life as contemplating this with a certain quantity of immediate knowledge, with certain convictions, intuitions, and deductions which by habit become of the nature of intuitions; he considers him as looking upon this complex scene of ideas and sensations, and finding everywhere objects that immediately excite in him sympathies which, from the necessities of his nature, are accompanied by an overbalance of enjoyment.[11]

This is a fundamental and universal act. The poet, 'singing a song in which all human beings join with him, rejoices in the presence of truth as our visible friend and hourly companion'.[12] He 'binds together by passion and knowledge the vast empire of human society, as it is spread over the whole earth, and over all time'.[13] It is illuminating to notice how the claims of universality and permanence bring the poet close to the maker of myths, and how the description of his relation to the external world anticipates the structuralist's epistemology of nature as sign: the poet considers the external world as sensation, but also as something which we approach with intuitions and sympathies. Earlier in the Preface, dealing with the subjects of poetry (the general passions and the thoughts and feelings of men) Wordsworth had emphasized their basic and primitive foundations:

> And with what are they connected? Undoubtedly with our moral sentiments and animal sensations, and with the causes which excite these; with the operations of the elements and the appearances of the visible universe; with storm and sun-shine, with the revolutions of the seasons, with cold and heat, with loss of friends and kindred, with injuries and resentments, gratitude and hope, with fear and sorrow.[14]

We may compare this with Rousseau's description, in the *Discours sur l'Origine de l'Inégalité*, of the process by which man develops from the animal stage:

> The differences of terrain, climate and season, must have had an effect on their ways of living. Unfertile years, long and hard winters, burning summers which destroyed everything, exacted from them new techniques. Beside the sea and the rivers they invented the fishing line and hook; and they became fishermen and fish-eaters. In the forests they made themselves bows and arrows, and became hunters and warriors; in cold countries they covered themselves with the skins of the beasts that they had killed. . . .
>
> The repeated application of various beings to himself, and of some to others, would naturally in the mind of man have stimulated the perceptions of certain relationships.[15]

Wordsworth is claiming for the poet the same kind of insight which

Rousseau is outlining as the understanding process of natural man: the apprehension of the physical world, and the gradual perception of relations. It is this conception which led Lévi-Strauss to single out Rousseau as the forerunner of modern structuralist anthropology; and both Rousseau and Wordsworth are basically concerned with the external world, and man's understanding of it. As we have seen, the first part of *The Prelude* (in the two-part form of 1799) is occupied with the child Wordsworth's experience of this: while *Lyrical Ballads* are concerned with the presentation of the simplest and most fundamental relationships between man and man and man and nature. The subjects which the poet deals with are 'the great and universal passions of men, the most general and interesting of their occupations, and the entire world of nature'.[16] Hence the emphasis on permanence, which W. J. B. Owen has noted as an important constituent of Wordsworth's poetic theory. In the Preface, this is presented as 'a deep impression of certain inherent and indestructible qualities of the human mind, and likewise of certain powers in the great and permanent objects that act upon it which are equally inherent and indestructible'.[17] In *Lyrical Ballads* these result in

> tracing the maternal passion through many of its subtle windings, as in the poems of the Idiot Boy and the Mad Mother; by accompanying the last struggles of a human being at the approach of death, cleaving in solitude to life and society, as in the Poem of the Forsaken Indian; by shewing, as in the Stanzas entitled We are Seven, the perplexity and obscurity which in childhood attend our notion of death, or rather our utter inability to admit that notion; or by displaying the strength of fraternal, or to speak more philosophically, of moral attachment when early associated with the great and beautiful objects of nature, as in *The Brothers*; or, as in the Incident of Simon Lee, by placing my Reader in the way of receiving from ordinary moral sensations another and more salutary impression than we are accustomed to receive from them.[18]

Such an interest in the fundamental emotions and desires of man is primary, though, like Rousseau, Wordsworth distinguishes between this and the state of the animal man or savage. In the Preface, Wordsworth speaks of 'a state of almost savage torpor'[19] which is the consequence of all the forces which he disliked conspiring to blunt the discriminating powers of the mind. The mind, therefore, is at its best in a pure and natural state: neither savage nor sophisticated, yet accustomed to viewing the external world and making signs from the myriad of impressions which it presents.

Thus the poet, as we have seen, is 'a man speaking to men'. The phrase is simple and reverberant: it indicates the shared humanity and the same kind of relationship which Buber adumbrates in his later, similar phrase, 'Between Man and Man'. The dialogue which Buber describes in that book, the unreserved communication between men which breaks down the normal barriers of self-hood, is perhaps what Wordsworth also unconsciously had in mind: it is curious that Buber should describe one such moment as happening when 'the fictitious fell away and every word was an actuality',[20] which is close to the 'matter-of-factness' of Wordsworth's poetry, his insistence that the words should represent some actuality, his stubborn adherence to uncomfortable facts and unpoetical excrescences like the ankles of Simon Lee. Wordsworth's vulnerability in *Lyrical Ballads*, too, is perhaps due to an unreserve, a preparedness to reveal his individuality and his limitations; for true communication, says Buber,

> Each must expose himself wholly, in a real way, in his humanly unavoidable partiality, and thereby experience himself in a real way as limited by the other, so that the two suffer together the destiny of our conditioned nature and meet one another in it.[21]

This corresponds, not only to the sense of raw exposure found in *Lyrical Ballads*, but also to the extraordinary awareness of the individual, the strong personality that is Wordsworth and those whom he meets, which infuses so much of his poetry. 'The destiny of our conditioned nature', too, is something which is found in many of the tragic *Lyrical Ballads*; and in a meeting like the one in 'Simon Lee', the poet and the old man confront each other in a sharing of their common humanity. This is one reason why it is such an unusual poem: it is a poem, like so much of Wordsworth, about relationship, and not about looking on. Wordsworth is not beholding Simon Lee, but acknowledging the fundamental transition from youth and strength to old age and feebleness; and he meets the old man across the years as one who understands this, and who awaits it himself as part of his conditioned nature. Of Buber's three categories, 'Observing, Looking On, Becoming Aware',

Wordsworth belongs to the third, I believe, in spite of Buber's assertion that 'All great artists have been onlookers'[22] and Coleridge's description of Wordsworth as *spectator ab extra*. Wordsworth is, indeed, an unusual artist, if only because at his greatest moments he is a poet of becoming aware. The observer, says Buber, is 'wholly intent on fixing the observed man in his mind. . . . He probes him and writes him up';[23] the onlooker 'sees the object freely, and undisturbed awaits what will be presented to him. . . . He gives his memory no tasks, he trusts its organic work which preserves what is worth preserving.'[24] Although this second figure sounds like Wordsworth, and has affinities with his use of memory, his central process is different, closer to Buber's 'Becoming Aware'. Buber distinguishes it from the other two as follows:

> It is a different matter when in a receptive hour of my personal life a man meets me about whom there is something which I cannot grasp in any objective way at all, that 'says something' to me. That does not mean, says to me what manner of man this is, what is going on in him, and the like. But it means, says something *to me*, addresses something to me, speaks something that enters my own life. It can be something about this man, for instance that he needs me. But it can also be something about myself. The man himself in his relation to me has nothing to do with what is said. He has no relation to me, he has indeed not noticed me at all. It is not he who says it to me, as that solitary man silently confessed his secret to his neighbour on the seat; but *it* says it.[25]

We may consider the poet's relationship to his characters in *Lyrical Ballads* as an unconscious anticipation of this: there is not only Simon Lee, who needs help; but the other characters, who are unaware of the poet contemplating them, and yet who mysteriously 'communicate' with him. A particularly clear example is 'The Thorn', where Martha Ray in her miserable situation says something to the poet, but nothing to the retired sea-captain, who views her situation through his telescope with unimaginative eyes.

Equally interestingly, for our purposes, Buber suggests that 'It by no means needs to be a man of whom I become aware. It can be an animal, a plant, a stone.'[26] And his assertion that 'I cannot depict or denote or describe the man in whom, through whom, something has been said to me' is the only way in which his description of 'becoming aware' differs from Wordsworth's memorable poetry of awareness. Even here, Wordsworth is capable of saying exactly the same thing:

> It was, in truth,
> An ordinary sight; but I should need
> Colours and words that are unknown to man
> To paint the visionary dreariness
> Which, while I look'd all round for my lost guide,
> Did at that time invest the naked Pool,
> The Beacon on the lonely Eminence,
> The Woman, and her garments vex'd and toss'd
> By the strong wind (*The Prelude*, XI. 308–16).

And something of the same idea may lie behind the jocular bafflement which interrupts the action of 'The Idiot Boy':

> I to the muses have been bound,
> These fourteen years, by strong indentures;
> Oh gentle muses! let me tell
> But half of what to him befel
> For sure he met with strange adventures.
>
> Oh gentle muses! is this kind?
> Why will ye thus my suit repel?
> Why of your further aid bereave me?
> And can ye thus unfriended leave me?
> Ye muses! whom I love so well (347–57).

Wordsworth is acknowledging some inability to describe Johnny to the full, to pierce to the centre of his nature and his reaction to the world around him (this is the section of the poem in which Johnny is alone; there is no 'mediator', as it were, between Johnny and the poet becoming aware); yet it is clear that Johnny 'says something' to the poet in a mysterious way which is very important.

III

The poet of *Lyrical Ballads*, therefore, is a prophet; the poems themselves are concerned, at the deepest level, with dialogue and with 'becoming aware'. For Wordsworth, this is a deeply serious task, and he goes on the the Preface to berate those who see poetry as 'amusement and idle pleasure; who will converse with us as gravely about a *taste* for Poetry, as they express it, as if it were a thing as indifferent as a taste for Rope-dancing, or Frontiniac or Sherry.'[27] His view is that of Aristotle, that 'poetry is the most philosophic of all writing'; and in the magnificent section of the Preface which follows, he speaks directly of dialogue and communication:

> Emphatically may it be said of the Poet, as Shakespeare hath said of man, 'that he looks before and after'. He is the rock of defence of human nature; an upholder and preserver, carrying every where with him relationship and love.[28]

The poet is a key figure in an ideal community, the figure who strives to preserve the best qualities of man in society. We may see how the loss of these poetic qualities accompanies, and perhaps causes, the disintegration of a good society, in Buber's dignified sorrow of 1929:

> Dialogue and monologue are silenced. Bundled together, men march without *Thou* and without *I*, those of the left who want to abolish memory, and those of the right who want to regulate it: hostile and separated hosts, they march into the common abyss.[29]

At this point we can observe the intersection of the individual, benevolently influenced by his upbringing and by the power of nature, and the community. The community requires the love which is inherent in dialogue; it also requires the prophecy which can develop from monologue. In the true process of 'becoming aware', there is a subtle relationship between the I and the Thou, in which there is a uniting of the self to the other, and yet at the same time a quickening and enhancing of the self. The poet, who 'rejoices more than other men in the spirit of life that is in him' and who is 'a man pleased with his own passions and volitions', is also able to entertain a dialogue with others and with the natural world. *Lyrical Ballads*, like *The Prelude*, enhances both individual and community, and stands at the centre of Wordsworth's poetry because it involves dialogue and monologue, poet and external world. Buber has a convenient description of this:

> It is not the solitary man who lives the life of monologue, but he who is incapable of making real in the context of being the

community in which, in the context of his destiny, he moves. It is, in fact, solitude which is able to show the innermost nature of the contrast. He who is living the life of dialogue receives in the ordinary course of the hours something that is said and feels himself approached for an answer. But also in the vast blankness of, say, a companionless mountain wandering that which confronts him, rich in change, does not leave him.[30]

Wordsworth would have understood the idea, and his poetry is a strenuous and continuous struggle towards the life of dialogue. Opposed to it is the life of monologue:

He who is living the life of monologue is never aware of the other as something that is absolutely not himself and at the same time something with which he nevertheless communicates. Solitude for him can mean mounting richness of visions and thoughts but never the deep intercourse, captured in a new depth, with the incomprehensibly real. Nature for him is either an *état d'âme*, hence a 'living through' in himself, or it is a passive object of knowledge, either idealistically brought within the soul or realistically alienated. It does not become for him a word apprehended with senses of beholding and feeling.[31]

An idea which is close to, if not identical to, this one lies behind the otherwise rather puzzling section of the Preface which follows, in which Wordsworth considers poetry and science. 'The Man of Science', he writes, 'seeks truth as a remote and unknown benefactor; he cherishes and loves it in his solitude' (i.e. 'monologue'). Whereas the poet, 'singing a song in which all human beings join with him, rejoices in the presence of truth as our visible friend and hourly companion' ('dialogue'). It is even suggested that it is the poet's duty to bring dialogue to accompany the monologue of science; he will, in the future, 'be ready to follow the steps of the Man of Science, not only in those general indirect effects, but he will be at his side, carrying sensation into the midst of the objects of the Science itself'.[32]

Here Wordsworth is discriminating between two kinds of perception: the scientific, which is 'monologue' in Buber's terms, and the poetic, which carries everywhere with itself relationship and love, the dialogue of the self with the external world which is the opposite of egotistical and yet enhances the self. We may, finally, notice the effect of this on Wordsworth's discussion of poetic language, where the concept of relationship or dialogue is more important than might be supposed. Low and rustic life was chosen, according to Wordsworth,

> because in that situation the essential passions of the heart find a better soil in which they can attain maturity, are less under restraint, and speak a plainer and more emphatic language;[33]

Wordsworth is talking about the conditions which are necessary for the life of dialogue. People in the country are 'less under the action of social vanity';[34] indeed, social life, as Buber saw, does not necessarily mean dialogue. 'I know people', he writes, 'who are absorbed in "social activity" and have never spoken from being to being with a fellow-man.'[35] Dialogue flourishes at moments of great simplicity, as he notes in a Lawrentian passage:

> When I was eleven years of age, spending the summer on my grandparents' estate, I used, as often as I could do it unobserved, to steal into the stable and gently stroke the neck of my darling, a broad dapple-grey horse. It was not a casual delight but a great, certainly friendly, but also deeply stirring happening. If I am to explain it now, beginning from the still very fresh memory of my hand, I must say that what I experienced in touch with the animal was the Other, the immense otherness of the Other, which, however, did not remain strange like the otherness of the ox and the ram, but rather let me draw near and touch it. When I stroked the mighty mane, sometimes marvellously smooth-combed, at other times just as astonishingly wild, and felt the life beneath my hand, it was as though the element of vitality itself bordered on my skin, something that was not I, was certainly not akin to me, palpably the other, not just another, really the Other itself; and yet it let me approach, confided itself to me, placed itself elementally in the relation of *Thou* and *Thou* with me.[36]

Buber goes on to describe how, as he became conscious of his own enjoyment and of his own hand, the spell was broken and the experience was not quite the same. There is a necessary total simplicity between the inner self and the outer world, a simplicity which Wordsworth often refers to by using the word 'naked', a simplicity akin to T. S. Eliot's, 'costing not less than everything';

and it is in this context that the theory of poetic diction in the Preface should be considered. When Wordsworth criticizes Gray's sonnet on the death of Richard West, he does so in what appears to be a high-handed way; critics have objected to the discrimination between five good lines and the remaining bad ones on numerous grounds. Yet the five lines which Wordsworth chose as good have one consistent feature: they show a simplicity of statement which interposes no self-consciousness between the poet and his subject. The virtue of prose, for Wordsworth (and the language of the five lines, he noted, differed in no respect from that of prose) was that it attempted to present the dialogue between the self and the Other in a manner which did not destroy that dialogue. Sometimes he is unsuccessful, in that the very simplicity becomes self-conscious: but the intention deserves respect. Throughout the aim is to create dialogue: this is the point of the citation of the Johnson parody, and the contrast with the 'Babes in the Wood' verse. Johnson's lines

I put my hat upon my head,
And walk'd into the Strand,
And there I met another man
Whose hat was in his hand.

are a very good example of a meeting which is not a dialogue. The hat-wearers pass each other physically, but have no real contact or relationship, and the reader also remains separated, a *spectator ab extra* who regards the whole scene with an amused detachment. The other verse which Wordsworth puts beside it is a very different matter:

These pretty Babes with hand in hand
Went wandering up and down;
But never more they saw the Man
Approaching from the Town.

Here there is no meeting, but the verse encourages relationship at every point. The description of the babes as 'pretty', and their going 'hand in hand' draws attention to their human qualities as little children; they are wandering, which attracts sympathy; and the man whom they do not see focuses interest and enquiry as to his relationship to them. Is he a man who has deserted them? do they trust him? what is the town? why are they where they are? In every way the four lines draw the reader in to a relationship with the children. This is perhaps why Wordsworth concludes the Preface with this comparison, and with the important consideration of subject-matter in poetry:

> Whence arises this difference? Not from the metre, not from the language, not from the order of the words; but the *matter* expressed in Dr. Johnson's stanza is contemptible. The proper method of treating trivial and simple verses to which Dr. Johnson's stanza would be a fair parallelism is not to say this is a bad kind of poetry, or this is not poetry, but this wants sense; it is neither interesting in itself, nor can *lead* to any thing interesting; the images neither originate in that sane state of feeling which arises out of thought, nor can excite thought or feeling in the Reader.[37]

The final sentence makes it clear that Wordsworth is not talking just about the subject of poetry. He is talking about its matter, the ability of poetry to express feeling that arises out of thought, and to excite thought or feeling in the reader. He is talking, in fact, about poetry as dialogue; and the Preface to *Lyrical Ballads* is a sustained essay about dialogue, and the conditions necessary for its expression in poetry.

6 *Lyrical Ballads*: Dialogue and Suffering

Lyrical Ballads is a book which is concerned at every point with the dialogue between man and man, and between man and the external world. In the narrative poems, such as 'Simon Lee', 'The Thorn', 'The Idiot Boy' and 'Goody Blake and Harry Gill', Wordsworth is exploring the relationship of the marginal individual to the society which surrounds him. In the earliest-written poem of the collection,[1] 'The Convict' (never reprinted after 1798) an individual is separated from society by the process of crime and punishment, and the result is degradation and misery:

> His black matted hair on his shoulder is bent,
>   And deep is the sigh of his breath,
> And with steadfast dejection his eyes are intent
>   On the fetters that link him to death.

He is contrasted, Godwinian-fashion, with the king in his luxury. The king is seen as another kind of criminal, is cossetted in comfort:

> When from the dark synod, or blood-reeking field,
>   To his chamber the monarch is led,
> All soothers of sense their soft virtue shall yield,
>   And quietness pillow his head.
>
> But in grief, self-consumed, in oblivion would doze,
>   And conscience her tortures appease,
> 'Mid tumult and uproar this man must repose;
>   In the comfortless vault of disease.

The stark contrast, the polar opposite of existences, is a feature of Wordsworth's poetry at this time. It is found in 'The Old

Cumberland Beggar' and the Salisbury Plain poems, and in 'The Ruined Cottage'; in each of these the suffering or aged protagonists mingle with, confront, or gain comfort from someone in an entirely different situation. The contrasts are absolute: between weak and strong, old and young, sane and mad, loving and harsh – Simon Lee and his former self, Martha Ray and the stolid, insensitive sea-captain, Goody Blake and Harry Gill, the forsaken Indian woman and the remainder of the tribe. Such contrasts make for dramatic intensity, and they also suggest a bare stage, a stark and primitive confrontation: 'Goody Blake and Harry Gill' – a direct opposition of the have-nots with the haves. In these poems the scene is bare and the incidents are few: we contemplate the characters without intervening distractions, and with a sharp and unavoidable attention to their plight. It is all reduced to essentials, like a play by Samuel Beckett. To this may be added the language, which prevents any escape into the poems as art: Wilfred Owen's assertion that he was not concerned with poetry, but rather with war and the pity of war, articulates the same idea. Nor is there much in the way of incident: like the hero of Sartre's *La Nausée*, Roquentin, the figures in *Lyrical Ballads* live lives in which 'there are no adventures'.

The most spectacular example of a lack of incident comes in 'Simon Lee', the full title of which is 'Simon Lee, the Old Huntsman, with an incident in which he was concerned'. The title arouses expectations which are never fulfilled, thus emphasizing the absence of plot or story line. This is also stressed by the one part of the poem which remained virtually untouched amid Wordsworth's many alterations:

> My gentle Reader, I perceive
> How patiently you've waited,
> And I'm afraid that you expect
> Some tale will be related.
>
> O reader! had you in your mind
> Such stores as silent thought can bring,
> O gentle reader! you would find
> A tale in every thing.
> What more I have to say is short,
> I hope you'll kindly take it;
> It is no tale; but should you think
> Perhaps a tale you'll make it (69–80).

At first sight these lines seem an awkward and unnecessary interruption, an obtrusive reminder of a disappointment that there will be no story. But let us put them beside another quotation:

Vladimir:	(*without anger*). It's not certain.
Estragon:	No, nothing is certain.
	Vladimir slowly crosses the stage and sits down beside Estragon.
Vladimir:	We can still part, if you think it would be better.
Estragon:	It's too late now.
	Silence.
Vladimir:	Yes, it's too late now.
	Silence.
Estragon:	Well, shall we go?
Vladimir:	Yes, let's go.
	They do not move.

Curtain

This end of Act I of *Waiting for Godot* is comic, particularly as it is repeated at the end of Act II. But it is also very sad: it summarizes the ineffectual attempts towards significant action made by the two tramps, their uncertainty, their dependence upon one another as they wait for what may never happen, their sense of lost possibilities and purpose in 'it's too late now'.

In both *Waiting for Godot* and 'Simon Lee' there is a sense of expectancy which is frustrated. Something is going to happen: we are going to hear a story, the tramps are going to do something, Godot may arrive today. But the action is denied us: the curtain falls on Vladimir and Estragon, still waiting – 'Nothing happens, nobody comes, nobody goes, it's awful.' In the same way Simon Lee is unchanged at the end, his pathetic gratitude for a small service emphasizing his powerless and feeble old age. We see a man who was once strong and good, now the victim of an irreversible process which allows no hope of relief, but only a passive waiting for the end. It is this which makes appropriate the lines about no tale. Nothing is altered, for nothing can be altered; and there is no tale because, at the level at which Wordsworth is writing, there can be no tale. Both Wordsworth and Beckett have stuck to the essentials of the human condition: two tramps stand by a tree; an old man hacks away at a tree root.

II

The very simplicity of 'Simon Lee' allows dialogue, the meeting of the self and the Other. The poet feels a natural compassion and extends his help, whereupon the old man bursts into tears, since he realizes his own pathetic dependence on others. Both figures in the poem reveal something of themselves: the poet shows the effect of pity (*'la pitié naturelle'*) and the old man his consciousness of his age and his frailty. The poet, at the end, is left with a new and striking idea: that there is a state which is even worse than ingratitude, a state in which man's own feebleness makes him pathetically grateful for each small service. And when this state comes after a life of healthy activity, it throws into relief the brevity of man's life, and the precarious nature of his happiness. All of this means that 'Simon Lee' is a poem of illumination, in which both the protagonists have a meeting which forces them to a deeper understanding of themselves as human beings. This is the significance which is carried by the word 'tale'. On one level it is a narrative, and not to be found in 'Simon Lee'; on another level it indicates a meaning, or understanding, an awareness of something profound in everyday happenings.

Throughout his poetry, Wordsworth is concerned to bring out the meaning, the 'tale', from ordinary moments:

> The dragon's wing, the magic ring,
> I shall not covet for my dower,
> If I along that lowly way
> With sympathetic heart may stray,
> And with a soul of power.
>
> These given, what more need I desire
> To stir, to soothe, or elevate?
> What nobler marvels than the mind
> May in life's daily prospect find,
> May find or there create (*Peter Bell*, 136–45)?

And in *Lyrical Ballads* especially, the subjects are strikingly unsensational. 'Mr. Wordsworth', wrote Coleridge, 'was to propose to himself as his object, to give the charm of novelty to things of every day, and to excite a feeling analogous to the supernatural, by awakening the mind's attention from the lethargy of custom, and directing it to the loveliness and the wonders of the world before us.'[2] The loveliness and wonders are human as well as natural, moments of compassion and understanding which look back to the primitive kindness of Wordsworth's childhood community. One poem which does this explicitly is 'The Old Cumberland Beggar', which is a link with his past life, a memory of what was fast disappearing. It was, Wordsworth noted, 'observed, and with great benefit to my own heart, when I was a child'.[3] The benefit to his heart came from observing the Lake District community caring for the old man, with a natural pity for the weak and helpless. New laws, with workhouses and organized relief, meant (in Wordsworth's view) that charity was 'being *forced* rather from the benevolent than given by them; while the avaricious and selfish, and all in fact but the humane and charitable, are at liberty to keep all they possess from their distressed brethren.'[4] The beggar himself, therefore, although the centre of the poem, is not its whole: he is one element of a community, who has established himself as so pathetic and helpless that he is shown unusual consideration. The horseman stops to give alms instead of throwing them; the toll-woman opens gates specially, and the post-boy goes to some trouble to avoid running over him. It is as though they all have some undefined and inexplicable affection and respect for the itinerant beggar, perhaps because of the sheer strangeness and precariousness of his mode of existence. He is recognizably human, particularly in the first portrait, when he is calculating the number of scraps given to him by the village women, and trying to stop the crumbs from spilling; yet he is also peculiarly remote, partly because he moves so slowly, and partly because of his restricted field of vision. He sees nothing of the world except the patch of ground before his feet, and what he sees is insignificant and fragmentary, a trivial and monotonous scattering of things, like dead leaves, or wheel marks. He goes so slowly that everything passes him by, and even the dogs grow weary of barking at him.

The point about the beggar is that he appears to be liminal, but in fact he is not: he is marginal to the community, certainly, but he has his place in the affections of all. He is an object of charity, and thus separated from the givers, but he meets them in the *communitas* which is inspired by his helplessness:

And while in that vast solitude to which
The tide of things has borne him, he appears

To breathe and live but for himself alone,
Unblamed, uninjured, let him bear about
The good which the benignant law of Heaven
Has hung around him (163–8):

What the reformers wish to do is institutionalize the beggar, which
would effectively destroy the meeting between giver and recipient,
the community of love which sees the beggar as someone to be loved
and cared for. As Wordsworth points out, the very action of loving
and caring makes people feel human, and it is important that the
very poor should have a chance to feel so:

             man is dear to man; the poorest poor
Long for some moments in a weary life
When they can know and feel that they have been,
Themselves, the fathers and the dealers-out
Of some small blessings; have been kind to such
As needed kindness, for this single cause,
That we have all of us one human heart (147–53).

The beggar is therefore not useless; he provides a focus and centre
for the *communitas*, the unstructured feeling of love and dialogue. He
keeps alive a natural compassion which would disappear, because
'lapse of years/And that half-wisdom half-experience gives' (92–3)
lead to neglect and selfishness. 'Half-experience' is the life of
monologue, the inability to enter into the state of true communication; and many of the *Lyrical Ballads* deal, in their direct
way, with full experience, the powerful confrontation with the
other. This is one reason why they are so startling.

'Animal Tranquillity and Decay', or 'Old Man Travelling' as it
was first called, was an overflow from 'The Old Cumberland
Beggar'; but the two are rightly separated. In 'The Old Cumberland Beggar' the emphasis is on the community, the unstructured
feelings of unity and love; in 'Old Man Travelling', the emphasis is
on the individual himself, 'a study of the inward state of the Old
Man expressed in his outward form', as Wordsworth put it.[5] Unlike
the beggar, who has his round of calls, the old man is 'travelling',
leaving any community he may have known. He is truly liminal,
between his home and Falmouth, where his son is in hospital: and in
his liminality he attains a state in which he seems to transcend the
limitations of his body:

>   every limb,
> His look and bending figure, all bespeak
> A man who does not move with pain, but moves
> With thought (4–7).

The effect is very strange: it is as though we are able to sense that movement *is* painful to the old man, but that his actual movements are governed not by the body but by the mind. He is approaching the condition of a shaman in his ability to disregard normal limits of physical behaviour and endurance, and in consequence he is able to go beyond customary needs:

>   he is one by whom
> All effort seems forgotten; one to whom
> Long patience hath such mild composure given,
> That patience now doth seem a thing of which
> He hath no need. He is by nature led
> To peace so perfect that the young behold
> With envy, what the Old Man hardly feels (8–14).

He has passed beyond patience and effort, into some state of perfect peace. The process resembles what Eliade calls 'the change in the organisation of sensory experience' in the initiation of shamans: it is designed to destroy the 'profane' kinds of sensibility and open the mind to the spiritual universe.[6] So full of possibilities is this conception, and so harmoniously described in Wordsworth's poem, that the original lines about going to Falmouth sit uncomfortably with them: the final lines seem too circumstantial, and to run counter to the direction of the earlier part of the poem.[7] Yet, in an extraordinary way they stand for something which is central to Wordsworth's poetry: the interaction of the mystical and sacred with the ordinary and profane. The old man is both an 'ec-static', one who stands outside normal conditions, yet also one who acknowledges the ties of family and human love. His state also permits him, as it permits the charismatic pedlar, to encounter suffering with patience and peace. His son is dying, a victim of a sea-fight: the old man has many miles to go before reaching Falmouth, and may well, one suspects, arrive too late. Yet he accepts everything – the loss of his son, the fact of war, the distance, with a matter-of-factness that is profoundly moving.

III

'The Idiot Boy' is a jubilant poem. It was composed, Wordsworth recalled, 'in the groves of Alfoxden', and he remembered the occasion with gratitude, 'for, in truth, I never wrote anything with so much glee'.[8] The assurance of the poem confirms this: 'rapid and impassioned' was Wordsworth's description of its style, and he declined to add a stanza describing Johnny as handsome because it would interrupt the rapidity and leave 'a deadness upon the feeling'.[9] The result is a poem which vibrates with a zest for living: it overflows into a comic mode which is not overlaid but which becomes an integral part of the poem's meaning. The general air of fuss, bother and comic confusion creates a context, as Mary Jacobus has written, 'in which smiling at Betty can be linked with loving her'.[10] It is a kind of affectionate and humane comedy which is found elsewhere in Wordsworth, most notably in his description of Ann Tyson in Book IV of *The Prelude*; here, as there, the laughter is the laughter of tenderness.

It requires an extraordinary leap of the imagination to conceive of 'The Idiot Boy'. The bewilderment of contemporary readers such as Southey, Dr Burney and John Wilson, shows how difficult they found the subject and its treatment. Faced with a distressing and inconclusive series of happenings treated in the manner of a comic ballad, they were unable to perceive either its exuberance or its seriousness. Wordsworth had to point out the seriousness to John Wilson:

> I have often applied to Idiots, in my own mind, that sublime expression of scripture, that *their life is hidden with God*. They are worshipped, probably from a feeling of this sort, in several parts of the East. Among the Alps where they are numerous, they are considered, I believe, as a blessing to the family to which they belong. I have, indeed, often looked upon the conduct of fathers and mothers of the lower classes of society towards Idiots as the great triumph of the human heart. It is there that we see the strength, disinterestedness, and grandeur of love, nor have I ever been able to contemplate an object that calls out so many excellent and virtuous sentiments without finding it hallowed thereby and having something in me which bears down before it, like a deluge, every feeble sensation of disgust and aversion.[11]

In the poem we have to perceive this noble conception through the fuss and bother, the trivial and matter-of-fact detail, the 'fiddle-faddle': Betty repeats her instructions again and again:

> And Betty o'er and o'er has told
> The boy who is her best delight,
> Both what to follow, what to shun,
> What do, and what to leave undone,
> How turn to left, and how to right (62–6).

Having seen Johnny on his way, she goes back to the ailing Susan, still all of a fluster and full of a pathetic hope:

> And Betty, now at Susan's side,
> Is in the middle of her story,
> What comfort Johnny soon will bring,
> With many a most diverting thing,
> Of Johnny's wit and Johnny's glory.
>
> And Betty's still at Susan's side:
> By this time she's not quite so flurried;
> Demure with porringer and plate
> She sits, as if in Susan's fate
> Her life and soul were buried.
>
> But Betty, poor good woman! she,
> You plainly in her face may read it,
> Could lend out of that moment's store
> Five years of happiness or more,
> To any that might need it (132–46).

The portrait of Betty changes from her as garrulous and flustered, to demure, sitting like a little child with her porringer and plate, and then to her as overflowing with happiness. The ever-changing point of view, and the repetitive style of the ballad, combine to give the impression of hectic activity. By midnight, Betty is worried, and by one o'clock 'she's in a sad quandary'. Her volatility of mood, and general excitability, are forcibly contrasted with the figure of the doctor. When he is knocked up by Betty, the doctor is a comic figure too:

> The doctor at the casement shews,

His glimmering eyes that peep and doze;
And one hand rubs his old night-cap (259–61).

Yet when he discovers what Betty wants (since she is so preoccupied
with Johnny that she forgets to ask him to call and see Susan) he
turns out, as he wakes up, to be too self-possessed to be comic:

'Oh Doctor! Doctor! where's my Johnny?'
'I'm here, what is't you want with me?'
'Oh Sir! you know I'm Betty Foy,
'And I have lost my poor dear boy,
'You know him – him you often see;

'He's not so wise as some folks be.'
'The devil take his wisdom!' said
The Doctor, looking somewhat grim,
'What, woman! should I know of him?'
And, grumbling, he went back to bed (262–71).

Since Betty has knocked him up in the middle of the night to ask
about her lost son, the doctor's irritation is understandable. Yet his
impatience, and his abrupt dismissal of Betty – 'What, woman!' – is
of great significance in the poem. It is reasonable enough, if
uncharitable and dismissive; it is the voice of a man who knows his
position in the community, whose brief appearance in the poem is a
reminder of all the features of society which the poem is *not* about.
The poem is not about a structured society, or about reasonable
action; it is about an idiot, and the human love which surrounds
him.

As an idiot, Johnny is an 'ec-static', one who stands outside
normal experience. As we have seen, there are many such figures in
Wordsworth's poetry, and they are usually suffering, outcasts of one
kind or another: the difference between them and Johnny is that he
has the best of both worlds. He is able to see further, to lead an
imaginative and happy life which is beyond the reach of ordinary
men; yet he also has the joy of being surrounded by human love.
The glee with which Wordsworth wrote the poem may perhaps
have come from this ideal conception: a child who is exceptional,
even charismatic ('hidden with God') but who is also a part of a
loving community. In this instance, the community is very small,
but it is authentic as an example of an *I–Thou* relationship, or the

spontaneous *communitas* of an unstructured society. In this community (using the words in Buber's sense) strange and marvellous things happen: it is a world of natural intuitions, primary affections, and spontaneous recovery from illness. By his rational conduct as a member of a structured society, the doctor cuts himself off from the happiness in which Johnny and Betty find the recovered Susan. It is, we are told, as merry a meeting 'As ever was in Christendom', and the narrator continues:

> The owls have hardly sung their last,
> While our four travellers homeward wend;
> The owls have hooted all night long,
> And with the owls began my song,
> And with the owls must end (442–6).

Four travellers, not three: in this world of natural happiness and love, the human and animal kingdoms are united in mutual joy. At this point Johnny, the divine fool, makes his only speech of the poem (unlesss we include 'burr, burr'):

> And thus to Betty's question, he
> Made answer, like a traveller bold,
> (His very words I give to you,)
> 'The cocks did crow to-whoo, to-whoo,
> 'And the sun did shine so cold.'
> – Thus answered Johnny in his glory,
> And that was all his travel's story (457–63).

Here Johnny is 'in his glory' in more than one sense. In a simple way he is being led home after the night's adventures, surrounded by love and affection, and sitting on the pony as he loves to do; in a deeper sense he is 'in his glory' because he has seen something marvellous and is able to capture it in words that are imaginative (and which were, said Wordsworth 'the foundation of the whole').[12] He has seen owls as the cockerels of the night, and the moon as the cold-shining sun; he has entered a world which is for ever closed to the doctor. Indeed, it is also closed to the reader and the poet, for the muses will not allow the poet to describe what happened to Johnny; but at the end of the poem there is a glimpse of the world which lies beyond the reach of reason and the ordinarily applied senses. What is more, this is obtained by Johnny without the loss of human love.

So that when Geoffrey Hartman says of Wordsworth in this poem
that 'we suspect deeper causes for his delight than he is willing to
acknowledge',[13] we may be tempted to supply a cause: that
Wordsworth was celebrating, in 'The Idiot Boy', an ideal state. It
was one that he had himself known in childhood, and to which he
hoped to return: a state in which the individual had his individual,
shamanic insight, and was, at the same time, surrounded by a loving
and caring community.

IV

'The Thorn' is the polar opposite of 'The Idiot Boy'. Instead of
celebrating insight and *communitas*, it confronts problems of
betrayal, separation, and despair. In both poems there are certain
shared qualities – the ballad style, the central figure who is mad, the
intrusive narrator – but these only serve to emphasize the contrasts
between Johnny, lapped in the warmth of Betty's love, and Martha
Ray, sitting alone on the mountain. The contrast is between Johnny
sitting on the pony 'in his glory', and the huddled figure by the
thorn; while the thorn itself is used with marvellous directness at the
beginning of the poem, as a symbol of stunted growth:

> There is a thorn; it looks so old,
> In truth you'd find it hard to say,
> How it could ever have been young,
> It looks so old and grey.
> Not higher than a two-years' child,
> It stands erect this aged thorn;
> No leaves it has, no thorny points;
> It is a mass of knotted joints,
> A wretched thing forlorn (1–9).

The mixture of the child's stature with the old and grey appearance
of the bush suggests a grotesque mixture of youth and age, and a
stunted life. It is a prey to parasites of all kinds:

> Like rock or stone, it is o'ergrown
> With lichens to the very top,
> And hung with heavy tufts of moss,
> A melancholy crop:
> Up from the earth these mosses creep,

And this poor thorn they clasp it round
So close, you'd say that they were bent
With plain and manifest intent,
To drag it to the ground (12–20);

The picture is one of natural misery, of one organism preying upon another. The thorn is barren, stunted, imprisoned, under attack from mosses and other hostile organisms. The woman who sits beside the thorn has many resemblances: she is barren, by the loss of her baby, and stunted in her natural growth towards happiness by the betrayal of Stephen Hill; as the moss tries to drag down the thorn in some combined effort, so the villagers condemn Martha and try to bring her to justice; as the thorn has to withstand the winter gales, so Martha has to abide the fierce breath of public opinion. Above all, perhaps, as the thorn is 'bound', so Martha herself is imprisoned, locked in the fixation of her own grief. She has a compulsive need to remain beside the thorn:

At all times of the day and night
This wretched woman thither goes,
And she is known to every star,
And every wind that blows (67–70);

The stars and the wind are free and beautiful in comparison with this woman who is obsessed with one place and one idea, fixed by her own grief into one hopeless pattern of living. She is chained to the thorn by what Blake called 'mind-forg'd manacles', just as the thorn itself is bound by the moss. She is static, as Johnny is a wanderer: 'there she sits' is a phrase that recurs in one form or another, just as the refrain does:

And there beside the thorn she sits
When the blue day-light's in the skies,
And when the whirlwind's on the hill,
Or frosty air is keen and still,
And to herself she cries,
'Oh misery! oh misery!
'Oh woe is me! oh misery!' (71–7).

The refrain, which is Martha's only speech in the poem, is evidence of the misery and fixation of her obsessed existence. All her normal energy and happiness has been thwarted and stunted into an attitude of mind which can only be expressed in one repeated way.

We learn about Martha from the narrator. In the *Advertisement* of 1798 he was described as 'loquacious', and in 1800 Wordsworth drew a thumbnail sketch:

> a Captain of a small trading vessel for example, who being past the middle age of life, had retired upon an annuity or small independent income to some village or country town of which he was not a native, or in which he had not been accustomed to live. Such men having little to do become credulous and talkative from indolence.[14]

Thus instead of the exuberant narrator of 'The Idiot Boy', the poet-observer, there is the superstitious narrator, described by Wordsworth as imaginative but lacking in fancy, and prone to 'cleave to the same ideas'. He is a man who seems very much to be the observer: he surveys the landscape with his telescope rather than entering into any relationship with the external world.[15] He is a man of monologue rather than dialogue, or *I–It* rather than *I-Thou*. Throughout the poem he accumulates information; he knows about measurement and spaces:

> Not five years from the mountain-path,
> This thorn you on your left espy;
> And to the left, three yards beyond,
> You see a little muddy pond
> Of water, never dry;
> I've measured it from side to side:
> 'Tis three feet long, and two feet wide (27–33).

The apparent poetical naivety of these lines has obscured what they have to tell us about the sea-captain. The lines are as they are because of the mind which Wordsworth is attempting to describe, the mind which is concerned with facts and the accumulation of information. Occasionally he laments the fact that his knowledge is incomplete – 'I cannot tell; I wish I could' – but he has managed to piece together all the major elements of the story. He has the evidence of his own eyes, when he stumbles across Martha Ray in the Storm, and Conversations with the villagers, such as old farmer Simpson.

The narrator makes no attempt to establish a relationship with the woman, but remains isolated in his world of *I–It*. This is made pointedly clear at the moment when they meet by accident. The sea-captain is caught in the mist and rain:

> I looked around, I thought I saw
> A jutting crag, and off I ran,
> Head-foremost, through the driving rain,
> The shelter of the crag to gain,
> And, as I am a man,
> Instead of jutting crag, I found
> A woman seated on the ground.
>
> I did not speak – I saw her face,
> Her face it was enough for me;
> I turned about and heard her cry,
> 'O misery! O misery!' (192–203).

The Shakespearian 'as I am a man' emphasizes the basic humanity which the sea-captain possesses but which has become overlaid with all those characteristics which cause him to turn away. He has sympathy with her, but is unable to enter into any true communication: Martha remains 'she', the figure sitting on the ground, unaffected by his arrival. The lack of communication is her fault as much as his: she is obsessed by her grief, and he is frightened by her appearance.

If they share the blame for the lack of a relationship, the community also appears inadequate. They are interested in Martha Ray, but only as a subject for speculation: they notice when she is pregnant, and farmer Simpson observes her calmness at the time of the child's birth; after that all is rumour, and very nasty rumour at that:

> 　　　　　some will say
> She hanged her baby on the tree,
> Some say she drowned it in the pond,
> Which is a little step beyond,
> But all and each agree,
> The little babe was buried there,
> Beneath that hill of moss so fair (214–20).

Farmer Simpson's observation of Martha's calm at the time of birth
makes these suggestions of macabre and unnatural death
improbable. Martha has, up to this point, behaved very naturally in
her reaction to Stephen's betrayal, and the whole idea of child-
murder has the air of nasty speculation by the ignorant and
insensitive. Soon they become self-righteous and legalistic; like the
spectators of the hanging sailor at the end of 'Adventures on
Salisbury Plain', they look with complacency on the processes of
justice. They intend to find the evidence by digging up the baby,
and the imagery of the spade seeking for the tiny bones is brutal and
horrifying:

> And some had sworn an oath that she
> Should be to public justice brought;
> And for the little infant's bones
> With spades they would have sought (232–5).

The image of a heavy implement digging into a tiny body is able to
give force to the insensitivity of the village mob. When they are
repulsed by nature, as the grass quivers around them, the sea-
captain's superstition becomes imaginative, as Wordsworth said it
would; yet the description of nature, beautifying and then protect-
ing the baby's grave, serves in this poem only to emphasize the
cruelty and insensitivity of man. The final image is not of the little
hill of moss with its lovely colours, but of the stunted thorn, and the
woman sitting alone.

V

'Goody Blake and Harry Gill' also deals with human justice, in this
case private justice administered by a tyrannical farmer. It is a
strange poem, close to 'The Ancient Mariner' in its employment of
the curse, and yet also full of circumstantial detail. Wordsworth
expands on the original story which he took from Erasmus Darwin's
Zoonamia:

> A young farmer in Warwickshire, finding his hedges broke, and
> the sticks carried away during a frosty season, determined to
> watch for the thief. He lay many cold hours under a haystack, and
> at length an old woman, like a witch in a play, approached, and
> began to pull up the hedge; he waited till she had tied up her

bottle of sticks, and was carrying them springing from his concealment, he seized his prey with violent threats.[16]

In the poem Wordsworth banishes all suggestions of witchcraft by giving Goody economic and social circumstances that are obviously, if painfully, human. She spins all day, and in the evenings too; she does not have the advantage of sharing a cottage, and so she has to bear all the cost of heating. In the summer she is able to sit at the door; but in the winter she has to go to bed to keep warm, and then lies awake because she is too cold to go to sleep. She longs for a storm, because it scatters rotten boughs over the ground, but even this does not give her fuel for more than three days; coal, too, is expensive, since it has to be carried from the north by sea. It is with all this information as a background that Goody is seen taking sticks from hedges, and even here Wordsworth softens Darwin's version. Darwin writes of the farmer 'finding his hedges broke'; Wordsworth only of 'an old hedge' which was alluring to Goody Blake. When Harry sets a trap for her, he is motivated by thoughts of revenge as well as of justice:

> Now Harry he had long suspected
> This trespass of old Goody Blake,
> And vow'd that she should be detected,
> And he on her would vengeance take.

He is delighted to catch her in the act of stealing. He seizes her by the arm and shakes her, crying 'I've caught you then at last!' Goody's response is to kneel down and pray:

> Then Goody, who had nothing said,
> Her bundle from her lap let fall;
> And kneeling on the sticks, she pray'd
> To God that is the judge of all.

Goody's silence, and her direct and immediate response, are impressive: in their dignity they contrast with the pathetic eagerness of Harry's attempts to catch her:

> – He hears a noise – he's all awake –
> Again? – on tip-toe down the hill
> He softly creeps –

When she is caught, Goody makes no attempt to defend herself: she immediately moves the proceedings to a different level by appealing to God 'that is the judge of all'. Suddenly the protagonists are seen, not as farmer and poor woman, but as creatures in the sight of God:

> She pray'd, her wither'd hand uprearing,
> While Harry held her by the arm –
> 'God! who art never out of hearing,
> 'O may he never more be warm!'

At the same time the world of the poem expands, away from the hedge, the barley rick and the two figures, to the night sky and the moon:

> The cold, cold moon above her head,
> Thus on her knees did Goody pray,
> Young Harry heard what she had said,
> And icy-cold he turned away.

And so 'Goody Blake and Harry Gill' turns into a curse poem. The consequences are that Harry is self-isolated from other men: he is like so many of the characters in *Lyrical Ballads*, except that in this case it is his own fault. He becomes cut off from society by his sheer physical debility, which is the result of his having thought himself warm and self-sufficient. He is the prototype of the man who is so concerned with his property and possessions, and so unmindful of the needs of others, that he never becomes fully human, living permanently in the world of *It*.

'Goody Blake and Harry Gill', therefore, restates in a different form the concern for those on the edge of society: the mad, the betrayed, the very old and the very poor. Only once, in 'The Idiot Boy', does Wordsworth portray the marginal man as happy: but in every case their relationship to society is able to sharpen our awareness of the individual and of the structure which surrounds him. In his essay 'Passages, Margins, and Poverty: Religious Symbols of Communitas',[17] Victor Turner points to 'the state of outsiderhood, referring to the condition of being either permanently and by ascription set outside the structural arrangements of a given social system, or being situationally or temporarily set apart'.[18] He relates this to 'structural inferiority', the people of lowest status, the outcasts and the very poor:

in religion and art, the peasant, the beggar, the *harijan*, Gandhi's 'children of God', the despised and rejected in general, have often been assigned the symbolic function of representing humanity, without status qualifications or characteristics. Here the lowest represents the human total, the extreme case most fittingly portrays the whole.[19]

Wordsworth certainly deals in extreme cases, and sees them as representative. The purpose of *Lyrical Ballads*, he said, was 'to follow the fluxes and refluxes of the mind when agitated by the great and simple affections of our nature':

> This object I have endeavoured in these short essays to attain by various means; by tracing the maternal passion through many of its more subtle windings, as in the poems of The Idiot Boy and the Mad Mother; by accompanying the the last struggles of a human being at the approach of death, cleaving in solitude to life and society, as in the Poem of the Forsaken Indian; by shewing, as in the Stanzas entitled We are Seven, the perplexity and obscurity which in childhood attend our notion of death, or rather our utter inability to admit that notion; or by displaying the strength of fraternal, or to speak more philosophically, of moral attachment when early associated with the great and beautiful objects of nature, as in The Brothers; or, as in the Incident of Simon Lee, by placing my Reader in the way of receiving from ordinary moral sensations another and more salutary impression than we are accustomed to receive from them.[20]

The emphasis in this summary is on the human feelings that exist in what Turner calls 'the interstices of structure':

> from the standpoint of structural man, he who is in communitas is an exile or a stranger, someone who, by his very existence, calls into question the whole normative order. That is why when we consider cultural institutions we have to look in the interstices, niches, intervals, and on the peripheries of the social structure to find even a grudging cultural recognition of this primordial human modality of relationship.[21]

In taking his stand on the primary human emotions, Wordsworth is challenging the normal structure, as early critics pointed out. Dr

Burney was worried, for instance, about the meaning of 'Goody Blake and Harry Gill': 'if all the poor are to help themselves, and supply their wants from the possessions of their neighbours, what imaginary wants and real anarchy would it not create?'[22] Yet Wordsworth is not advocating direct political action as such, but asserting the value and nature of primary human relationships which are obscured or stifled by the demands of a structured society. Simpler societies, as Turner points out, 'seem to feel that only a person temporarily without status, property, rank, or office is fit to receive the tribal gnosis or occult wisdom which is in effect knowledge of what the tribespeople regard as the deep structure of culture and indeed of the universe'.[23] He goes on to remind the reader of Lévi-Strauss's argument that the savage mind has much in common with our own, and then draws in the main lines of difference:

> Now men who are heavily involved in jural-political, overt, and conscious structure are not free to meditate and speculate on the combinations and oppositions of thought; they are themselves too crucially involved in the combinations and oppositions of social and political structure and stratification. They are in the heat of the battle, in the 'arena', competing for office, participating in feuds, factions, and coalitions. This involvement entails such effects as anxiety, aggression, envy, fear, exultation, an emotional flooding which does not encourage either rational or wise reflection. But in ritual liminality they are placed, so to speak, outside the total system and its conflicts; transiently, they become men apart – and it is surprising how often the term 'sacred' may be translated as 'set apart' or 'on one side' in various societies. If getting a living and struggling to get it, in and despite of a social structure, be called 'bread' then man does not live 'by bread alone'.[24]

We are at this point close to one of Wordsworth's most explicit statements about man in nature and man in society:

> The world is too much with us; late and soon,
> Getting and spending, we lay waste our powers:
> Little we see in Nature that is ours;
> We have given our hearts away, a sordid boon!
> This Sea that bares her bosom to the moon;

The winds that will be howling at all hours,
And are up-gathered now like sleeping flowers;
For this, for everything, we are out of tune;
It moves us not (Miscellaneous Sonnets, I. xxxiii).

If this is connected with *Lyrical Ballads*, it can be seen that Wordsworth is not just extolling a country life, but stating the deep cultural opposition between *communitas* and structure. Although the figures of *Lyrical Ballads* are not in a state of ritual liminality, they are liminal in their relation to the rest of society. They are also free from the effects which are listed by Turner as accompanying the struggle to live in the social and political structure: anxiety, aggression, envy, fear and exultation. In their poverty and low status, the people of humble and rustic life – whose 'essential passions of the heart find a better soil in which they can attain their maturity, are less under restraint, and speak a plainer and more emphatic language'[25] – are free to partake in the primordial human modality of relationship.

What is involved in this is not just the relationship of man with man, the state of an *I–Thou* perception; it is a more complex phenomenon, involving a different kind of awareness of nature, a view of the external world which has some further connections with the savage mind. These connections are explored in some of the other Lyrical Ballads, though before approaching them we shall need to start again at the point where we began, with the opening scene of *The Prelude*.

Part II

On Nature

I do not know much about gods; but I think that the river
Is a strong brown god – sullen, untamed and intractable,
Patient to some degree, at first recognised as a frontier;
Useful, untrustworthy, as a conveyor of commerce;
Then only a problem confronting the builder of bridges.
The problem once solved, the brown god is almost forgotten
By the dwellers in cities – ever, however, implacable,
Keeping his seasons and rages, destroyer, reminder
Of what men choose to forget. Unhonoured, unpropitiated
By worshippers of the machine, but waiting, watching and waiting.

T. S. Eliot, 'The Dry Salvages'

7 Childhood (II)

To return to the beginning of this study: the first picture of the two-part *Prelude* is of the river and the child bathing, 'A naked savage in the thunder shower'. In this portrait the child is in an ideal state of relationship with the earth, the water, the sky and the rain. He is free to stand still, to run and to sport; he is naked, for he needs no protection against nature or man. In time he will have to join the structured society, to grow into adulthood; but at the moment he is pre-conscious of all this, running over the fields in a state of happy innocence. He is unaware of his future place in society, or of difficulties to come. His situation is that of the savage in the primitive myths of paradise: he enjoys a blessedness and freedom which existed before the fall from primordial innocence and grace. In these myths, Heaven and Earth were either joined before the fall, or were in close proximity: men knew nothing of death, understood the language of animals and lived at peace with them, and did no work, since there was an abundance of food.[1] Because of the fall, Heaven became separated from Earth, man became corrupted, and in the process he lost the powers and delights of the primordial time (except for certain individuals or at certain times and places).

Wordsworth chooses to begin the poem on the growth of his own mind with a description of this state of free primitivism, during which the child enjoys the perfection of the beginning of things. He is aware only of his ability to run, of the rain and the thunder, of the water and sunshine, as he

> stood alone
> Beneath the sky, as if I had been born
> On Indian plains, and from my mother's hut
> Had run abroad in wantonness, to sport
> A naked savage, in the thunder shower (I. 300–4).

The sky and the thunder are important: the god speaks in the voice of the thunder, and the sky, as Eliade points out, 'reveals transcendence, force, eternity':

> Simple contemplation of the celestial vault already provokes a religious experience. The sky shows itself to be infinite, transcendent. It is pre-eminently the 'wholly other' than the little represented by man and his environment. . . . The higher regions inaccessible to man, the sidereal zones, acquire the momentousness of the transcendent, of absolute reality, of eternity. There dwell the gods; there a few privileged mortals make their way by rites of ascent; there, in the conception of certain religions, mount the souls of the dead.[2]

As Wordsworth recalls his earliest childhood, therefore, he does so in terms which emphasize that childhood's state of relationship with the primary forms of nature: a relationship which is trusting, enjoying, experiencing to the full. In *The Prelude* Wordsworth sees his childhood in terms of myth, the myth of paradisal happiness and its loss: the child of Cockermouth is unconsciously aware of a proximate transcendence. Much of the power of the first part of *The Prelude* (Books I and II particularly) comes from its closeness to primary cosmic myth without losing sight of the actual possibilities of life as a child would have known it in the Lake District in the 1770s. In this childhood, the sky can become transfigured, a property of nature that speaks of other things than earthly:

> Oh, when I have hung
> Above the raven's nest, by knots of grass
> Or half-inch fissures in the slippery rock
> But ill sustained, and almost, as it seemed,
> Suspended by the blast which blew amain,
> Shouldering the naked crag, oh, at that time,
> While on the perilous ridge I hung alone,
> With what strange utterance did the loud dry wind
> Blow through my ears; the sky seemed not a sky
> Of earth, and with what motion moved the clouds (i. 57–66)!

The strange utterance of the wind, the unspecified motion of the clouds, and the unearthly sky, all speak of transcendent powers. The repeated 'what' is both exclamation and question, an acknowledgement of the indescribable and an enquiry into the origin of the noise of the wind and the movement of the clouds. The scene is full of power: the blast suspends the child, the wind blows with a strange utterance, and the clouds move with a wonderful motion.

This is one of several passages in the first part of *The Prelude* in which something remarkable is revealed: a moment out of the ordinary, in which the child is made aware of a particular power, or a particular beauty, in the external world. They are manifestations of something wonderful, and are akin to the manifestations of the sacred – hierophanies – in primitive religion. Buber, who relates this to the *I-Thou* mode, connects it with the widespread conception of *mana*, a power in the universe as seen by primitive man:

> The appearances to which he ascribes the 'mystical power' are all elementary incidents that are relational in character, that is, all incidents that disturb him by stirring his body and leaving behind in him a stirring image. The moon and the dead, visiting him by night with pain or pleasure, have that power. But so, too, have the burning sun and the howling beast and the chief whose glance constrains him and the sorcerer whose singing loads him with power for the hunt. Mana is simply the effective force, that which has made the person of the moon, up there in the heavens, into a blood-stirring Thou. The memory of it left its track when the image of the object was separated out from the total stirring image; although it itself, indeed, never appears other than in the doer and bringer of an effect.[3]

This is the power which Wordsworth finds in the universe, in the blood-stirring moments which occurred in his childhood. In the two-part *Prelude* he follows the description of the birds'-nesting with a hypothesis about the origin of the kinds of hierophany which he knew as a child:

> I believe
> That there are spirits which, when they would form
> A favoured being, from his very dawn
> Of infancy do open out the clouds
> As at the touch of lightning, seeking him
> With gentle visitation – quiet powers,
> Retired, and seldom recognized, yet kind,
> And to the very meanest not unknown –
> With me, though, rarely in my boyish days

They communed. Others too there are, who use,
Yet haply aiming at the self-same end,
Severer interventions, ministry
More palpable – and of their school was I (i. 68–80).

The event which follows – the boat-stealing – is the most powerful of
the hierophanies which the poet remembers from his childhood. He
begins it with the spirits – 'They guided me' (i. 81) – and describes
the action as full of life and meaning:

            from the shore
I pushed, and struck the oars, and struck again
In cadence, and my little boat moved on
Just like a man who walks with stately step
Though bent on speed. It was an act of stealth
And troubled pleasure. Not without the voice
Of mountain-echoes did my boat move on, . . (i. 86–92).

The boat moves like a man, and the mountain-echoes have a voice;
Wordsworth is here beginning to animate his universe, in prepar-
ation for the terrifying appearance of the huge cliff. This seems alive
and menacing, for it

As if with voluntary power instinct,
Upreared its head. I struck, and struck again,
And, growing still in stature, the huge cliff
Rose up between me and the stars, and still
With measured motion, like a living thing
Strode after me (i. 109–15).

The cliff is active – part of the 'active universe' which H. W. Piper
has related to eighteenth-century currents of thought – yet it is more
than just active: it is a manifestation, according to Wordsworth, of
the spirits 'who use . . . /Severer interventions'. In the two-part
Prelude he returns to the animistic forces in the external world at the
end of the boat-stealing passage:

Ah, not in vain ye beings of the hills,
And ye that walk the woods and open heaths
By moon or star-light, thus, from my first dawn
Of childhood, did ye love to intertwine
The passions that build up our human soul (i. 130–4).

In turn this is followed by the skating episode. Thus the examples of moments of insight or relation, or moments of hierophany, are intertwined with theoretical statements about the originating spirits, the forces behind the natural world. The poet turns to them again after the skating description:

> Ye powers of earth, ye genii of the springs
> And ye that have your voices in the clouds,
> And ye that are familiars of the lakes
> And of the standing pools, I may not think
> A vulgar hope was yours when ye employed
> Such ministry – when ye through many a year
> Thus, by the agency of boyish sports,
> On caves and trees, upon the woods and hills,
> Impressed upon all forms the characters
> Of danger or desire, and thus did make
> The surface of the universal earth
> With meanings of delight, of hope and fear,
> Work like a sea (i. 186–98).

Mana, it will be remembered, exists in the memory as the relational force, although it never appears except in the thing itself: in Wordsworth's summation, the spirits minister to the child with meanings. Nature is seen as sign, directed and animated by the spirits which allow relation, the confrontation of the self with the Other in the true *I-Thou* meeting. Moments of such meeting are of great importance: they are (to use Eliade's term) kratophanies, or manifestations of force. When the child sees the mountain coming after him, as he thinks, he sees a manifestation of a force in the universe; he is made forcibly aware of a power guiding and ministering to man. Hence the importance of the 'spots of time', which follow in the first part of the two-part *Prelude*: they remain in the memory as evidence of moments of kratophany, so that as the child grows older he can remain certain of the power that he once knew. The 'blood-stirring *Thou*' remains in the memory, to counteract the inexorable augmentation of the world of *It*.

II

Together with the spectacular moments of the 'ministry/More palpable', Wordsworth celebrates a more consistent happiness in

the first part of the two-part *Prelude*, a state of pleasure in the 'joys/
Of subtler origin' than the intense moments of visionary excitement.
These are not so much 'blood-stirring' as

>   hallowed and pure motions of the sense
> Which seem in their simplicity to own
> An intellectual charm, that calm delight
> Which, if I err not, surely must belong
> To those first-born affinities that fit
> Our new existence to existing things,
> And, in our dawn of being, constitute
> The bond of union betwixt life and joy (i. 381–9).

This is another approach to the *I–Thou* mode of relationship,
through the preservation of the 'first-born affinities'; as always in
this version of *The Prelude*, Wordsworth goes on to give an example.
As a child of ten, he

>   held unconscious intercourse
> With the eternal beauty, drinking in
> A pure organic pleasure from the lines
> Of curling mist, or from the level plain
> Of waters coloured by the steady clouds (i. 392–6).

and throughout 'The earth/And common face of Nature spake to
me/Rememberable things' (i. 416–18). So, throughout Part i,
nature is active and speaking, and this, for the later Wordsworth, is
a manifestation of transcendent power and a proof of the child's
state of paradisal happiness. This is the meaning of the final lines of
Part i, with their recall of this state:

> Those recollected hours that have the charm
> Of visionary things, and lovely forms
> And sweet sensations, that throw back our life
> And make our infancy a visible scene
> On which the sun is shining (i. 458–62).

which include both the kratophanic moments and the steady
happiness in a single vision of prelapsarian joy. In a moving moment
near the beginning of Part ii, Wordsworth contrasts this with a later
condition in which he is no longer preconscious of the structure in
which he has to live:

Ah, is there one who ever has been young
And needs a monitory voice to tame
The pride of virtue and of intellect (ii. 17–19)?

I take this to mean that any adult pride which may be associated
with virtue and intellect will quickly disappear if once we recall our
earliest years, when virtue was natural and the intellect unnecessary
because both were supplied by the active power of nature, with
which the child was able to enjoy an *I–Thou* relationship.
Wordsworth looks back at this state, in probing, subtle lines that
speak an authenticity: he knows he no longer exists in the condition
of pure happiness, and yet the condition lives on within him as he
recreates it through memory:

A tranquillizing spirit presses now
On my corporeal frame, so wide appears
The vacancy between me and those days,
Which yet have such self-presence in my heart
That sometimes when I think of them I seem
Two consciousnesses – conscious of myself,
And of some other being (ii. 25–31).

Part ii is concerned primarily to establish the child Wordsworth as
part of a community, to emphasize that he is by no means extraordinary in his circumstances, and that the experiences of Part i
do not separate him from his fellow schoolboys. Yet at one point he
turns back to discuss further the origin of his deepest feelings,

those first-born affinities that fit
Our new existence to existing things,
And, in our dawn of being, constitute
The bond of union betwixt life and joy (i. 385–8).

This is the forerunner of the important 'Blessed the infant babe'
section of Part ii, which explores the earliest sensations of infancy
and their relationship to the paradisal vision of the world. We have
seen already (in Chapter 1) how the child is involved with the
world, in the state of relation: the child grows and explores the world
under the guidance and influence of his mother's love. We may now
observe how the natural bond which the babe feels towards his
mother is part of a much wider feeling of connection:

> Along his infant veins are interfused
> The gravitation and the filial bond
> Of Nature that connect him with the world (ii. 292–4).

Without rejecting his own mother, the poet is here alluding to another feature of the primitive religious sense, the myth of the *terra genetrix*, or the earth as mother. This belief, which is of universal distribution, sees the mother as the representative of the great Earth Mother, and permits the newly-born child to be related to the earth, thus giving expression to the obscure but powerful sense of autochthony, of having sprung from the soil, in man. Thus the babe feels attached to the earth with the filial bond, the resonant 'gravitation' suggesting a continual need to return to the earth-mother. He feels the earth as active and giving, and a mutual relationship exists between them:

> Emphatically such a being lives,
> An inmate of this *active* universe.
> From Nature largely he receives, nor so
> Is satisfied, but largely gives again (ii. 295–8);

Hence the mind becomes 'creator and receiver both' and this is seen as the 'first/Poetic spirit of our human life', the sense of a bond between man and the earth to which he feels joined. When man has this sense of autochthony, he naturally feels an attachment to one particular place, his native country; so, in this second part of the two-part *Prelude*, there is a paraphrase of the first poem in Wordsworth's collected poems, 'Dear native regions'. When he was fourteen, the poet recalls that he said

> That in whatever region I should close
> My mortal life I would remember you,
> Fair scenes – that dying I would think on you,
> My soul would send a longing look to you, (ii. 166–9).

This is more than a sentiment of affection; it is a deeply-held sense of the link between himself and the earth which Wordsworth claims for the young child, and which corresponds to the myth of the *terra genetrix* in archaic societies.

III

According to Buber, the memory of *mana*, the force behind hierophany, 'left its track when the image of the object was separated out from the total stirring image'.[4] That is to say that the object remains in the memory, and so does the knowledge that something was felt about it, even when the actual feeling has passed. Wordsworth, who spoke of poetry and its composition as 'emotion recollected in tranquillity', described his own listening to the sounds of the earth:

> Thence did I drink the visionary power.
> I deem not profitless these fleeting moods
> Of shadowy exaltation; not for this,
> That they are kindred to our purer mind
> And intellectual life, but that the soul –
> Remembering how she felt, but what she felt
> Remembering not – retains an obscure sense
> Of possible sublimity, to which
> With growing faculties she doth aspire,
> With faculties still growing, feeling still
> That whatsoever point they gain they still
> Have something to pursue (ii. 360–71).

The fleeting moments are those in which the soul perceives what it had once known and which, with a returning movement, it still continues to seek. It has a nostalgia for the paradise which it once knew, and is fortunate in being able to retain 'an obscure sense/Of possible sublimity'. This is explored explicitly in the 'Immortality Ode', but also in *The Prelude*: it involves the profoundly religious sense that lives which are centred on the material world and are limited by its time have chosen to neglect the spiritual values which give significance to man's existence. Wordsworth's exploration of this in *The Prelude* involves the reader in a characteristic response to the poetry which demands an understanding which is aware of its religious implications. We have seen how the first portrait of the child as savage leads into a striking awareness of transcendent powers; we may now turn to other aspects of the sacred, manifested in primitive religious experience and found also in Wordsworth. The most important of these are sacred time and sacred space.

For religious man, time is not clock time, a succession of moments; although he lives in this historical time, there is a more important way of experiencing time – as sacred time. According to this perception, certain moments or experiences (often connected with recurring religious festivals) have much greater value than others; time is no longer homogeneous, a succession of moments, but broken up by periods of great significance or value. In these moments man can draw near to God, can approach again or even experience again the unfallen condition that he once knew. 'Religious man', says Eliade,

> periodically finds his way into mythical and sacred time, re-enters the *time of origin*, the time that 'floweth not' because it does not participate in profane temporal duration. Religious man feels the need to plunge periodically into this sacred and indestructible time. For him it is sacred time that makes possible the other time, ordinary time, the profane duration in which every human life takes its course.[5]

During this sacred time, the religious man experiences a heightened awareness of himself and his possibilities, because he feels for a moment 'the sanctity of human existence as a divine creation'.[6] Hence 'the elevated mood, by form/Or image unprofaned', moments of such exalted experience that they cannot even be linked to material things. At other times these moments give Wordsworth a kind of extra perception, in which the world takes on momentarily a new and wonderful face. This is what happens during the boat-stealing, and during the skating episode, when the child

> Stopped short – yet still the solitary cliffs
> Wheeled by me, even as if the earth had rolled
> With visible motion her diurnal round (i. 180–2).

To experience this, the child has deliberately ignored the claims of ordinary time –

> And in the frosty season, when the sun
> Was set, and visible for many a mile
> The cottage windows through the twilight blazed,
> I heeded not the summons. Clear and loud
> The village clock tolled six; I wheeled about

Proud and exulting, like an untired horse
That cares not for its home (i. 150–6).

In his physical exuberance, he enters another world, and the whole
experience becomes meaningful and important, a moment in which
the ordinary progression of profane time is interrupted. In these
moments he felt that

> The earth
> And common face of Nature spake to me
> Rememberable things – (i. 416–18)

In these moments of sacred time, the earth is invested with an
extraordinary power, and the poet is privileged to see it. In a great
passage at the end of the two-part *Prelude* he sees the whole
worshipping creation alive with joy and delight:

> I was only then
> Contented when with bliss ineffable
> I felt the sentiment of being spread
> O'er all that moves, and all that seemeth still,
> O'er all that, lost beyond the reach of thought
> And human knowledge, to the human eye
> Invisible, yet liveth to the heart,
> O'er all that leaps, and runs, and shouts, and sings,
> Or beats the gladsome air, o'er all that glides
> Beneath the wave, yea, in the wave itself
> And mighty depth of waters (i. 448–58).

The discontent which Wordsworth feels at other moments, the dim
longing for something greater than the ordinary profane vision, is
authentically the discontent of the religious man. So, for some of the
time at Cambridge, he succeeded in carrying his own world with
him:

> To every natural form, rock, fruit or flower,
> Even the loose stones that cover the highway,
> I gave a moral life: I saw them feel,
> Or linked them to some feeling: the great mass
> Lay bedded in a quickening soul, and all
> That I beheld respired with inward meaning (III. 134–9).

With great perception, Wordsworth detects this as a primitive religious phenomenon: he sees it as inspiration and prophecy, but also as a return to the primordial experience of happiness and closeness to the gods:

> Some called it madness – such indeed it was,
> If child-like fruitfulness in passing joy,
> If steady moods of thoughtfulness matured
> To inspiration, sort with such a name;
> If prophecy be madness; if things viewed
> By poets of old time, and higher up
> By the first men, earth's first inhabitants,
> May in these tutored days no more be seen
> With undisordered sight (III. 147–55).

Such divine wisdom begins in the experiences of childhood, and is continued because the poet-prophet is determined to testify to the authenticity and value of those experiences. Moreover, he has others in later life, which confirm him in his beliefs and encourage him to go on. One of these occurs after the dance in Book IV. All night long he had been gay, enjoying the noise, the talk, and the perceptible beginnings of sexual excitement; afterwards the walk home comes as a strong contrast, a moment of release from these things into another world and another dimension of feeling. It is one of the most pictorial of Wordsworth's landscapes, with a Constable-like freshness and sparkle:

> The sea was laughing at a distance; all
> The solid mountains were as bright as clouds,
> Grain-tinctured, drenched in empyrean light;
> And in the meadows and the lower grounds
> Was all the sweetness of a common dawn –
> Dews, vapours, and the melody of birds,
> And labourers going forth into the fields (IV. 333–9).

This is sometimes known as the 'dedication' passage, which is misleading, for at the time there was no conscious act of dedication on Wordsworth's part. The process was one which he later learned to wait for with a wise passiveness, but which here came unbidden:

>   I made no vows, but vows
> Were then made for me; bond unknown to me

Was given, that I should be, else sinning greatly,
A dedicated Spirit. On I walked
In blessedness, which even yet remains (IV. 341–5).

As Mary Moorman has pointed out, this is not necessarily a dedication to poetry, though it has often been assumed to be so.[7] No doubt poetry, which was Wordsworth's prophecy, was the result of it: but the actual experience is concerned rather with the poet's ontological state as *homo religiosus*. He had found his status threatened at Cambridge: however much he was able to carry his own world with him, he was nevertheless aware of the forces which were inimical to his deepest needs. The sustaining of these needs by a renewed experience of sacred time had to wait until his return to the Lake District during his long vacation. The glimpse of the wonderful morning is a reassurance, a confirmation, as well as a dedication: it attests to the validity of the early experiences, and looks forward to a life which continues to acknowledge them – the life of a religious man, not a non-religious man.

The fact that this experience takes place in the Lake District is relative to the allied religious concept of sacred space. From earliest times, certain places where man experiences the sense of closeness to the gods have taken on a sacred quality. In the profane mode of being, space is neutral, and no single place has more value or meaning than another; but in the sacred mode of being, certain places become holy because they have witnessed an hierophany. Wordsworth, as we have seen, began by enjoying a relationship with the earth in which he was naked and unprotected, yet aware of the transcendent power. Then other childhood experiences allow him to preserve his awareness of the sacred. When he returns from Cambridge to Hawkshead, he walks round the lake of Esthwaite at twilight, and

> Gently did my soul
> Put off her veil, and self-transmuted, stood
> Naked as in the presence of her God (IV. 140–2).

The sense of once again being naked before a transcendent power is striking as a moment of rediscovery. The poet returns to the sacred place, and putting off the veil of profane things that has begun to envelop him, rediscovers his true self. He had, of course, not been conscious of the insidious advance of the profane in his life, but now

> Strength came where weakness was not known to be,
> At least not felt; and restoration came,
> Like an intruder, knocking at the door
> Of unacknowledged weariness (IV. 145–8).

The language which Wordsworth goes on to use leaves no doubt of the nature of the experince as a religious one:

> I had hopes and peace
> And swellings of the spirit, was rapt and soothed,
> Convers'd with promises, had glimmering views
> How Life pervades the undecaying mind,
> How the immortal Soul with God-like power
> Informs, creates, and thaws the deepest sleep
> That time can lay upon her (IV. 152–8);

This sleep is the product of profane time; for Wordsworth it is significantly interrupted by moments of sacred time, which take place in association with certain places. Thus the attachment to the country of his birth is not just a sentimental one; it is an instinctive return of a religious man to a place where he has experienced moments of hierophany. Man receives a sign in the sacred place, which thus acquires meaning; he desires to live in that place, because for him, 'the sacred is pre-eminently the *real*, at once power, efficacity, the source of life and fecundity'[8] – in Wordsworth's case of poetic creativity. Eliade's description of the religious man's motives has some remarkable affinities with the processes described in *The Prelude*:

> Religious man's desire to live *in the sacred* is in fact equivalent to his desire to take up his abode in objective reality, not to let himself be paralyzed by the never-ceasing relativity of purely subjective experiences, to live in a real and effective world, and not in an illusion.[9]

Seen in this light, the crisis of Book x of *The Prelude* can be understood, not as a 'breakdown' and 'recovery', but as an encounter with the chaos that lies outside the sacred space. During it the poet was deflected from his natural course, 'turn'd aside/From Nature by external accidents' (x. 885), and he recovers only after

> Nature's Self, by human love
> Assisted, through the weary labyrinth
> Conducted me again to open day,
> Revived the feelings of my earlier life,
> Gave me that strength and knowledge full of peace,
> Enlarged, and never more to be disturb'd (x. 922–7).

The strength which the poet receives brings him back to a situation in which he can experience the manifestation of the sacred; indeed this is what the 'credal lyrics', as Hartman calls them, are celebrating. 'Tintern Abbey', too, is a poem of celebration, as we shall see. Together with *The Prelude*, they are evidence of a particular sacred mode of being, one which desires the real and abhors the chaos. 'Religious man', says Eliade, 'thirsts for *being*':

> His terror of the chaos that surrounds his inhabited world corresponds to his terror of nothingness. The unknown space that extends beyond his world – an uncosmicized because unconsecrated space, a mere amorphous extent into which no orientation has yet been projected, . . . – for religious man, this profane space represents absolute nonbeing. If, by some evil chance, he strays into it, he feels emptied of his ontic substance, as if he were dissolving in Chaos, and he finally dies.[10]

We may surmise that for Wordsworth the London experience was this state of nonbeing, and that it was through the love and encouragement of Dorothy and Coleridge that he was drawn away from the labyrinth of chaos to a condition in which he could once again believe in the sacred as a mode of being. Whatever the agency, however, it seems clear that Wordsworth passed from a period in which he knew the reality of the sacred, into the chaos, and then returned to the life-giving cosmos.

IV

In the eighth book of *The Prelude*, entitled 'Retrospect', Wordsworth is much more explicit about the paradisal element of his childhood. Comparing his native regions to a Chinese garden, he used Miltonic phraseology and grandeur to make his point:

> But lovelier far than this, the paradise
> Where I was reared; in Nature's primitive gifts
> Favoured no less, and more to every sense
> Delicious, seeing that the sun and sky,
> The elements, and seasons in their change,
> Do find their dearest fellow-labourer there –
> The heart of man, a district on all sides
> The fragrance breathing of humanity,
> Man free, man working for himself, with choice
> Of time, and place, and object; by his wants,
> His comforts, native occupations, cares,
> Conducted on to individual ends
> Or social, and still followed by a train
> Unwooed, unthought-of even – simplicity,
> And beauty, and inevitable grace (VIII. 144–58).

Intuitively, Wordsworth turns to the simple gifts of nature, the sun and sky, the elements and seasons, and connects them with the workings of the human heart. Avoiding the profane and superficial, he celebrates the union between internal and external as one which leads to beauty and grace, and to the benevolent organic community. He continued to associate childhood with paradise. In the poem about his French daughter written at Calais in 1802, the poet walks on the sands with her on a beautiful evening:

> Dear Child! dear Girl! that walkest with me here,
> If thou appear untouched by solemn thought,
> Thy nature is not therefore less divine:
> Thou liest in Abraham's bosom all the year;
> And worshipp'st at the Temple's inner shrine,
> God being with thee when we know it not.
>   (Miscellaneous Sonnets, I. xxx)

There is an element of piety in the imagery here, which is happily missing from the descriptions of childhood in *The Prelude*. There the predominant force is a 'natural piety', although the paradise is equally present and real. The boys of Hawkshead were

> A race of real children, not too wise,
> Too learned, or too good; but wanton, fresh,
> And bandied up and down by love and hate,

Fierce, moody, patient, venturous, modest, shy;
Mad at their sports like wither'd leaves in winds;
Though doing wrong, and suffering, and full oft
Bending beneath our life's mysterious weight
Of pain and fear; yet still in happiness
Not yielding to the happiest upon earth (v. 436–44).

The passage makes it clear that the childhood paradise does not
depend upon ordinary happiness or unhappiness, but is concerned
with a deeper relationship with the external world. In primitive
societies, certain individuals, the shamans, are particularly able to
preserve the features of the sacred time, or have access to it.
Wordsworth's own claim to be a poet-prophet rests upon his
awareness of certain shamanic qualities within himself, as he
celebrates in verse the primordial time of origins, the paradisal time
of closeness to the gods. In the same Book v, moreover, there is a
signal example of the shamanic, in the picture of the child hooting to
the owls –

                    and they would shout
Across the watery vale, and shout again,
Responsive to his call, with quivering peals,
And long halloos and screams, and echoes loud,
Redoubled and redoubled, concourse wild
Of mirth and jocund din (v. 397–404);

In the sacred time of origins one of the powers of man was the ability
to communicate with birds; and here, as E. B. Greenwood has
pointed out, 'is the case of a poet who had no theoretical or abstract
knowledge of such a motif discovering it in his own experience'.[11]
The child is in paradise: even when the owls did not answer, other
things spoke to him:

Then sometimes, in that silence while he hung
Listening, a gentle shock of mild surprise
Has carried far into his heart the voice
Of mountain torrents; or the visible scene
Would enter unawares into his mind,
With all its solemn imagery, its rocks,
Its woods, and that uncertain heaven, received
Into the bosom of the steady lake (v. 406–13).

In MS JJ the boy is Wordsworth himself. The transference to another (Wordsworth later mentioned a William Raincock) is important because it allows the poet to describe the boy as dead. In his death the boy attains a peculiar magnificence: he has been an ordinary boy, and then dies before he can step out of the childhood paradise. The terms in which his death is recounted tell us that

> This Boy was taken from his mates, and died
> In childhood, ere he was full ten years old (v. 414–15).

By whom was he taken? Why 'from his mates'? The answer to the first question is that he has been taken by nature, or by the active earth; and the emphasis on 'mates' sharpens the contrast between the sociable life of a village schoolboy and the return to the earth, while also suggesting that he is a 'normal' boy, with an ordinary enjoyment of the pleasures of youth. Yet he is also shamanic in his ability to communicate with the owls; and when he dies his power is undimmed. He returns to the earth, the *terra genetrix* from which he came, without ever having left the paradise of childhood.

The poet stands beside the dead boy's grave in commemoration and perhaps in a kind of communication:

> Fair are the woods, and beauteous is the spot,
> The vale where he was born; the churchyard hangs
> Upon a slope above the village school,
> And there, along that bank, when I have passed
> At evening, I believe that oftentimes
> A full half hour together I have stood
> Mute, looking at the grave in which he lies (v. 416–22).

All Francis Jeffrey could manage in response to this was a derisory and uncomprehending exclamation mark: ' . . . for the sake of this one accomplishment, we are told, that the author has frequently stood mute, and gazed on his grave for half an hour together!'[12] F. W. Bateson agrees: 'There is really no excuse for its last nine lines,' he writes of 'There was a Boy'; 'as Jeffrey rightly says, the last nine lines are the sort of sentimental nonsense from which Crabbe is absolutely free.'[13] This, like Jeffrey's dismissal of the pedlar, is a crucial misunderstanding: it indicates a rationalist view of Wordsworth which is disinclined to listen to the strange voice of feeling which comes through these lines. For Wordsworth is describing emotions which lie far below the rational or explicable. The child who is dead returns to the earth in the place where he is born (and the nostalgia for a return to the earth-mother is one feature of the search for the lost paradise) so that his life has a kind of unspoiled perfection about it. The child who is living communicates with this by his half-hour of silence: he suspends his normal active life, and becomes mysteriously united with the child under the earth, who is also still and silent. Perhaps he understands, unconsciously, that

> what the dead had no speech for, when living,
> They can tell you, being dead: the communication
> Of the dead is tongued with fire beyond the language of the living.

(T. S. Eliot, Little Gidding, 1)

The whole episode is mysterious and powerful: there is a ritual element in the boy's standing by the grave (compare the modern enfeebled ritual of the two minutes' silence on Remembrance Sunday) which is explicable only in terms of the dead child as being in touch with the primordial world. In his awareness of this, the living child reaches out towards such a perfection with an awareness of his own loss and his own possibilities.

V

In his autobiography, *Sowing*, Leonard Woolf describes his departure for Ceylon to begin his career in the Civil Service as a second birth, a cutting of the umbilical cord that bound him to his mother, and his family and friends. The journey to Cambridge in October 1787 similarly marks a new epoch in Wordsworth's life, an end and a beginning. The account in *The Prelude* suggests that it was a moment of some importance: if not as traumatic as Woolf's departure, it was a point of farewell to all known and familiar things, and perhaps unconsciously a cutting of the umbilical cord that bound him to his native earth. Certainly the farewell salute to the Lake District includes a reference to the poet's birth there:

> ye mountains and ye lakes,
> And sounding cataracts! ye mists and winds

That dwell among the hills where I was born.
If in my youth I have been pure in heart,
If, mingling with the world, I am content
With my own modest pleasures, and have lived
With God and Nature communing, removed
From little enmities and low desires,
The gift is yours (II. 440–8);

From the moment at the beginning of Book III when he saw the roof
of King's College Chapel, the poet was in a different world; an
agreeable world, certainly, but one which sharpened his awareness
of more mysterious things by its very difference. His own phrase for
this is that 'the under soul' was hushed – 'locked up in such a calm,/
That not a leaf of the great nature stirred' (III. 540–1). The agents of
imprisonment were the pleasures of Cambridge and also its official
duties – examinations, compulsory chapel – which made the poet
prefer idleness to duty. The dons, too, were men whose academic
egotism and senility made them a sharp contrast to the shepherds
whom Wordsworth had known as a child. After nearly three years at
Cambridge, his final response to all this was an extreme one, the
walking tour with Robert Jones which was undertaken as 'An open
slight/Of college cares and study' (VI. 342–3). What that walking
tour led to, in the mind's awareness of itself, has been brilliantly
discussed by Geoffrey Hartman in his *Wordsworth's Poetry, 1787–
1814*; its relation to the life of duty and the life of Cambridge has
been less frequently considered. Wordsworth's Cambridge friends
thought it 'mad and impracticable',[14] but its response to the
situation of 1790 was fundamental and vital to Wordsworth. The
clearest statement of that vitality came later, and is found in some of
the 1798 *Lyrical Ballads*.

8 *Lyrical Ballads*: Time, Place and Nature

The four poems which have been called 'the credal lyrics' present some problems. The stanza from 'The Tables Turned'

> One impulse from a vernal wood
> May teach you more of man;
> Of moral evil and of good,
> Than all the sages can.

was described by A. C. Bradley as 'outrageous',[1] and if its meaning is paraphrased it certainly seems to be so. It is true that the stanza appears in a somewhat jocular poem: the title, 'The Tables Turned', suggests a certain amount of japing, and the tone of the first verse seems facetious and exaggerated:

> Up! up! my friend, and clear your looks,
> Why all this toil and trouble?
> Up! up! my friend, and quit your books
> Or surely you'll grow double.

Yet this is followed by a serious second verse, with its description of the yellow sunlight over the long green fields; and even though this is succeeded by the overstatement of the third verse, with its colloquial 'on my life', the poem later returns to a tone which demands to be taken seriously as a whole:

> Come forth into the light of things,
> Let Nature be your Teacher.

> She has a world of ready wealth,
> Our minds and hearts to bless –
> Spontaneous wisdom breathed by health,
> Truth breathed by cheerfulness.

The vernal wood stanza which follows takes its place in a poem which, although it contains both playful and serious elements, combines them to make the same point. Thus the playful cannot be dismissed as exaggeration. As Bradley remarked, to explain such things away or water them down 'is the road round Wordsworth's mind, not into it'.[2] What is required is a context for these lines which allows the poem, together with its companion 'Expostulation and Reply', and 'To my Sister' and 'Lines written in Early Spring', to stand for something credible and valuable.

The four poems are linked by similarities of metre, tone, and vocabulary, and by a common awareness of the overwhelming beauty of nature. Their affinity with each other is all the more obvious when they are read in the 1798 *Lyrical Ballads* in their original places beside 'Simon Lee', 'The Thorn' and 'Goody Blake and Harry Gill'. In their affirmative, hymn-like statements, they express what can only be seen as a set of positives, over against the destructive *I–It* relationships of the narrative poems in the collection. Émile Legouis remarked upon 'the spiritualized and almost religious expression'[3] of these poems. It can be seen in the sonorous language of a verse of 'To my Sister' which is reminiscent of Isaac Watts:

And from the blessed power that rolls
About, below, above,
We'll frame the measure of our souls:
They shall be tuned to love.

The exalted and solemn tone of this verse (which may be sung to the hymn tune 'St Anne', used for 'O God our help in ages past') suggests an enveloping awareness of the transcendent which is investing the earth. It is a power, love, which is everywhere – 'About, below, above' – and the poet becomes aware of this power on a beautiful morning. Time and place are neatly noticed:

It is the first mild day of March:
Each minute sweeter than before,
The red-breast sings from the tall larch
That stands beside our door.

In the ordinary time and place, the poet becomes powerfully aware of joy and blessing. He is recording a moment of hierophany, a manifestation of the sacred:

There is a blessing in the air,
Which seems a sense of joy to yield
To the bare trees, and mountains bare,
And grass in the green field.

Everything suggests a new beginning: the trees and mountains are bare, as if first created, and the poet records the grass as a simple, original property of nature – 'grass in the green field'. In this first mild day of spring, the world seems as if it were but newly created. This corresponds exactly to the primitive sense of hierophany as a new beginning, and the urge to return to the beginning, to the sacred time of origins, when all was pure and man was in close contact with the gods. In primitive rituals, mythical time is built around the conception of renewal: 'for religious man, of the archaic cultures', Eliade writes, '*the world is renewed annually*; in other words, *with each new year it recovers* its original sanctity, the sanctity that it possessed when it came from the Creator's hands'.[4] This sense of renewal comes when the rituals of hierophany suggest to primitive man that the world is reborn; and each rebirth takes man back to the time of origins, the first creation when all was new and pure: 'this *rebirth*', writes Eliade, 'is a *birth*, . . . the cosmos is reborn each year because, at every New Year, time begins *ab initio*'.[5] So for Wordsworth this moment of beauty and power becomes the first day of his year:

No joyless forms shall regulate
Our living calendar:
We from to-day, my Friend, will date
The opening of the year.

Ordinary human time, measured by hours and months, and running from January to December, is profane time; Wordsworth proposes instead a living calendar, which begins the year at the moment of nature's renewal. Life is about to be given to the bare trees and bare mountains, and the rebirth of spring becomes the annual re-enacting of the first day, the start of a new time. Thus he feels an impulse to date the new year from this first mild day of March – for 'Since the New Year is a reactualization of the cosmogony, it implies *starting time over again at its beginning*, that is, restoration of the primordial time, the "pure" time, that existed at the moment of Creation.'[6] The purity of the moment is something which Wordsworth conveys partly by the natural images – the robin singing, the tall larch, the blessing in the air – but also by his insistence on the 'now' of the moment: 'Love, now a universal birth', 'One moment now', which are linked with the repeated 'this one day'. The poem begins with a simple present tense, 'It is', followed by 'There is' in verse two, and later 'It is the hour of feeling'. The hour of feeling is Wordsworth's phrase for Eliade's sacred time, in which 'the participants experience the sanctity of human existence as a divine creation'.[7] It is also the time of purification and exaltation, which is why the poet calls upon his sister to 'Come forth and feel the sun'. By participating ritually in this new creation, man is born anew: he begins life again 'with his reserve of vital forces *intact*, as it was at the moment of his birth'.[8] The words 'Come forth' suggest a movement from darkness and confinement to light and freedom. It is a movement which is traditionally associated with the process of rebirth in conversion experiences, because the unregenerate state is thought of as darkness and bondage. Conversion is followed by an emphasis on 'all-embracing love, light, joy, expectation; deliverance from anxiety; a sense of security and completeness'.[9] In this poem Wordsworth is urging his sister towards the same kind of release. She is to abandon her work, come forth, and feel the sun. She is also to dress herself in tune with nature for the rebirth, by putting on her woodland dress, and she is urged to do this quickly. Every moment is important, and she must not miss the sacred time: 'One moment now may give us more/Than years of toiling reason.' From the darkness and cold of winter the earth is turning to the fertility and life of spring, feeling the generative power of the sun's warmth; for man to fail to respond would be for him to miss the sacred time, the moment of all-embracing love and joy in the interaction between man and nature, the *I–Thou* experience:

> Love, now a universal birth,
> From heart to heart is stealing,
> From earth to man, from man to earth:
> – It is the hour of feeling.

The exuberance (Hartman's word) of all this is not, therefore, simple exaggeration: it is a consequence of the mood which accompanies rebirth, described by William James as including the loss of anxiety, the sense of perceiving truths not known before, and of 'clean and beautiful newness within and without'.[10] At this moment, too, the poet frames the 'silent laws' which will guide him until the next return of the sacred time, which is looked forward to in the phrase 'the year to come':

Some silent laws our hearts will make,
Which they shall long obey:
We for the year to come may take
Our temper from to-day.

If the apprehension of sacred time is vital to this poem, the sense of sacred space is also present, though in a subordinate role. The original title in the 1798 *Lyrical Ballads* was 'Lines written at a small distance from my house, and sent by my little boy to the person to whom they are addressed'. This draws attention to the circumstantial details: the lines are written near the house, sent by the little boy, with sentiments addressed to the poet's sister who is working indoors. The robin sings by his door, and it is his morning meal that is finished. By such apparently trivial notes, Wordsworth establishes the place and circumstances: he seems to be trying to pin down the moment as exactly as possible, since sacred time and sacred place imply 'an irruption of the sacred that results in detaching a territory from the surrounding cosmic milieu and making it qualitatively different'.[11]

The poem ends with a modified repetition of verse 4, which exhorts the poet's sister to put on her woodland dress and join the poet in celebrating the moment. The act of self-surrender which accompanies conversion is here found in agreeable form: she must give up the household chores, neglect her books, and come forth. It suggests a total yielding to the demands of the time: Dorothy must give up her normal life, the occupations she pursues in the profane time, and surrender the day to idleness. In this way she will be concentrating, with all possible power, on the moment of hierophany; and by it she will be renewed, even born again, into a life of love.

II

'Expostulation and Reply' and 'The Tables Turned' are companion poems which are closely related to the religious experience of 'To my Sister'. In them William, the paradise-struck dreamer,

confronts Matthew, the representative of busy and active profane
man. While Matthew is industrious, William is idle; Matthew
recommends study and books, William prefers to dream his time
away. William, as Matthew unconsciously perceives, is encounter-
ing a particular moment of sacred time, 'the paramount *time of
origins*, . . . the instant that saw the appearance of the most
immense of realities, the world . . . if sacred time is that in which
the gods manifested themselves and created, obviously the most
complete divine manifestation and the most gigantic creation is the
creation of the world'.[12] In the poem Matthew stumbles upon this
unwittingly:

> You look round on your Mother Earth,
> As if she for no purpose bore you;
> As if you were her first-born birth,
> And none had lived before you!

Matthew intends this as a joke, to the effect that William is behaving
as if he were Adam at the creation of the world: the irony is that in
his moment of hierophany William is exactly in the position of
Adam. He feels newly born, and in the moment of sacred time he
feels as if the world had been newly created, like Dylan Thomas at
Fern Hill:

>   it was Adam and maiden,
>   The sky gathered again
>   And the sun grew round that very day.
> So it must have been after the birth of the simple light
> In the first, spinning place, the spellbound horses walking warm
>   Out of the whinnying green stable
>   On to the fields of praise.

With his reference to 'Mother Earth', Matthew also touches on the
widespread primitive belief, the idea that human beings were born
from the Earth. Together, these observations provide powerful
evidence that William's mode of being is that of myth, that he is
homo religiosus. For such a man, as William's reply indicates, the
surrender to such an experience is involuntary:

> 'The eye – it cannot choose but see;
> We cannot bid the ear be still;

Our bodies feel, where'er they be,
Against or with our will.

What the religious man perceives is the world as a meaningful cosmos, with powers before which man has to be passive and receptive. In Eliade's words:

> The world stands displayed in such a manner that, in contemplating it, religious man discovers the many modalities of the sacred, and hence of being. Above all, the world exists, it is there, and it has a structure; it is not a chaos but a cosmos, hence it presents itself as creation, as work of the gods. This divine work always preserves its quality of transparency, that is, it spontaneously reveals the many aspects of the sacred. The sky directly,'naturally,' reveals the infinite distance, the transcendence of the deity. The earth too is transparent; it presents itself as universal mother and nurse. The cosmic rhythms manifest order, harmony, permanence, fecundity.[13]

It is the active properties of such a world which are emphasized by the poem; the religious man attains his insight by a passiveness before such a manifestation of the sacred:

Nor less I deem that there are Powers
Which of themselves our minds impress;
That we can feed this mind of ours
In a wise passiveness.

Think you, 'mid all this mighty sum
Of things for ever speaking,
That nothing of itself will come,
But we must still be seeking?

The 'mighty sum' is a powerful and original phrase, suggesting not only the adding together of all things, but also the power of accumulated nature, the transformed world speaking to the poet. These are 'things', yet they speak; and William describes himself as 'Conversing as I may', suggesting a dialogue with this speaking nature which echoes the interaction in 'To my Sister' – 'From earth to man, from man to earth'. The interaction between 'heart and heart' described in that verse is the holy conversation of religious man and nature, and this is William's occupation as he sits on the old grey stone. The stone itself becomes part of the mighty sum, though Matthew sees it only as an old stone, just as he sees William as dreaming his time away. In his day-dreaming William is significantly abstracting himself from profane time, and the stone is, by implication, far more than just a stone. In the final verse, William's repetition of 'old grey stone' is deliberately ironic, reflecting Matthew's ignorance rather than the actual nature of the stone. 'For those', says Eliade,

> to whom a stone reveals itself as sacred, its immediate reality is transmuted into a supernatural reality. In other words, for those who have a religious experience all nature is capable of revealing itself as cosmic sacrality. The cosmos in its entirety can become a hierophany.[14]

In 'The Tables Turned' William becomes active rather than passive. The morning/evening opposition which makes this a companion-piece to 'Expostulation and Reply' is echoed in the reversal of rôles. Here Matthew is sitting, and William is up: he seems, after his conversation with the sacred powers of nature, to be charged with exultation, so that he adopts an exuberant and jocular tone. In its exhortation to Matthew to 'Come forth into the light of things' the poem echoes 'To my Sister', but in its emphasis on Matthew's books and his trust in the intellect, it is much more aware of forces which threaten the religious view of nature:

> Our meddling intellect
> Mis-shapes the beauteous forms of things: –
> We murder to dissect.

Matthew here is profane man, who refuses the idea of transcendence, and declines to accept the need to pay attention to the manifestations of power in the created universe. For him the world is to be studied in books: he is an early example of modern non-religious man, who 'regards himself solely as the subject and agent of history', and 'refuses all appeal to transcendence':

> Man *makes himself*, and he only makes himself completely in proportion as he desacralizes himself and the world. The sacred is the prime obstacle to his freedom. He will become himself only

when he is totally demysticized. He will not be truly free until he has killed the last god.[15]

Outside Matthew's study, the evening sun is throwing a fresh light on the green fields; the spring birds are singing; the leaves which are spreading on the trees are, in a witty antithesis, fruitful, as opposed to the barren leaves of the books. The wit here is important. Together with the initial 'Up! up!' and the cheerful exaggerations – 'Books! 'tis a dull and endless strife:' – it contributes to the poem's air of boisterous heartiness and good-fellowship. It is as though William, though aware of the role which science, dissection and books play in the desacralization of the universe, is entirely and jubilantly convinced that he is right: that he has spent the day more valuably than Matthew. This is suggested by the whole tone and structure of the poem, which imply an overflowing physical and spiritual energy. This is what has come from the 'wise passiveness' of the morning poem; it is evidenced in the facetiousness of high spirits:

> Up! up! my Friend, and quit your books;
> Or surely you'll grow double:
> Up! up! my Friend, and clear your looks;
> Why all this toil and trouble?

which continues throughout the poem, and which is delicately balanced by the serious portrayal of the beauty of the evening scene which Matthew is ignoring.

It is in this context that the impulse from a vernal wood appears. It is part of the remarkable poise of the poem, hanging delicately between the exaggerated ('you'll grow double') and the serious. The first line of the poem, for instance, with 'Up! up!' suggests the drill sergeant or gym instructor, only to qualify this with 'my Friend'. In the same way the 'impulse from a vernal wood' verse has the over-emphasis of high spirits, and yet is deeply serious. It indicates a moment of hierophany which William urges Matthew to come forth and behold: this will lead to an awareness that there is such a thing as sacred time and place, and not the mechanical existence of routine and work, in which everything becomes relative. The poem expresses this in its own very individual way, for its tone re-enacts the benefits of a participation in the natural world at the primordial time. Books therefore become, facetiously, a dull and endless strife rather than the repositories of knowledge and moral enquiry; and the alternative, as so often in this poem, is jocular but also desperately serious:

> Come, hear the woodland linnet,
> How sweet his music! on my life,
> There's more of wisdom in it.

Here 'on my life' may not be just an exclamation: for religious man it may have its other meaning of total commitment, and concern for the foundations of his spiritual existence.

III

'Line written in Early Spring' is, despite its title, a poem of later date than 'To my Sister'; the bare trees and mountains have been covered by periwinkles and primrose tufts, and the first green leaves are spreading out from their buds like a fan. This poem, like the others, is concerned with a moment of beauty, providing a 'sweet mood' ('sweet' or 'sweeter' is a word which occurs in all these four poems). The sanctity of the natural world is presented undeniably to the poet: the birds sing, the flowers grow, and both appear to take a joy in living. This is the poet's faith and belief:

> Through primrose tufts, in that green bower,
> The periwinkle trailed its wreaths;
> And 'tis my faith that every flower
> Enjoys the air it breathes.
>
> The birds around me hopped and played,
> Their thoughts I cannot measure: –
> But the least motion which they made,
> It seemed a thrill of pleasure.

Without being able to prove anything, the poet reiterates his belief in the universe as alive and in a state of continuous pleasure. The budding twigs are animate, spreading out their leaf-fans with a conscious intention of catching the healthy, fresh, breezy air; the sense of natural delight is so overwhelming that it compels belief, in spite of any evidence to the contrary:

> The budding twigs spread out their fan,
> To catch the breezy air;

And I must think, do all I can,
That there was pleasure there.

The odd 'do all I can' is perhaps best interpreted as Wordsworth's gesture towards a residual rationalism which is being driven out by the hierophantic power of nature, in the same way as converts are known to stress the force and stubbornness of their unregenerate nature. In both cases, the attempt to cling to the non-religious or the pre-conversion state serves only to emphasize the power of the regenerative process. Wordsworth reminds us, in this verse, that the evidence of the scientist or the botanist, which he is bound to accept as empirically true, would be that there is no such thing as pleasure in nature. The poet, however, is forced by the power of the moment into believing more than the scientific evidence would normally permit. The delight of the moment throws into sharp focus something which Wordsworth has not mentioned in the three previous poems of this group, but which he was very concerned with in other poems written during this spring: the cruelty of man, as found in 'The Thorn' or 'Goody Blake and Harry Gill'. From the moment of sacred time, the poet observes the addition of man:

If this belief from heaven be sent,
If such be Nature's holy plan,
Have I not reason to lament
What man has made of man?

The birds hopping and playing, the flowers interwining, the twigs opening their buds to the spring air, all suggest a natural life of harmless enjoyment which contrasts with the life of man. To record it, the poet assumes a double identity. He is man, the participator in guilt and sorrow, receiver of the belief and plan, whose ideas about animate nature are held by faith; yet he is also, by his participation in the hierophantic moment, the man who becomes momentarily close to the gods. He acquires a semi-divine status during the sacred time, and becomes, in Eliade's phrase, 'contemporary with the gods':

The intention that can be read in the experience of sacred space and sacred time reveals a desire to reintegrate a primordial situation – that in which the gods and the mythical ancestors were *present*, that is were engaged in creating the world, or in organizing it . . . the nostalgia for origins is equivalent to a religious nostalgia. Man desires to recover the active presence of the gods; he also desires to live in the world as it came from the Creator's hands, fresh, pure, and strong.[16]

In this light, Wordsworth's lament for man has a two-fold origin. In the first place it is a lament by a man, for himself and other men. This is, to some extent, the force of the first occurrence of 'What man has made of man' in verse 2. On this occasion the poet has placed himself in a recognizably human situation, in a grove listening to the birdsong, and has emphasized 'The human soul that through me ran':

> I heard a thousand blended notes
> While in a grove I sate reclined,
> In that sweet mood when pleasant thoughts
> Bring sad thoughts to the mind.

> To her fair works did Nature link
> The human soul that through me ran;
> And much it grieved my heart to think
> What man has made of man.

This is a moment of great sadness, for the hierophany has made the poet more than usually aware of the sufferings of mankind; he is experiencing the nostalgia for the time of origins, when all was pure as it came from the creator's hand. Yet this blends in the poem with another approach, since the poet is capable of a raised ontological status. The line 'What man has made of man', in its second appearance, implies some overlooking glance, an authority which comes from having been close to the gods – or contemporary with them – in the sacred time. Thus the poet surveys the human situation from two points of view: the moment of hierophany has left him with a nostalgia for a purer world and made him, as a man, feel sad and guilty; but as a participant in the regenerative experience he also has a god-like over-view, an ability to pass judgment.

IV

The precise recording of time and place which is found in 'To my Sister' is also present in 'Tintern Abbey'. The full title of the poem with its exact date – 13 July 1798 – and its other circumstantial details, suggests that this is an important moment to be set down. The poem is a record of a certain time and a certain place. It is also a poem of celebration. It celebrates the survival of the poet's ability to feel the meaningful relationship with nature which he had felt five years previously, and the two points of contact with the scene (1793 and 1798) make convenient measuring marks for him to assess this. The all-pervading joy of the poem comes from the poet's thrilled awareness that he has not lost his power to experience the kind of *I– Thou* relationship with nature. Confronting the scene five years later, he is still capable of experiencing the 'blood-stirring *Thou*'. The delighted reiteration in the first paragraph of 'again . . . Once again . . . again . . . Once again' suggests a return to the place accompanied by a renewal of feelings, of the excitement of the moment of relation. Lovingly, therefore, the poet enumerates the various parts of the landscape, with exact qualification and detail:

> Once again
> Do I behold these steep and lofty cliffs,
> That on a wild secluded scene impress
> Thoughts of more deep seclusion; and connect
> The landscape with the quiet of the sky.
> The day is come when I again repose
> Here, under this dark sycamore, and view
> These plots of cottage-ground, these orchard-tufts,
> Which at this season, with their unripe fruits,
> Are clad in one green hue, and lose themselves
> 'Mid groves and copses. Once again I see
> These hedge-rows, hardly hedge-rows, little lines
> Of sportive wood run wild: these pastoral farms,
> Green to the very door; and wreaths of smoke
> Set up, in silence, from among the trees (4–18)!

The poet catalogues these elements, as if reassuring himself that all is complete. Returning to the scene, he finds that his memory has not been false, and that he was justified in his feelings about what it was and what it did for him. In rediscovering it, he is able to confirm himself and his vital relationship to nature.

This relationship is unchanged, and Wordsworth celebrates its survival in the poem; though he himself is changed, as he freely admits ('though changed, no doubt, from what I was when first/I

came among these hills;'). There is, in 'Tintern Abbey', the same
provision of double time – inner and outer time – that Herbert
Lindenberger has found in *The Prelude*: Wordsworth makes it clear
that he is five years older than when he first visited the place, and
that this means that he is different:

> I cannot paint
> What then I was. The sounding cataract
> Haunted me like a passion: the tall rock
> The mountain, and the deep and gloomy wood,
> Their colours and their forms, were then to me
> An appetite; a feeling and a love,
> That had no need of a remoter charm,
> By thought supplied, nor any interest
> Unborrowed from the eye. – That time is past,
> And all its aching joys are now no more,
> And all its dizzy raptures (75–85).

The visit to Tintern Abbey is poised between this past and a future
which is also plainly acknowledged:

> and, in after years,
> When these wild ecstasies shall be matured
> Into a sober pleasure; when thy mind
> Shall be a mansion for all lovely forms,
> Thy memory be as a dwelling-place
> For all sweet sounds and harmonies; oh! then,
> If solitude, or fear, or pain, or grief,
> Should be thy portion, with what healing thoughts
> Of tender joy wilt thou remember me,
> And these my exhortations (137–46)!

so that time is carefully recorded and admitted to the poem. In
counterpoint to this outer time, however, is the inner time, which
makes the experience of the first visit recoverable in the memory. It
is a time which is not homogeneous, but filled with value: the first
visit to the place becomes invested with meaning and power, for it is
an example of sacred time, a moment of closeness to the primordial
time. Through the memory, this moment can be recovered:

These beauteous forms,
Through a long absence, have not been to me
As is a landscape to a blind man's eye:
But oft, in lonely rooms, and 'mid the din
Of towns and cities, I have owed to them
In hours of weariness, sensations sweet,
Felt in the blood, and felt along the heart (22–8);

The memory here performs the same function which ritual festivals do in primitive societies: it brings back the moment of sacred time, makes it present, so that the poet can exist in mythical time rather than profane time. Eliade describes sacred time thus:

> *by its very nature sacred time is reversible* in the sense that, properly speaking, it is *a primordial mythical time made present.* Every religious festival, any liturgical time, represents the reactualization of a sacred event that took place in a mythical past, 'in the beginning'. Religious participation in a festival implies emerging from ordinary temporal duration and reintegration of the mythical time reactualized by the festival itself. Hence sacred time is indefinitely recoverable, indefinitely repeatable.[17]

For Wordsworth, the landscape of his first visit becomes repeatable through memory, and significant because of the power of that original visit. At that time the sounding cataract haunted him like a passion,

when like a roe
I bounded o'er the mountains, by the sides
Of the deep rivers, and the lonely streams,
Wherever nature led

and the peculiar circumstances of the first visit probably heightened this awareness. We have seen (Chapter 4) how Wordsworth entered a 'liminal' state during his solitary journey over Salisbury Plain, and how during it he was able to achieve an *I–Thou* relationship with the external world. It is this *I–Thou* moment of *communitas* which the memory returns to, even in times and places which are inimical to *communitas*, 'in lonely rooms, and 'mid the din / Of towns and cities'. Since *communitas* breaks down the usual barriers between man and

man created by structure, it is not surprising to find Wordsworth
claiming for these moments of memory that they have

> no slight or trival influence
> On that best portion of a good man's life,
> His little, nameless, unremembered, acts
> Of kindness and of love (32–5).

These acts are unconscious: the poet is not talking here about
deliberate actions but about the tenor of his life, his dim awareness
that the best moments of his existence are those in which he was in a
state of *communitas* with others. But the memory does not only affect
his relations with his fellow men; it also brings forward and makes
present the sacred time. This is the other gift 'Of aspect more
sublime':

> that blessed mood
> In which the burthen of the mystery,
> In which the heavy and the weary weight
> Of all this unintelligible world,
> Is lightened: –that serene and blessed mood,
> In which the affections gently lead us on, –
> Until, the breath of this corporeal frame
> And even the motion of our human blood
> Almost suspended, we are laid asleep
> In body, and become a living soul:
> While with an eye made quiet by the power
> Of harmony, and the deep power of joy,
> We see into the life of things (37–49).

This is a state akin to the mystical, in which the soul is made free so
that, like a shaman, it can see further than ordinary men into the
nature of existence. Buber described it in terms of 'religious
experience' which was

> the experience of an otherness which did not fit into the context of
> life. It could begin with something customary, with consideration
> of some familiar object, but which then became unexpectedly
> mysterious and uncanny, finally lighting a way into the light-
> ning-pierced darkness of the mystery itself.[18]

The image of light is close to the Wordsworthian one of seeing: both suggest the brightness of perception which is the result of religious experience. Moreover, Wordsworth's vision is not concerned with the supernatural, but with seeing into the life of things. Similarly, in his opening definition of religion in *The Elementary Forms of the Religious Life*, Durkheim refutes the idea that religion, in primitive manifestations, is concerned with the supernatural, or the mysterious, the unknowable. In primitive religions, the practiser is much more concerned to understand and influence the natural world around him, than to go beyond it. In Wordsworth's case he is 'laid asleep in body' not in order to leave the world behind, but in order to allow the soul to have existence. The soul is, of course, a vital concept for the religious man: according to Durkheim, all religions have the sense of the human body possessing an interior being, 'the principle of the life which animates it'.[19] Similarly the sense of the soul coming into independent existence is related to the experience described by Wordsworth:

> Today, as formerly, the soul is what is best and most profound in ourselves, and the pre-eminent part of our being; yet it is also a passing guest which comes from the outside, which leads in us an existence distinct from that of the body, and which should one day regain its entire independence. In a word, just as society exists only in and through individuals, the totemic principle exists only in and through the individual consciousness whose association forms the clan. If they did not feel it in them it would not exist; it is they who put it into things. So it must of necessity be divided and distributed among them. Each of these fragments is a soul.[20]

In Wordsworth the process by which the soul becomes active is through the body's sleep, the quietening of the active eye, the suspending, almost, of the motions of the blood. This corresponds to a primitive's deduction of the soul from dreams,[21] suggesting a wider and richer existence than the waking one, bound by material things. Thus the landscape – or the spontaneous relationship of dialogue which the poet has with it – serves to activate the religious sense. The soul becomes a 'living soul' as opposed to something dead or impaired; the moment has something in common with the re-awakening and divesting of the soul by the lake of Esthwaite when Wordsworth returned from Cambridge. In both cases the poet is able to move from structure into liminality – in the first case by his return in the flesh to a beloved place, in 'Tintern Abbey' by a return in the memory. The conditions inimical to this are further outlined in the poem:

> In darkness and amid the many shapes
> Of joyless daylight; when the fretful stir
> Unprofitable, and the fever of the world,
> Have hung upon the beatings of my heart – (51–4)

It is against this that the memory has caused the *I–Thou* relationship to survive: the poet's return to the original gives him cause to celebrate the power of the imagination to keep it alive in the intervening years. The sacred time is one in which he feels the world sanctified, aware of the presence of *mana* in and through all things:

> a sense sublime
> Of something far more deeply interfused,
> Whose dwelling is the light of setting suns,
> And the round ocean and the living air,
> And the blue sky, and in the mind of man:
> A motion and a spirit, that impels
> All thinking things, all objects of all thought,
> And rolls through all things (95–102).

and because this has been kept alive, he is able to continue his relationship with the physical world. An important word which expresses this is 'still', held for a perceptible moment at the end of the line:

> Therefore am I still
> A lover of the meadows and the woods,
> And mountains; and of all that we behold
> From this green earth; of all the mighty world
> Of eye, and ear, – both what they half create,
> And what perceive; well pleased to recognise
> In nature and the language of the sense
> The anchor of my purest thoughts, the nurse,
> The guide, the guardian of my heart, and soul
> Of all my moral being (102–11).

The last lines emerge with an admirable and appropriate clarity, as the poet emerges from his characterizing of sacred time to declare its importance to him. How this sacred time is apprehended has already been discussed (Chapter 1); it should be sufficient here to record the first occurrence of the idea that the mind is both creator and receiver. The half creating and perceiving add up to a total apprehension which combines the awareness of nature as stimulus with the understanding of nature as sign.

The completeness of such an apprehension does not avoid suffering, as we have seen in the case of the pedlar; it is aware of unhappiness as a condition of man in profane time:

> The still, sad music of humanity,
> Nor harsh nor grating, though of ample power
> To chasten and subdue (91–3).

But here as elsewhere Wordsworth sees this against a background of something more important, the external world in moments of transformation. His awareness of sacred time, and the function of memory in recalling it, are confirmed as a vital truth when the poet stands again before the landscape. If he does not feel as passionate as he did on the first occasion, he nevertheless recognizes the scene which he saw then and which he was able to revive later. The revival is a revival of relation, and the second visit is a reassurance that the original relationship did exist and was not an invention or wishful thinking. It was a genuine *I–Thou* relation, an interaction through love in spontaneous dialogue. Its presence in the world is evidence of the love that can exist between man and man, and between man and nature; and it is this love which triumphs over the destructive forces,

> that neither evil tongues,
> Rash judgements, nor the sneers of selfish men,
> Nor greetings where no kindness is, nor all
> The dreary intercourse of daily life,
> Shall e'er prevail against us, or disturb
> Our cheerful faith, that all which we behold
> Is full of blessings (128–34).

The list of human ills is penetrating: they are all things which act against the free and spontaneous relationship between man and

man. They may be seen as an early nineteenth-century version of
Eric Berne's *Games People Play*, and at least one of them (greetings
where no kindness is) appears in Berne's book as spinal cord
shrivelling. The important thing to realize is that these are all
human negations: beyond them is the far more important truth, for
Wordsworth, that the human mind is capable of moments of sacred
time, of the *I–Thou* interaction between man and man and between
man and nature. It is this which allows the cheerful faith: the
confirmation which the Wye valley landscape brings that time is not
profane time and place is not just relative and undistinguishable
space, but that the world does contain sacred moments and sacred
places. This will remain, whatever happens, as the final section of
the poem asserts. It turns towards the future, foreseeing this as a
permanent truth:

> when thy mind
> Shall be a mansion for all lovely forms,
> Thy memory be as a dwelling-place
> For all sweet sounds and harmonies; oh! then,
> If solitude, or fear, or pain, or grief,
> Should be thy portion, with what healing thoughts
> Of tender joy wilt thou remember me,
> And these my exhortations (139–46)!

In these lines there is a combination, a simultaneous existence of two
states, which is crucial to an understanding of Wordsworth's poetry,
and especially his tragic poetry. The mind can suffer solitude, pain
and the other ills, while also being 'a mansion for all lovely forms'.
Tragedy is not evaded, but side by side with it there is the awareness
of the existential nature of man – that he lives in a world which is not
profane, in which his existence is given purpose by its moments of
relation. Hence the poem becomes an assertion of love, the dialogue
which results in spontaneous *communitas* between the poet and his
sister; and the place which confirms this is the landscape of the Wye
valley. Thus Wordsworth returns to it at the end, in the beautiful
conclusion which begins with love, 'With warmer love – oh! with far
deeper zeal/Of holier love' (154–5) and which concludes with the
return to the place itself, with which the poem began:

> Nor wilt thou then forget,
> That after many wanderings, many years

Of absence, these steep woods and lofty cliffs,
And this green pastoral landscape, were to me
More dear, both for themselves and for thy sake (155–9)!

The validity of the poem thus depends, not on circumstances, but on a view of the existential nature of the world. It asserts triumphantly the reality and importance of sacred place, as the poet, after 'many wanderings', homes again on a landscape of vital importance to him. The 'wanderings' seem not just physical, but the wanderings of a mind that is now restored: the wanderings are associated with the kind of chaos which religious man finds away from the sacred space. The return to the sacred space, on the other hand, is a return to the real, the life-giving; and it is the existence of such life and such reality that Wordsworth's poem is demonstrating. It survives permanently, as a truth about man and the external world: this is why Wordsworth (as evidenced in the Duke of Argyle's story)[22] could go on reading the poem with such enthusiasm even after Dorothy's illness. He was remembering the visit of 1798, not just as a happy memory, but as an example of a mode of being.

9 The Lucy Poems

Wordsworth was not very helpful about the Lucy poems. In the notes which he dedicated to Isabella Fenwick he gave the barest circumstantial details of composition: 'Composed in the Hartz Forest'; 'Written in Germany'; 'The next three poems were written in Germany, 1799'.[1] De Quincey observed that 'he always preserved a mysterious silence on the subject of that "Lucy" ',[2] and there has been much speculation about whether she represents Annette, or Dorothy, or Mary Hutchinson. Wordsworth's silence on the subject is of great interest, particularly as he was usually ready and forthcoming with information about his poems; not because this silence suggests a concealed love-affair, but because of the way our lack of knowledge about the identity of Lucy affects any reading of the poems.

The poems themselves tell us very little, apart from the fact that Lucy died young, that she lived in a cottage working at her spinning wheel, and that the cottage was in a lonely place near the river Dove (which does not help much, as there are several). The result is that Lucy herself, though named in all the poems except 'A slumber did my spirit seal', is curiously insubstantial and elusive. She is the goal of the lover's journey and the object of his grief, and yet she remains shadowy; at the centre of the Lucy poems the reader's experience is like that of Donne, imagining a spirit of love before it had taken human shape:

> Still when, to where thou wert, I came,
> Some lovely glorious nothing I did see.

('Aire and Angels')

Lucy herself has something of this quality of being a 'lovely glorious nothing', a spirit, yet also a young girl – 'A Spirit, yet a Woman too!' This line, and the poem from which it comes, 'She was a Phantom of delight', underline the characteristics which Wordsworth most admired in women – the combination of human (and especially simple domestic) living with something more divine and spiritual:

A perfect Woman, nobly planned,
To warn, to comfort, and command;
And yet a Spirit still, and bright
With something of angelic light.

This is a more mature version of the Lucy figure; in this the ideal is realized and completed, whereas in the Lucy poems it is lost. Yet both demonstrate the combination of human and other-worldly qualities which stand at the centre of the Lucy poems: 'She seemed a thing that could not feel/The touch of earthly years.' And yet the touch of earth is exactly what she does feel, as she is rolled round in the diurnal course with rocks, and stones and trees. The union of natural and supernatural, and the transience of the human, is what binds together the Lucy poems, whether they are considered as a group or as separate works dealing with the same theme – the growth of love for a pure young girl, and the loss of that love.[3]

II

There are several possible ways of dividing the Lucy poems. One is to consider that Wordsworth himself included two under 'Poems of the Imagination' and three under 'Poems Founded on the Affections', but this is not usually thought to be significant, except that it could be seen as an indication that he did not feel strongly that they were a group. Another, better division, is between 'I travelled among unknown men' and the others; not only because it was composed later but because it makes the narrator into a returned traveller, which none of the others does. Although this is better, it is still not a very helpful division; more useful, perhaps, would be a grouping of the poems into two, according to what the critics of the novel would call 'point of view'. In three of the poems, 'Strange fits of passion have I known', 'I travelled among unknown men', and 'A slumber did my spirit seal', the emphasis is primarily on the experiencing and remembering mind of the poet; we see Lucy, as it were, at one remove, which is one reason why she seems insubstantial. She remains in the poet's past, and she appears in the poems only as a product of his memory; he is not interested in painting a portrait, but in remembering certain moments, so that Lucy appears without ever being seen. She is like a figure in an anecdote, whom we have never met; a figure without a face, like the portrait of Virginia Woolf by Vanessa Bell. In the other two poems, 'She dwelt among the untrodden ways' and 'Three years she grew in sun and shower', the portrayal is more direct, and the poet appears only in the final verse. The result of this variation in technique, this double point of view, is that although Lucy is elusive, we have a stereoscopic view of her: we see her relationship to nature, and to the simple life; and we also see her as the poet's ideal, as his loved one.

In 'She dwelt', Lucy is connected with nature, partly by her mode of living, and partly by the imagery used to describe her. She lives in an unfrequented place, near the river Dove; her life is obscure: there were 'none to praise', indicating that she did not lead the kind of public life which invites praise; and 'very few to love', suggesting an intimate society, where there were not many people who knew Lucy well enough to love her – carrying in addition, the suggestion that to know Lucy was to love her. Having placed Lucy thus, as a retired and lovable figure, the poet turns to see her as natural:

> A violet by a mossy stone
>   Half hidden from the eye!
> – Fair as a star, when only one
>   Is shining in the sky.

The contrast is not only between the star and the violet, the brilliant and isolated juxtaposed to the beautiful and half-hidden; it is also between the 'Maid' of the first verse, and these natural phenomena. From the shining, remote star and the half-hidden violet, we return to the human in the final verse, with the domestic 'She lived alone'; the simplicity is a surprise, because so much of the imagery up to this point has been suggestive, carrying the kind of emotional reverberations that are discussed by F. W. Bateson in his examination of the poem, where he points to the unobtrusive contradictions of the language.[4] Now the contradictions, and the need for what Bateson calls 'silent corrections' disappear. 'She lived alone' takes us right back to 'She dwelt', with the 'alone' simplifying and modifying the complexities of the lines between. Similarly the phrase 'few to know' echoes 'few to love', and establishes the continuity of Lucy's humanness across the natural images of violet and star. It is this human quality which is responsible for Lucy's death, when she 'ceased to be'; the words 'ceased to be' have reverberations, however, which return us to Lucy's naturalness, as well as emphasizing her transience. When she 'was', she existed as a star or as a violet, as a part of the natural world. Now she has 'ceased to be', and the last two lines present two moments of surprise: 'But she is in her grave, and, oh,/The difference to me!' The first shock comes from the blunt severity of the statement that she is in her grave; it is a shock because Lucy has, up to this point, been elusive, half-hidden like the violet or remote like the star. Now the image is of Lucy in a fixed and determinate place, from which she will never move. The second surprise comes with the introduction of the poet; the 'oh' at the end of the penultimate line catches the reader unawares, because it refers to a depth of feeling and a personal involvement with Lucy which has been hitherto unstated. The effect of the last line is complex: the 'oh', the caught breath of deep emotion, is counterbalanced by the understatement of 'difference', and yet 'difference' itself is given profound weight and substance by the preceding 'oh'. The result is that emotion seems controlled, but only just; 'The difference', with the stress thrown by the second syllable of the line on to 'diff', suggests a whole world of feeling and emotion. This is given credibility and substance by the final 'to me', in which, for the first time, the poet comes out into the open. He does so with a vengeance: the 'to me' strikes with a surprise and force which throw a new light on all that has gone before; the poet is one of the 'very few' who has loved Lucy, and one of those who has trodden the untrodden ways beside the springs of Dove. For him her death signifies a loss also of a way of life, an intimacy and simplicity which flourished in remote places; and also the loss of an ideal beauty, of a girl who was like a violet and a star. The 'difference' is indeed a world of difference.

The same process of portrayal followed by bereavement is found in 'Three years she grew in sun and shower', though nature in this poem is a much more prominent and positive force. Nature, in fact, is a presence throughout, speaking and acting, and Lucy is nature's creature. She is chosen by nature after growing for three years 'in sun and shower', which suggests the same kind of natural existence as a flower (or the very natural existence of a country child, like the infant Wordsworth basking in the sun and sporting 'A naked savage, in the thunder shower'). Nature actually calls Lucy a flower in her first words, thus beginning a sequence in which Lucy is referred to sometimes as a flower or a faun, and sometimes as a child or a girl. The sense that Lucy is a natural creature is overwhelming, much stronger than in the other poem. There, although she is likened to a violet and a star, she is recognizably human; in this poem she has a special relationship with nature which almost prevents this. Yet the poem succeeds in making Lucy credible as a girl, if only because it acknowledges her physical growth, as she becomes tall and her breasts develop; such acknowledgments of her physical presence counterbalance the sense that she belongs, truly, in another world. Her life, however, is one long response to nature. She is one of the 'elect', who is chosen to feel 'an overseeing power/ To kindle or restrain'. The life which results includes two things which are also found in the life of the child Wordsworth, an animal-like gladness and activity and also a knowledge of stillness:

> She shall be sportive as the fawn
> That wild with glee across the lawn
> Or up the mountain springs;
> And hers shall be the breathing balm,
> And hers the silence and the calm
> Of mute insensate things.

Just as she enters into a natural state here, so a reciprocal process occurs, and nature lends her most beautiful qualities to the girl:

> The floating clouds their state shall lend
> To her; for her the willow bend;
> Nor shall she fail to see
> Even in the motions of the Storm
> Grace that shall mould the Maiden's form
> By silent sympathy.

> The stars of midnight shall be dear
> To her; and she shall lean her ear
> In many a secret place
> Where rivulets dance their wayward round,
> And beauty born of murmuring sound
> Shall pass into her face.

Here, through these graceful and beautifully-modulated stanzas, the qualities blend to make up a Wordsworth ideal, a human being

in whom the most wonderful characteristics of the natural world
live, and move, and have their being. Lucy is, in fact, nature
incarnate, the most beautiful parts of the natural world made flesh,
and that very flesh moulded and shaped by the power of nature:

> And vital feelings of delight
> Shall rear her form to stately height,
> Her virgin bosom swell;
> Such thoughts to Lucy I will give
> While she and I together live
> Here in this happy dell.

Sadly, we are never permitted to see such a figure in action. The last
verse is shocking because it compresses time so ruthlessly, and we
pass abruptly from Lucy growing to Lucy dead. There is no present
tense in this poem: from the future of nature's intentions we are
rushed into the past. The happy dell is no longer inhabited by Lucy
and nature, but by the poet, solitary and bereaved:

> Thus Nature spake – The work was done –
> How soon my Lucy's race was run!
> She died, and left to me
> This heath, this calm, and quiet scene;
> The memory of what has been,
> And never more will be.

The appalling thing is that between the perfection of Lucy's growth
and her death there is nothing: the completion of the work is
followed immediately by the end of her earthly race. There is
perhaps a sense in which the process is inevitable, that such
perfection is always followed by death, as a flower grows, and
blossoms and dies. In this possibility, the intention of nature at the
beginning, 'This child I to myself will take' has something
prophetic, and even sinister about it; certainly it is something very
powerful, and the poet's own claim to Lucy, asserted in the final
verse, appears feeble in comparison – 'How soon my Lucy's race was
run!'. She is not his Lucy, but nature's. At the end of the poem she
has been taken back into nature: hers is now for ever 'the silence and
the calm/Of mute insensate things'. The poet is left with her
memory, and her bequest to him, which is the remote and quiet
place where she lived, now empty of her presence:

She died, and left to me
This heath, this calm, and quiet scene;
The memory of what has been,
And never more will be.

The last verse, and the introduction of the bereaved poet,
emphasize the remoteness and fragility of Lucy, her characteristics
of beauty that are almost non-human. She has access to a perfection
that is denied to most people: the poet is left behind, with only a
memory of what was.

III

The closest parallel to Lucy in the poetry of Wordsworth is the boy
hooting to the owls in Book v of *The Prelude*. Like Lucy, he is close to
the earth in childhood, and his cycle of birth, maturing and early
death is soon complete like hers. Lucy's race is run, and the boy is
interred in the earth in the place where he was born. In both cases
the unconscious centre of reference is the myth of the *terra genetrix*. Eliade, for instance, writes of 'a mystical solidarity with *the
place*'

> which was intense enough to have survived till now in folk-lore
> and popular traditions. The mother did no more than bring to
> completion the creation of the Earth-Mother: and, at death, the
> great desire was to return to the Earth-Mother, to be interred in
> the native soil – that 'native soil' of which we can now see the
> profound meaning.[5]

The boy dies, still in an innocent childhood simplicity which can be
recognized, through the communication with the owls, as being
genuinely sacred time; Lucy's rural simplicity, and her close
relationship to nature, show her to be another such figure. The poet,
on the other hand, is not. He is excluded from the perfect cycle, in
both cases: when he stands by the boy's grave he attempts some
communication with the dead, some mute identification with the
silent boy. Yet he can never escape from his exclusion: by being
human he has to accept the imperfect, and to acknowledge that he
can never regain the relationship with the boy which he knew when
alive. By introducing the poet standing by the grave, Wordsworth

makes this part of *The Prelude* marvellously complex: it is both a record of an ideal and a lament for the transience of human happiness.

Similarly, in the Lucy poems the attention is directed not only to Lucy herself, but also to the figure who is left behind, the poet for whom the 'difference' indicates a world of difference, and the lover, left only with the calm, and quiet scene – 'The memory of what has been,/And never more will be.' He is faced with the painful fact of human transience, and the mystery of a beauty that is so quickly destroyed; in Geoffrey Hartman's words, 'The voice we hear shares in the still sad music of humanity, and the mystery it depicts is the commonplace mystery of humanization.'[6] Another way of putting this would be to say that the Lucy poems are powerful because they show, as 'There was a Boy' shows, a human voice, faced with pain and loss, calling and searching for an ideal. Like Browning's lover in 'Two in the Campagna', it discerns 'Infinite passion, and the pain/ Of finite hearts that yearn' and the yearning in Wordsworth is towards a state of natural and physical perfection; it is a nostalgia for paradise, the paradise from which man has fallen, to which Lucy herself is still linked. It is this nostalgia which is present in all the Lucy poems: Wordsworth's description of the girl acknowledges her natural power, and the poet's own distance from it, and from the primordial vision which it embodies. The three Lucy poems in which the poet is present from the beginning, are particularly concerned with this nostalgia.

The opening line of 'Strange fits of passion have I known' directs the attention straight to the surviving poet, and in this poem Lucy is seen through his memory. The mood here is at once odd and involuntary: a fit is something which occurs suddenly and unpleasantly, and here strangely as well. It is not any kind of fit, but a fit of passion, suggesting an upsurge of intense feeling, an unexplained and unforeseen explosion. The word 'dare' in the second line increases the element of foreboding, and the sense of menace. This opening of the poem remains like a time bomb ready to go off throughout the remainder of the poem, with its placid description of the poet-lover on his way to Lucy's cottage, making a familiar journey along well-loved paths. The language quietens, becoming less spectacular and exciting:

When she I loved looked every day
Fresh as a rose in June,

I to her cottage bent my way,
Beneath an evening moon.

Here the suggestion found in an earlier version, that the loved one is
no longer well ('Once when my love was strong and gay') has almost
disappeared, and there is only the faintest hint of future sadness to
disturb the happiness of the moment – though it could be claimed, I
suppose, that 'Fresh as a rose in June' is not a commonplace image
for beauty, but contains the suggestion of beauty rapidly turning to
decay.

As he travels on, the lover on his horse watches the moon sinking
in the evening sky. Like him, the moon is coming 'near, and nearer
still' to the cottage. Human and natural converge, with Lucy at the
centre. Here the cottage is, for a moment, the significant or sacred
space, the centre of the world to which everything is directed. As the
lover falls into a sweet trance, the horse continues of its own accord;
the lover becomes passive, suspended in time at a moment of
expectation like Keats's lover on the Grecian Urn, 'winning near
the goal'. In this case, however, the equilibrium is upset, and the
trance broken. When the moon disappears, the lover discovers that
it was not as he had thought in his sweet dream: everything is not
converging on Lucy's cottage, and the cottage is not the significant
centre, at least not permanently. The lover had thought that he had
regained the lost paradise, and now realizes, on wakening, that it is
a human happiness which he possesses, a happiness which is subject
to time and mischance. Thus, when the moon goes, he sees
everything as threatened:

What fond and wayward thoughts will slide
Into a Lover's head!
'O mercy!' to myself I cried,
'If Lucy should be dead!'

The poem is thus a poem of nostalgia for a paradise that is
permanent. In a verse of 1799 which Wordsworth later omitted, the
lover's fear of losing paradise is seen to be all too justified:

I told her this: her laughter light
Is ringing in my ears:
And when I think upon that night
My eyes are dim with tears.

The omission of this verse treads the ground less heavily, but nevertheless makes the point that the lover's impression of stability and permanence is misplaced. The natural world changes, and the possibility of death must be admitted. The sudden arrival of fear has no specific cause – it is a 'fond and wayward' thought – but it is understandable; it is related to the upsetting of a perfect moment of equilibrium and happiness, in which the moon, and the horse and rider, are converging on the loved one. As in the other poems, the fact that both man and nature are so moving indicates Lucy's half-human, half-natural mode of being: she acts as a loadstone for the moon as well as the lover. Both are caught in a single moment of unity; then the balance is upset, and the limitations of human life reassert themselves: *et in arcadia ego*.

'I travelled among unknown men' is often separated from the other Lucy poems; the fact that it was written after the poet's return to England, rather than in Germany, and that it deals with an exile's feeling for his country, are two reasons for this. Yet it has close affinities with 'A slumber did my spirit seal', very different though that poem may seem, for both deal with Lucy's relationship with the earth on which she lives. 'I travelled' stresses the place, and its importance; 'A slumber' shows Lucy lying in the earth. Both poems draw for much of their power on the myth of the *terra genetrix*, and show Lucy's attachment to a certain place, and her return to the earth from which she came and to which she is bound.

The first eight lines of 'I travelled among unknown men' treat of the poet's love of his country. Only in the third verse is this joined to his love:

Among thy mountains did I feel
The joy of my desire;
And she I cherished turned her wheel
Beside an English fire.

The effect of the first line is one of distancing. The travelled lover, returned from 'lands beyond the sea', has experienced the far-off view of the loved place, seeing it from afar as the centre of the world. There, among the mountains, was the scene of his love, the cherishing of the simple Lucy. Lucy belongs strongly to the place: she turns her wheel beside an English fire, and her nights and days are particularly local ones:

Thy mornings showed, thy nights concealed,
The bowers where Lucy played;
And thine too is the last green field
That Lucy's eyes surveyed.

The understatement of the last couplet – like 'the difference to me' –
is effective because it underlines the finality of Lucy's death through
invoking the spirit of place – the spirit which possesses the green
fields. Lucy dies, as it were, as she had lived, affected by this spirit,
surveying its landscape to the last; and the singular 'the last green
field' suggests one particular place, beloved as a special piece of
ground.

'A slumber did my spirit seal' has been interpreted in ways that
are diametrically opposed. For F. W. Bateson the poem is a climax
of 'pantheistic magnificence'; for Cleanth Brooks it suggests 'dead
lifelessness' and 'earthly time in its most powerful and horrible
image'. Such different interpretations suggest that the centre of the
poem is indeed strange and elusive; its quietness of tone and
regularity of metre tend to obscure the very real strangeness of its
experience. It begins with 'A slumber' that 'seals' the poet's spirit,
which could mean either that the poet's spirit was closed up, sealed
like an envelope or a tomb; or that it was completed, given a seal of
approval and fulfilment by the slumber which came upon it. The
slumber is related to the sweet dream in 'Strange fits of passion'; it is
associated with a timeless period, a moment of supposed
permanence, when the poet had 'no human fears' and his loved
seemed to be immortal:

A slumber did my spirit seal;
I had no human fears:
She seemed a thing that could not feel
The touch of earthly years.

The whole of this verse raises elusive and suggestive ideas. Does 'I
had no human fears' mean that the poet was quite free from anxiety?
Or that, possibly there were other, stranger fears than human ones?
Does the word 'seemed' include a sense of deceptive appearances, or
not? Does it, in other words, just mean 'I used to think . . . '? Or
does it suggest, following the slumber, that Lucy 'seemed' in the
sense of having a dream-like presence, a reality which is not the
flesh-and-blood reality of the waking encounter of person with

person? In this connection, what sort of 'thing' could she be? And what is the 'touch' of earthly years, and how does one feel it? Clearly the last image refers to the coming of old age; but the language which Wordsworth uses opens up fugitive possibilities of other meanings and other worlds of thought.

If the first verse is elusive, dream-like and ethereal, the second is material, precise. It uses the language of physics to indicate Lucy's death: 'No motion has she now, no force;/She neither hears nor sees.' Here we are reminded of fields of force, and laws of motion, and, by implication, of Lucy's stillness and lack of power, contrasting with her movement and force when alive. The double hammer blows of 'motion' and 'force' are parallelled by two more in the next line, 'hears' and 'sees'. These are succeeded, after a pause, by the thudding last line, where the three blows are like nails in a coffin: 'Rolled round in earth's diurnal course,/With rocks, and stones, and trees.' The difficulty with these amazing last two lines has always been to capture the divergent yet simultaneous and connected meanings included in them. On the one hand, Lucy is a lifeless corpse, an object turning with the earth in its everyday motion. On the other hand she is now a part of nature, one with the rocks and stones and trees; the trees are obviously beautiful, moving and growing things, and this suggests that Lucy is one with a living nature. Given Wordsworth's views on the animism of stones, also, her link with them is another union with something living. In ancient mythology, stones were habitually thought of as the bones of the earth-mother; and the power of this Lucy poem depends, I suggest, upon its direct, almost stark portrayal of the *terra genetrix* myth. Lucy has been buried in the earth; she who was like a violet and a star, who seemed a thing 'that could not feel/The touch of earthly years' is now 'in her grave', rolled round 'With rocks, and stones, and trees'. At this point she has returned to the nature from which she sprang, and has again become a part of the ever-moving universe. To some extent she never lost this and became fully human: she was always a 'child of nature', close to the storm, and the willow, and the stars of midnight, and the floating clouds.

IV

The degree to which Lucy is an elusive figure of myth may be appreciated by comparing her with a fully human subject. When

Tennyson thought of the body of Arthur Hallam, being brought
back by sea from Vienna, he wrote

> O to us,
> The fools of habit, sweeter seems
>
> To rest beneath the clover sod,
> That takes the sunshine and the rains,
> Or where the kneeling hamlet drains
> The chalice of the grapes of God;
>
> Than if with thee the roaring wells
> Should gulf him fathom-deep in brine;
> And hands so often clasped in mine,
> Should toss with tangle and with shells.

(In Memoriam, x)

Later the poet receives some consolation from Hallam's burial in his
native earth:

> 'Tis well; 'tis something; we may stand
> Where he in English earth is laid,
> And from his ashes may be made
> The violet of his native land.
>
> 'Tis little; but it looks in truth
> As if the quiet bones were blest
> Among familiar names to rest
> And in the places of his youth.

(In Memoriam, xviii)

The poet thinks of the way in which the Severn tides wash by the
churchyard of Clevedon where Hallam is buried, and sings 'to him
that rests below'. Yet in all this a stubborn rationalism undercuts the
primitive feeling. We are 'The fools of habit' to prefer to bury
someone in his native soil, rather than at sea; there is an element of
surprise in 'it looks in truth/As if the quiet bones were blest' to be
buried near his birthplace. The phrases suggest a modern de-
sacralized consciousness contemplating the primitive belief. For
Wordsworth, on the other hand, the death of Lucy is treated as a
man for whom the sacred was his mode of being would treat it: he
sees her as autochthonous, springing from the soil and returning to
it. When she does become a human being, she carries with her a

natural perfection; in her day-to-day living, this is seen in her simple life, with its cottage in a remote valley, her wheel beside the fire, and her distance from the hurly-burly of public life. Yet these are only temporary symptoms of her inner condition, her close connection with nature, by whom she is guided and to whom she returns. As she is a daughter of nature, so nature becomes, in these poems, the *terra genetrix* figure; and Lucy's place in the myth (as opposed to Hallam's in the physical reality) is one reason why it is unnecessary – or it might even be harmful – to identify the original of Lucy. If a manuscript were discovered which proved that Lucy was Dorothy, or Annette, or Mary Hutchinson, or which described the illness she had, this would detract from her mythological kind of reality by confusing it with a physical reality.

Thus Wordsworth's silence on the subject of the Lucy poems, apart from the bare circumstances of their composition, was probably instinctive and deliberate. In the poems she remains the half-natural, half-human figure, whose face is indistinct and who is, as F. W. Bateson saw, curiously sexless. The poems have as their subject Lucy's simple perfection, and also the poet's sense of separation from it. He is separated from Lucy because she belongs, ultimately, to nature; any moments in which the poet thinks he has achieved a stable and permanent relationship are seen to be preludes to a rude awakening. He is separated from her also because of his human condition: Lucy is close to the original, pure state, and receives joy, and love, and her growth and development, from the earth. The poet's glimpse of this is an opportunity for him to encounter the kind of perfection which Lucy has; and his loss of her is a forcible reminder of the distance which he has travelled from the sacred time. His moments of transient happiness are the prelude to a deeper realization of loss, and human imperfection, and the separation from paradise.

Part III
On Human Life

For him the poet, using no bible but nature, was the *Seer* whose keener senses and fresher and more integral imagination make him the supreme teacher, whose office it is to render men better and happier by revealing to them their own nature and that of the universe in which they dwell.

Emile Legouis, *The Early Life of
William Wordsworth*, p. 472.

10 The Growth of Tenderness

As we have seen, the 1805 text of the passage describing the child bathing in the stream is an expansion of the original text, as follows: the child

> stood alone
> Beneath the sky, as if I had been born
> On Indian Plains, and from my Mother's hut
> Had run abroad in wantonness, to sport,
> A naked Savage, in the thunder shower (I. 300–4).

The child is attached to his home and family, in a manner described by Rousseau:

> The first developments of the heart were the effect of a new situation, which united in a common dwelling husbands and wives, fathers and children. The habit of living together gave birth to the sweetest feelings known to man, married love and fatherly affection. Every family became a little society, the more united because mutual attachment and freedom were its only ties.[1]

Wordsworth is deeply conscious of the effects of maternal love on the infant:

> blest the Babe
> Nurs'd in his Mother's arms, the Babe who sleeps
> Upon his Mother's breast, who, when his soul
> Claims manifest kindred with an earthly soul
> Doth gather passion from his Mother's eye (II. 239–43)!

He anticipates modern psychologists in understanding that a child's willingness to explore the external world is dependent on a secure base. The mother's love allows a condition in which

> his mind spreads,
> Tenacious of the forms which it receives.
> In one beloved presence, nay and more,
> In that most apprehensive habitude
> And those sensations which have been deriv'd
> From this beloved Presence, there exists
> A virtue which irradiates and exalts
> All objects through all intercourse of sense (II. 253–60).

In the second book of *The Prelude* this develops into the unconscious awareness of the myth of the *terra genetrix*, as the child feels bound to the earth through the mediation of his mother's love. For the infant this is the time of origins, the sacred time; and it is significant that Wordsworth holds back the information about his mother's death until Book V. Throughout the joyous excitement of the first two books there is no indication of the child bereaved; when we do learn about her death, it is with a moving and controlled pathos:

> Early died
> My honoured Mother, she who was the heart
> And hinge of all our learnings and our loves:
> She left us destitute, and, as we might,
> Trooping together (v. 256–60).

Here the 'honoured Mother' suggests the fifth commandment, and a family brought up with a certain care and correctness; its formality gives way to the images of closeness and integration, 'heart and hinge', and then to the surprising 'destitute', which suggests the total poverty of emotional life, the loss of love and security caused by her death, so that the little ones have to band together for support, 'trooping together'. The quality of his mother's character which Wordsworth singles out is a tranquil faith, which led her to a simple acceptance of things as they were:

> and therefore she was pure
> From feverish dread of error or mishap,
> And evil, overweeningly so called;
> Was not puffed up by false unnatural hopes,
> Nor selfish with unnecessary cares,
> Nor with impatience from the season asked
> More than its timely produce; rather loved

The hours for what they are, than from regards
Glanced on their promises in restless pride (v. 276–84).

This has unmistakable echoes of St Paul – 'charity envieth not;
charity vaunteth not itself, is not puffed up, /Doth not behave itself
unseemly, seeketh not her own, is not easily provoked, thinketh no
evil' (I Corinthians 13; 4, 5). Its celebration of the highest kind of
human love looks forward to the later description of Mary
Hutchinson (xi. 199 ff). In both cases the poet sees an ideal
humanity, an incarnation of love and goodness –

God delights
In such a being; for her common thoughts
Are piety, her life is blessedness (xi. 221–3).

The grandeur of this conception is complemented by the more
simple goodness of Ann Tyson. All three women, however, are
figures of love: their effect on the poet's life is to confirm and
strengthen his central beliefs, his sense of the ideal relationship
which can exist between man and man, and his feeling that man can
exist in close proximity to God. Ann Tyson does so in a way which is
endearing because it is so guilelessly human, devoid of anything but
the best intentions:

With new delight,
This chiefly, did I view my grey-haired Dame;
Saw her go forth to church or other work
Of state, equipped in monumental trim;
Short velvet cloak (her bonnet of the like)
A mantle such as Spanish Cavaliers
Wore in old time (iv. 205–13).

Here the comic juxtaposition of 'monumental trim' with the picture
of the little old lady on her way to church is delightful; so too is the
incongruity of her cloak being like that of a Spanish cavalier. Yet
this is the gentle comedy of endearment, as one smiles at the
idiosyncrasies of a loved one. The same loving comedy appears in
the description of Ann Tyson's Sunday afternoons:

With thoughts unfelt till now I saw her read
Her Bible on the Sunday afternoons,

And loved the book, when she had dropped asleep
And made of it a pillow for her head (IV. 218–21).

Sleeping in public, as Christopher Ricks has observed, is embarrassing because we are defenceless, no longer in control of our features; yet 'it is love which makes it feel altogether proper to watch somebody sleeping without any possibility of embarrassment on either side should he awake'.[2] Here, the young poet's tenderness is a moving demonstration of his love, moving partly because he is so aware that Ann Tyson is no ideal figure. She is an ordinary human being, with her limitations. Her religion is not the elevated closeness to God of the shamanic or prophetic figures of Wordsworth's poetry, but a 'clear though shallow stream of piety/That ran on Sabbath days a fresher course (IV. 216–17). Her presence in the poem is a typical Wordsworth stroke, ensuring that the creative and accumulating energies of love are anchored in human kindness as well as in the loftier moments of interaction between man and the 'something other'. Indeed, side by side with the awareness of sacred place and sacred time, and the conception of the ideal community, there is also the growth of tenderness, a sense of the ordinary work done by human agents. This is, of course, linked to the idea of community; but it is essentially an awareness of what qualities also go to make up the good individual. And in the growth of the poet's mind the human agency complements and reinforces the religious awareness in the development of the fully integrated prophet-poet.

II

Throughout *The Prelude* the poet is aware of a human agency working side by side with the influence of place and time. An episode such as the card games in Book I seems at first sight to be out of place, like the food in *Paradise Lost*, amid so much sublimity. Yet its ordinariness is reassuring and complementary: it indicates that the boy who has experienced such intense moments as the boat-stealing or skating is also capable of simpler pleasures. Just as Ann Tyson's practical kindness balances the sense of blessedness which the poet feels in connection with his mother and his wife, so the cottage episodes provide a counterweight to the magnificence which the child discovers outside; yet the two areas of experience are integrated with great skill. The language of the introductory paragraph, for instance, contains words which have a religious significance and resonance:

> Ye lowly cottages in which we dwelt,
> A ministration of your own was yours,
> A sanctity, a safeguard, and a love!
> Can I forget you, being as ye were
> So beautiful among the pleasant fields
> In which ye stood? or can I here forget
> The plain and seemly countenance with which
> Ye dealt out your plain comforts (1. 525–32)?

Thus, however trivial the homework with slates and the playing at cards may appear, we remember that the poet has spoken of this life in terms of sanctity and ministration. The actual card game is described in terms that are deliberately comic, but which, like the description of Ann Tyson, hold feelings of tenderness and endearment.

Boldly, Wordsworth challenges comparison with Pope in this episode, as phrases like 'plebeian cards' make clear; and in any comparison Wordsworth seems sure to lose, since Pope's account of the game in *The Rape of the Lock* is so intricate and sure-fingered. But Wordsworth risks the comparison because he is then able to point up the difference between Hampton Court and the lowly cottage. His game is played on 'the naked table' instead of Belinda's 'verdant field' or 'level green'; and instead of having coffee served on lacquered tables, the children sit 'in close array' warmed by the peat fire. The pack of cards, too, is old and dirty: some court cards have been lost, and have been replaced by ordinary ones with faces drawn on them. The pack is

> A thick-ribbed Army; not as in the world,
> Neglected and ungratefully thrown by
> Even for the very service they had wrought,
> But husbanded through many a long campaign (1. 544–7).

The compound epithet 'thick-ribbed' (perhaps from Shakespeare, *Measure for Measure*, III. i. 123 – 'thick-ribbed ice') probably refers to the thick pasteboard cards stacked and forming layers – the thicker the card, the poorer the quality. The fact that the cards are now looked after and carefully husbanded makes a difference to the description which follows, which is mock-heroic in an affectionate way:

> Uncouth assemblage was it, where no few
> Had changed their functions, some, plebeian cards,
> Which Fate beyond the promise of their birth,
> Had glorified, and call'd to represent
> The persons of departed Potentates.
> Oh! with what echoes on the Board they fell (1. 548–53)!

Words like 'glorified' and 'Potentates' are deliberately sonorous and inappropriate for this patching up. The real condition of the pack is more pitiable than grand, as the next couplet suggests – 'Ironic Diamonds, Clubs, Hearts, Diamonds, Spades, /A congregation piteously akin'(554–5). The diamonds are ironic because they no longer sparkle – indeed, the cards are so dirty that all four suits look similar. The original pictures peer through their coating of grime:

> Those sooty knaves, precipitated down
> With scoffs and taunts, like Vulcan out of Heaven;
> The paramount Ace, a moon in her eclipse,
> Queens gleaming through their splendour's last decay,
> And Monarchs surly at the wrongs sustain'd
> By royal visages (1. 556–62).

It is the dirtiness of these cards which gives point to the extraordinary piece of *discordia concors*, the likening of the knaves to Vulcan, who was thrown out of heaven by Jupiter: the god was usually represented with a blackened forehead, dirty from his work at the forge. Similarly the figure of the paramount ace (the ace of spades) is so indistinguishable from the white surround, that it looks like a moon in eclipse.

It is clear Wordsworth was not trying to emulate Pope, since he describes no actual hand or game; however, the initial echoes, and the general resemblance of the poetic card game, allow Wordsworth to emphasize the differences between the cottage boys and Belinda and the Baron. The cosiness of the room, and its homely simplicity, are everywhere evident: and these qualities are further stressed by the magnificent passage which follows, describing the winter weather outside, and ending with the 'noise of wolves' 'howling round the Bothnic Main' (569–70). But Wordsworth is interested in

more than cosiness and happiness: the care which the boys take over
the cards is an example of consideration, even love. I have suggested
elsewhere,[3] in fact, that the card games passage should be taken in
conjunction with the description of the discharged soldier in Book
IV. The cards are described with a military metaphor –

> not, as in the world,
> Neglected and ungratefully thrown by
> Even for the very service they had wrought,
> But husbanded through many a long campaign (I. 544–7).

The soldier, on the other hand, has his own history:

> That in the Tropic Islands he had serv'd
> Whence he had landed, scarcely ten days past,
> That on his landing he had been dismiss'd,
> And now was travelling to his native home (IV. 446–9).

He is a clear case of one who has been neglected and ungratefully
thrown by, even for the very service he has wrought. The prompt
help which the young Wordsworth gives him is an example of the
continuing power of the mind which was formed in his youth. As we
have seen, he knows the area well enough to be sure of a cottage
where the soldier will be welcome, takes the soldier there, and then
returns home. The return home is, significantly, to the same cottage
where he first learned the virtues which accompany lowliness and
simplicity, especially the importance of care and love for things and
people that others would throw away.

III

The companionship and human love which is associated in
Wordsworth's mind with the growth of tenderness is necessarily
transient and subject to time. In this it differs fundamentally from
the recurring moments of sacred time and sacred place, and it is
valuable as asserting the poet's companionableness and humanity,
so that the moments of hierophany and the visions of the ideal
community are connected to ordinary experience. The effects of
time, for instance, are found throughout *The Prelude*: in Book II, as a
small example, Wordsworth describes how before school he would

walk round the lake of Esthwaite with John Fleming, and regrets that he and Fleming have now lost touch. Time becomes very important as a theme in Book v, which opens with a discourse on transience:

> Even in the steadiest mood of reason, when
> All sorrow for thy transitory pains
> Goes out, it grieves me for thy state, O Man,
> Thou paramount Creature! and thy race, while ye
> Shall sojourn on this planet; not for woes
> Which thou endur'st; that weight, albeit huge,
> I charm away; but for those palms atchiev'd
> Through length of time, by study and hard thought,
> The honours of thy high endowments, there
> My sadness finds its fuel (v. 1-10).

Wordsworth goes on to emphasize the difference between what he has been considering in the first four books, and the works of man. Man, as the first four books have shown, has such wonderful possibilities, but his works, like himself, pass away. This is the meaning of the dream, which immediately follows. The Arab possesses the stone, standing for geometry, and the shell, standing for poetry. He goes, half-Arab, half-Don Quixote, on his futile errand of preservation, and the last we see of him is riding over the desert sands, pursued by 'the fleet waters of the drowning world' (v. 136). The impression given is that this is a quixotic attempt to save the highest works of man, an attempt that is doomed to failure (the waters seem to be gaining on him). For his attempt, however, the poet feels reverence, not pity or scorn: it is an attempt to preserve all that is most worth-while in the human range of achievements.

At this point in the poem, therefore, Wordsworth is concerned with immortal qualities – friendship, poetry, geometry – but also with the fact that they are contained within frail and mortal vessels – people, and books. Poetry is something that can be held in the hand – 'Poor earthly casket of immortal verse,/Shakespeare, or Milton, labourers divine!' (v. 164-5) – and friends are parted, or die. The effect of this part of *The Prelude* is governed by the switch from the mythological mode to the historical. The first four books are concerned with the construction of a myth – the work of the '*bricoleur*'; now the poet acknowledges the other mode of being. He is going to 'stoop/To transitory themes' (v. 223-4), and discuss the effects of human agencies in the formation of the character of man. As we have seen, these have been allowed in to the first four books as part of the composite experience of childhood; now they are explored more fully, and placed in relation to the first understandings of life and its values. In the first place, Wordsworth records his thanks for a freedom of choice in reading; he adds to this a recognition of the early infulence of his mother, in a conjunction which is not at first obvious, as the poet himself admits (v. 290–1). He explains it by contrasting his own childhood with 'the monster birth/Engendered by these too industrious times' (v. 292–3). The character which he paints of the 'dwarf man' is opposite to his own: gone is the enthusiasm, the delight in nature, the physical excitment, the animal high spirits, all the qualities which Rousseau recognized. Instead there is a cold, disciplined intellectual, incapable of experiencing any kind of hierophany:

> He is fenced round, nay armed, for aught we know,
> In panoply complete; and fear itself,
> Natural or supernatural alike,
> Unless it leap upon him in a dream,
> Touches him not. (v. 314–18)

In a brilliant image, Wordsworth conveys both his introspection and self-centredness, and the sense that knowledge is his life-blood:

>   he must live
> Knowing that he grows wiser every day
> Or else not live at all, and seeing too
> Each little drop of wisdom as it falls
> Into the dimpling cistern of his heart (v. 341–5):

'The cistern contains', wrote Blake: 'the fountain overflows'; 'Except poison from the standing water'. Wordsworth's character is equally dead, and equally poisonous; pre-Gradgrind, he is replete with facts, 'Can string you names of districts, cities, towns,/The whole world over' (v. 335–6), and neglects the natural world around him. At this point, to point his argument more sharply, Wordsworth draws again upon the primitive sense of autochthony, in which man has his roots in the earth. The intellectual monster which he is imagining is guilty of disregard for the maternal love and provision of earth:

Meanwhile old grandame earth is grieved to find
The playthings, which her love designed for him,
Unthought of: in their woodland beds the flowers
Weep, and the river sides are all forlorn (v. 346–9).

Here the *terra genetrix* is ignored and her gifts spurned: the Lycidas-like response of the flowers and streams is evidence that the man of intellect is dead. Bring him out into the light of common sense, and he is nothing; his moving passion is vanity, and he has nothing to love but himself. This awful spectacle makes Wordsworth wish again for fairy tales,[4]

                          the wishing cap
Of Fortunatus, and the invisible coat
Of Jack the Giant-killer, Robin Hood,
And Sabra in the forest with St. George!
The child, whose love is her, at least, doth reap
One precious gain, that he forgets himself (v. 364–9).

With a masterly sense of timing and contrast, the section which follows, on the evils of a confining and mechanical education, is followed by one of the great distinctive presentations of the sacred. This is the passage beginning: 'There was a Boy: ye knew him well, ye cliffs/And islands of Winander' (v. 389–90)! Here the shamanic technique, the power of communicating with birds, presents itself with an immense power after the catalogue of modern educational methods. After the cold and lifeless man of intellect, the noise is one of rejoicing:

       he, as through an instrument,
Blew mimic hootings to the silent owls,
That they might answer him; and they would shout
Across the watery vale, and shout again,
Responsive to his call, with quivering peals,
And long halloos and screams, and echoes loud,
Redoubled and redoubled, concourse wild
Of mirth and jocund din (v. 397–404).

Even when the owls did not answer, the surprise of the silence made him aware of other things into his heart, unlike the dimpling cistern, comes the waterfall.

Then sometimes, in that silence while he hung
Listening, a gentle shock of mild surprise
Has carried far into his heart the voice
Of mountain torrents; or the visible scene
Would enter unawares into his mind,
With all its solemn imagery, its rocks,
Its woods, and that uncertain heaven, received
Into the bosom of the steady lake (v. 406–13).

The boy dies young, and returns to the earth-mother; only the poet
strives to communicate with him by standing mute beside his grave.
Yet throughout this description we are aware of ordinary profane
time. The village church, beside which the boy rests, forgets him,
and so do the village boys:

Even now, methinks, I have before my sight
That self-same village church; I see her sit
(The throned Lady spoken of erewhile)
On her green hill, forgetful of this Boy
Who slumbers at her feet, – forgetful, too,
Of all her silent neighbourhood of graves,
And listening only to the gladsome sounds
That, from the rural school ascending, play
Beneath her and about her. May she long
Behold a race of young ones like to those
With whom I herded (v. 423–33)!

The poet is here distinguished from the rest of the village by the fact
that he remembers the boy, and stands silent by his grave; yet he also
takes his place in the society of village boys, who are then described
in all their robust and imperfect humanity:

A race of real children; not too wise,
Too learned, or too good; but wanton, fresh,
And bandied up and down by love and hate;
Fierce, moody, patient, venturous, modest, shy;
Mad at their sports like withered leaves in winds;
Though doing wrong and suffering, and full oft
Bending beneath our life's mysterious weight
Of pain and fear, yet still in happiness
Not yielding to the happiest upon earth (v. 436–44).

There seems to be a double agency at work (as there was with Wordsworth's mother and wife, and the less sublime Ann Tyson) in which the influence of the shamanic boy blends with the society of the more ordinary children; yet Wordsworth's point is that, in an ideal community, the sacred and the ordinary can exist side by side, that there can be a kind of society in which a normal boy can have apprehensions of a 'something other', as the hooting boy does with the owls and the other imagery of nature. The life of the children is transient and imperfect (a nice detail of this is the one in which the poet and a friend failed to complete their saving up to buy a full edition of the *Arabian Nights*); it includes pain and fear, yet it is also happy because it includes the *I–Thou* apprehension of the external world. Just as Margaret's suffering is embraced by the pedlar, and yet he is happy, so the boys are aware of failure and loss, yet also of the primary meaningful relation to the external world; and Rousseau would have agreed that this is in every way better than the artificial goodness of the over-managed child. Where Wordsworth gives new meaning to Rousseau is by extending his ideas to include an awareness of the vital *I–Thou* relation; so that what for Rousseau is natural goodness, is for Wordsworth the power that relates man to the external world and which gives a purpose to life that even tragedy cannot destroy.

IV

The child who is brought up in a restricted manner loses many advantages: one of them is that he does not experience fear. Fear often accompanies an hierophany, as it does in the boat-stealing episode, and this cannot touch the 'dwarf man', whose imagination is stultified and narrowed by too much learning. The openness to experience which Wordsworth recommends allows the child, either through books or through events, to survive moments of terror. One example is the episode of the drowned man, when the child Wordsworth, during his first week at Hawkshead, saw the clothes lying beside the lake and witnessed the bringing up of the body – 'with his ghastly face, a spectre shape/Of terror even' (v. 472–3) – and it did not frighten him, because he had seen such sights with the inner eye, through the tales of romance.[5] In this way the reading of books acts with nature in the formation of a stable mind; and to establish their co-operation the poem returns to the river Derwent,

and the child fishing and reading. This is the scene of the first
picture of the child as savage; now a new image is superimposed on
the old one, showing the development of the human heart. Books
and nature unite to provide a nobility of mind:

> A gracious spirit o'er this earth presides,
> And o'er the heart of man: invisibly
> It comes, directing those to works of love
> Who care not, know not, think not what they do (v. 516–19).

Freedom, physical and intellectual, allows this spirit to work:

> Dumb yearnings, hidden appetites, are ours,
> And they must have their food. Our childhood sits,
> Our simple childhood, sits upon a throne
> That hath more power than all the elements (v. 530–3).

This is given more emphasis in the 1850 text by the underlining of
'must have', which implies an almost desperate insistence upon the
need for romance. It is at this stage that the youthful imagination
needs books, not to control, but to increase or reinforce its wildness.
We are, says the poet,

> Uneasy and unsettled, yoke-fellows
> To custom, mettlesome, and not yet tamed
> And humbled down; oh! then we feel, we feel,
> We know when we have friends. Ye dreamers, then,
> Forgers of lawless tales! we bless you then,
> Impostors, drivellers, dotards, as the ape
> Philosophy will call you: then we feel
> With what, and how great might ye are in league,
> Who make our wish, our power, our thought a deed,
> An empire, a possession, – ye whom time
> And seasons serve; all Faculties; to whom
> Earth crouches, the elements are potter's clay,
> Space like a heaven fulled up with northern lights,
> Here, nowhere, there, and everywhere at once (v. 544–57).

In this marvellous description of imaginative literature, the mind is
given a number of shocks: words like 'Forgers', 'Impostors' and
'drivellers' are turned on their heads to become signs of approval.

This 'my enemy's enemy is my friend' technique, gives way to a gradual enlarging of the nature and function of literature. It takes wishes, powers, thoughts, and makes of them something that we can possess, that can exist in its own right ('a deed') and that we can feel royal in ruling over ('An empire'); and then, paradoxically, it is the external world which serves literature, rather than the other way round: the earth, times and seasons, the elements, space, all join to make up the great creating and sustaining body of writing, the books that release and do not confine, that liberate the child by sustaining his most potent imaginings.

Blake's expression of this theme is found in the figure of Lyca in 'The Little Girl Lost', who wishes to sleep under the tree (being a child of nature) and thereby causes her parents much distress. Lyca sympathizes with their feelings but knows in her innocence that there is nothing to fear. When she lies down to sleep, the wild beasts come and play round her; she is undressed, thus losing the artificiality she has been bound in and returning to the natural life to which her innocence entitles her. When her parents look for her, they find a lion, of whom they are afraid; but it turns into a fairy prince, and they find their child and live with her happily in a state of nature. Wordsworth approaches the same area of misunderstanding between adult and child in 'Anecdote for Fathers' and 'We are Seven', and his treatment is instructively different. The 'matter-of-factness' which Coleridge observed shows itself clearly in the way in which the confrontation has become local and personal: instead of Lyca in the desert, there is a simple domestic scene – a father with his child walking in front of the house on a fine morning and thinking back to a former house by the sea. The father is a foolish and over-insistent questioner, who drives his little boy to a nonsensical and untruthful answer; it is a lesson in how not to bring up children, for it is an anecdote 'shewing how the art of lying may be taught' (as the title has it).

The poem begins quietly, with the father and son strolling in front of the house. Written a month or so after 'To my Sister', it again celebrates a beautiful morning, though not in this instance one of sacred time:

A day it was when I could bear
To think, and think, and think again;
With so much happiness to spare,
I could not feel a pain.

He begins to question the little boy 'In very idleness', without any
serious motive, and purely for something to do;

'My little boy, which like you more,'
I said and took him by the arm –
'Our home by Kilve's delightful shore,
'Or here at Liswyn farm?'

Three times the father takes the little boy by the arm while asking
the question. This introduces the element of compulsion and alters
the whole relationship; at the beginning it was one of love – 'And
dearly he loves me', but now it is one in which the adult holds the
child captive. The child, who has answered carelessly that he prefers
Kilve, is embarrassed when he is asked to provide a reason, and
hangs his head. The question is repeated five times, during which
the child is in a state of verbal captivity as strong as the grasp on the
arm. Searching for an answer, he sees the weather-cock; anything
will do to get out of this situation, so he invents an unlikely story that
he prefers Kilve because it has no weather-cock. A feature like this is
usually so attractive to children that his fabricated reason is
obviously inadequate; and it is at this point that the parent-cum-
gaoler-cum-inquisitor unties the knot and releases the child with an
exclamation of love. As love returns in the last verse, it does so with
the realization that it is the adult who has been wrong, and that it is
he who needs the child's teaching:

Oh dearest, dearest boy! my heart
For better lore would seldom yearn,
Could I but teach the hundredth part
Of what from thee I learn.

The ending is surprising, like the one in 'Simon Lee', where the poet
takes a normal reaction and turns it upside down. It is also an
acknowledgment of the natural way in which a child feels,
undisturbed by the requirements of adult justification; by asking for
such justification, the poet immediately destroys the dialogue which
exists at the beginning of the poem, and which is restored so fully at
the end with the expressive 'Oh dearest, dearest boy'. Though the
restoration of dialogue, the poet now understands more about the
nature of human behaviour, and the wisdom of children.
    The same illumination through a child's wisdom is found in 'We

are Seven'. Like the encounter with the original of Peter Bell, the meeting with this little girl took place during Wordsworth's liminal journey of 1793. In her innocent happiness she is like Johnny in 'The Idiot Boy', an 'ec-static': she stands outside the constraints of normal understanding of death, and is therefore released from its threat. The adult seeks to make her understand, and he is wrong to do so: the child, who 'feels its life in every limb' has an inexplicable sense of the continuing life of her dead brother and sister. The poem, although it is question and answer, is without dialogue, for the poet adopts an *I–It* mode of perception: he goes in for simple arithmetic, explaining that two from seven equals five. The child remains unconvinced, and the skilful handling of the poem ensures that her way of perceiving things exists side by side with the adult way, and even uses the same evidence. As the poet points out, she is able to run about and they are not; but to the child her activity near their graves is what joins her to them. She sits beside the graves knitting stockings or hemming a handkerchief, singing to the children, or she takes her supper and eats it 'with' them. She is quite unconscious that her statements, to an adult, actually point up the contrast between the living and the dead: to her they are evidence of something quite different. Her mind is inviolable, and the adult is seen as excluded from her vision.

Is she wrong? This is a difficult a question to answer, because from one point of view she clearly is. The two children are dead. From another point of view she is not wrong – from the point of view of the *I–Thou* as a mode of relation. In her simplicity the child has preserved an innocent faith in the goodness of the world, and in the oneness of all things, living and dead, in love. By the side of this the adult seems negative, carping, anti-life. So, in *The Prelude*, Wordsworth pleads for freedom, because

> at such time no vulgar power
> Was working in us, nothing less, in truth,
> Than that most noble attribute of man,
> Though yet untutor'd and inordinate,
> That wish for something loftier, more adorn'd,
> Than is the common aspect, daily garb
> Of human life (v. 595–601).

If this seems to contradict what Wordsworth says elsewhere about ordinary things and ordinary life being sufficient for him, the answer is that to some degree they are: but it is through this ordinary life, as led by the poet himself, or the child of 'We are Seven', that the 'something other' can be perceived. What *The Prelude* asks for in Book v is that the child shall be left alone to perceive and retain it, as it is found both in books and in nature.

V

A further expression of these views is found in the 'Reply to Mathetes', published in *The Friend* in December 1809 and January 1810. 'Mathetes' (John Wilson) had emphasized the importance of an enlightened teacher or friend, and Wordsworth counters with a strong plea for a morality that originates from within:

> Protection from any fatal effect of seductions and hindrances which opinion may throw in the way of pure and high-minded Youth can only be obtained with certainty at the same price by which every thing great and good is obtained, namely, steady dependence upon voluntary and self-originating effort, and upon the practice of self-examination sincerely aimed at and rigorously enforced.[6]

Wordsworth develops this by suggesting questions which youth can ask itself, and profit from the answers, seeing Reason and Nature as united in leading youth onward (p. 16). But because the education is actively from within, progress is often more in the manner of a river than of a road. But the pupil who is too carefully supervised may find his powers degenerating into 'passiveness and prostration of mind' (p. 23). This figure establishes his own strength:

> He will not long have his admiration fixed upon unworthy objects; he will neither be clogged nor drawn aside by the love of friends or kindred, betraying his understanding through his affections; he will neither be bowed down by conventional arrangements of manners producing too often a lifeless decency; nor will the rock of his Spirit wear away in the endless beating of the waves of the World: neither will that portion of his own time, which he must surrender to labours by which his livelihood is to be earned or his social duties performed, be unprofitable to himself indirectly, while it is directly useful to others: for that time

has been primarily surrendered through an act of obedience to a moral law established by himself, and therefore he moves them also along the orbit of perfect liberty (p. 24).

This independent, self-discovering character has a connection with the developing youth in *The Prelude*, whose mistakes – Godwinism and the picturesque, for instance – help him to discover himself and the world:

> Long time in search of knowledge desperate,
> I was benighted heart and mind; but now
> On all sides day began to reappear,
> And it was proved indeed that not in vain
> I had been taught to reverence a Power
> That is the very quality and shape
> And image of right reason, that matures
> Her processes by steadfast laws, gives birth
> To no impatient or fallacious hopes,
> No heat of passion or excessive zeal,
> No vain conceits, provokes to no quick turns
> Of self-applauding intellect, but lifts
> The Being into magnanimity;
> Holds up before the mind, intoxicate
> With present objects and the busy dance
> Of things that pass away, a temperate shew
> Of objects that endure, and by this course
> Disposes her, when over-fondly set
> On leaving her incumbrances behind
> To seek in Man, and in the frame of life,
> Social and individual, what there is
> Desirable, affecting, good or fair
> Of kindred permanence, the gifts divine
> And universal, the pervading grace
> That hath been, is, and shall be (*The Prelude*, XII. 20–44).

The most spectacular mistake in *The Prelude* is the moment when Wordsworth and Jones took the wrong path, thinking that they still had to go upward to cross the Alps. The whole description seems to emphasize that they made the wrong decision: there were two paths, and they took the wrong one –

The only track now visible was one
Upon the further side, right opposite,
And up a lofty Mountain. This we took
After a little scruple, and short pause,
And climb'd with eagerness (*The Prelude*, vi. 504–8).

The fact that this mistake leads to a great moment of illumination, as the poet realizes the possibilities inherent in the human imagination, is a central moment in the growth of his mind; for growth is no straightforward progress, but a subtle and wavering process of loss and gain – symbolized in the 'Reply' by the river image –

> Which both in its smaller reaches and larger turnings, is frequently forced back towards its fountains, by objects which cannot otherwise be eluded or overcome; yet with an accompanying impulse that will ensure its advancement hereafter, it is either gaining strength every hour, or conquering in secret some difficulty, by a labour that contributes as effectually to further it in its course, as when it moves forward uninterrupted in a line, . . . (p. 11).

It is this process which is contained in *The Prelude*, and it may have been to accommodate this that the poem was developed from a two-part celebration of childhood to a more complex and detailed study of the poet's growth in later years. The result of the whole process is seen in the final book, which describes the *I–Thou* state which is the consequence of the natural organic education which has been the subject of this chapter. As we have seen, it depends on love, and it involves the ordinary human accidents – mistakes, and unexpected discoveries. There is an element of the unexpected in the Snowdon passage: as the poet is leading the way

> at my feet the ground appear'd to brighten,
> And with a step or two seem'd brighter still;
> Nor had I time to ask the cause of this,
> For instantly a Light upon the turf
> Fell like a flash: I looked about, and lo!
> The Moon stood naked in the Heavens (xiii. 36–41).

At the end of this magnificent section, the poet muses on the ability of nature to present a dominating idea to the mind, so that 'even the grossest minds must see and hear/And cannot chuse but feel' (83–4). Such a power

> which Nature thus
> Thrusts forth upon the senses, is the express
> Resemblance, in the fulness of its strength
> Made visible, a genuine Counterpart
> And Brother of the glorious faculty
> Which higher minds bear with them as their own (85–90).

The focus is on the contrast between the grossest minds and the higher minds: the former can, in moments of natural splendour, be affected by the same power of relation which is present always in the higher minds; and it is clear from what follows that the poet is concerning himself with an *I–Thou* mode of preception, or what Eliade would consider a sacred mode of being:

> Them the enduring and the transient both
> Serve to exalt; they build up greatest things
> From least suggestions, ever on the watch,
> Willing to work and to be wrought upon,
> They need not extraordinary calls
> To rouze them, in a world of life they live,
> By sensible impressions not enthrall'd,
> But quicken'd, rouz'd, and made thereby more apt
> To hold communion with the invisible world.
> Such minds are truly from the Deity,
> For they are Powers; and hence the highest bliss
> That can be known is theirs, the consciousness
> Of whom they are habitually infused
> Through every image, and through every thought,
> And all impressions; hence religion, faith,
> And endless occupation for the soul
> Whether discursive or intuitive;
> Hence sovereignty within and peace at will
> Emotion which best foresight need not fear
> Most worthy then of trust when most intense.
> Hence chearfulness in every act of life
> Hence truth in moral judgements and delight
> That fails not in the external universe (97–119).

The whole of this extended quotation points to an awareness of the natural world as sanctified. The higher minds catch the smallest hints and suggestions from nature, build up their consciousness of a higher power within it, and are able to lead lives of inner peace, cheerfulness and delight. Similarly Eliade writes:

> For religious man, nature is never only 'natural'; it is always fraught with a religious value . . . . The world stands displayed in such a manner that, in contemplating it, religious man discovers the many modalities of the sacred, and hence of being. Above all, the world exists, it is there, and it has a structure; it is not a chaos but a cosmos, hence it presents itself as creation, as work of the gods. This divine work always preserves its quality of transparency, that is, it spontaneously reveals the many aspects of the sacred.[7]

It is this comprehensive vision which Wordsworth has arrived at in the conclusion to his great autobiographical poem. He goes on to expand his ideas, with reference to human love and divine love – 'a love that comes into the Heart/With awe and a diffusive sentiment' and which 'proceeds/More from the brooding Soul, and is divine' (162–5). This love, says Wordsworth, cannot exist without Imagination, and he describes how he has traced the course of this power, from its early mysterious beginnings, following it as it became evident and open, losing sight of it,

> Then given it greeting, as it rose once more
> With strength, reflecting in its solemn breast
> The works of man and face of human life,
> And lastly, from its progress have we drawn
> The feeling of life endless, the great thought
> By which we live, Infinity and God (179–84).

So the Imagination has been, in Eliot's words, 'lost/And found and lost again and again'; and Eliot's 'fight to recover' the poetic vision has the same kind of relation to his apprehension of the divine love that is found in Wordsworth's connection between the Imagination and the *agape* of awe and diffusive sentiment – the divine love made manifest in nature, the continuous hierophany which is to be discovered in the visible universe by the higher mind.

11 The Stability of Home

It is easy to make fun of Wordsworth's domestic felicity in his later years: of the poet of Grasmere and Rydal, surrounded by admiring women. Yet his love of home life, of domestic peace and harmony, is a natural consequence of the instability of his childhood. Book IV of *The Prelude* is concerned with a return to the only home which the poet had known since infancy, and as early as *An Evening Walk* Wordsworth was imagining a home with Dorothy, a distant scene of simple happiness. When the opportunity first came for them to set up house together (at Windy Brow in 1794), the experience included more than just a roof over their heads: it involved an ideal life of simplicity, of frugality and economy – 'our breakfast and supper are of milk and our dinner chiefly of potatoes and we drink no tea', wrote Dorothy.[1] Later, at Racedown and Alfoxden, Dorothy (with the help of Coleridge) preserved the poet's confidence in himself and his art; and in their companionship may be seen the forerunner of the community of family and friends which became so important in later years. In the companionship of Dorothy, Mary and Sara Hutchinson, the ideal became actual: there was a restoration of a loving community in the presence of a surrounding nature.

'Home at Grasmere', which celebrates the inauguration of the residence with Dorothy there, is a curious and fascinating poem, principally because it blends so intricately the human and the charismatic or prophetic. It is liminal in two ways, directions which neatly correspond to the two previous sections of this study. It is liminal in that it deals with a threshold experience in relation to the community: the poet and his sister arrive as newcomers, and hope to become integrated into it. It is also liminal in that it deals with a transformation from ordinary man into prophet.

We may take the community first. The vale is 'This small Abiding-place of many Men' (146), and in it the poet and his sister are strangers. They identify themselves with two swans, who came

> to sojourn here in solitude,
> Chusing this Valley, they who had the choice
> Of the whole world (241–3).

Although they resemble the swans in many ways, the swans have disappeared, and the poet conjectures that they may have been shot by the dalesmen. Such a conjecture suggests a community which is far from perfect, and although the poet immediately recalls the thought as ungenerous, it remains as a possibility. Indeed, the idea of a perfect community is seen as pleasing but as wishful thinking:

> Ah, if I wished to follow where the sight
> Of all that is before my eyes, the voice
> Which speaks from a presiding Spirit here,
> Would lead me, I should whisper to myself;
> They who are dwellers in this holy place
> Must needs themselves be hallowed, they require
> No benediction from the Stranger's lips,
> For they are blest already. None would give
> The greeting 'peace be with you' unto them,
> For peace they have, it cannot but be theirs,
> And mercy, and forbearance (273–83).

Such an idea is not to be blamed; indeed, such a contemplation of the ideal is good for the soul of man, even though it involves a 'forgetfulness' of the actual. It involves a surrender to the 'presiding Spirit', the 'visible Presence' of the place, which can deceive

> And lap in pleasing rest, and bear us on
> Without desire in full complacency,
> Contemplating perfection absolute
> And entertained as in a placid sleep (305–8).

As so often in Wordsworth, the dream is vivid, exciting in its possibilities of man living in brotherhood in the beautiful vale; but once again the realism takes over, and we understand that this is no ideal community but an actual one:

> But not betrayed by tenderness of mind
> That feared, or wholly overlook'd the truth,
> Did we come hither, with romantic hope

To find, in midst of so much loveliness,
Love, perfect love; of so much majesty
A like majestic frame of mind in those
Who here abide, the persons like the place (309–15).

Although it is denied, the ideal is stated with an insistence that
shows how fascinated the poet is by the possibility. He denies it
strongly:

I came not dreaming of unruffled life,
Untainted manners; born among the hills,
Bred also there, I wanted not a scale
To regulate my hopes. Pleased with the good,
I shrink not from the evil with disgust,
Or with immoderate pain. I look for Man,
The common Creature of the brotherhood,
Differing but little from the Man elsewhere,
For selfishness, and envy, and revenge,
Ill neighbourhood – pity that this should be –
Flattery and double-dealing, strife and wrong (347–57).

Yet in spite of this theoretical denial that man is any different here,
the poet goes on to indicate certain crucial ways in which there are
special advantages. In this vale men are independent, and free from
cold, poverty and hunger; they are allowed to feel the human
emotions which might be stifled in other places. An example is the
shepherd's widow, described with beautiful economy. She has 'a
gentle Spirit/Of memory faithful to the call of love' (387–8); she
remembers her husband and herself planting the grove of fir trees for
the sheep, and their care for 'the patient creatures' (they are seen as
loving and caring, the sheep as humanized). As Wordsworth points
out, this is different from 'pastoral fancies'; the widow is now old,
'withering in her loneliness', and her husband is dead, while in their
prime the business of looking after sheep was hard work. Yet there is
in this life dignity and grace; the realities of good and evil, in this
place, are part of a true humanity. It is this which will unite himself
and his sister to the community: they will be like the Grasmere folk,
as yet unknown, in that they are able to live in harmony with their
environment:

Look where we will, some human heart has been
Before us with its offering; not a tree

Sprinkles these little pastures but the same
Hath furnished matter for a thought; perchance
For some one serves as a familiar friend (440–4).

The result is that the whole valley becomes somehow related to the
human life that is lived there, whether good or bad:

Joy spreads, and sorrow spreads; and this whole Vale,
Home of untutored Shepherds as it is,
Swarms with sensation, as with gleams of sunshine,
Shadows or breezes, scents or sounds (445–8).

All the inhabitants can partake of this, the poet most of all, since he
and Dorothy are free from the preoccupation with the everyday
necessities of living; but for everyone the mountain sanctuary may
be

Diffusing health and sober chearfulness,
And giving to the moments as they pass
Their little boons of animating thought
That sweeten labour, make it seen and felt
To be no arbitrary weight imposed,
But a glad function natural to Man (465–70).

Actually to be living in such a place is a wonderful opportunity for
all men, but above all for the poet. He knows that he cannot, like a
traveller, avoid 'unwelcome things, which unawares/Reveal
themselves' (494–5), but he is not depressed by this,

But confident, enriched at every glance.
The more I see the more delight my mind
Receives, or by reflexion can create.
Truth justifies herself, and as she dwells
With Hope, who would not follow where she leads (497–501)?

The final part of the poem, from line 500 onwards, is concerned with
what this state of mature and tempered hopefulness means for the
poet. In the first place it means a love for created things, for animals
and birds; it means a delighted recognition of the seen landscape,
both of the minute details (562–7) and the general effect (567–79);
and it involves a sense of belonging to a community which is quite
different from the solitude of a city:

From crowed streets remote,
Far from the living and dead wilderness
Of the thronged World, Society is here
A true Community, a genuine frame
Of many into one incorporate (612–6).

In this community man and beast live together, under God, in a
state which is not Arcadian (625) but full of hope: and now the
poem returns to the home, to Dorothy, John Wordsworth and
Coleridge – to the society within a society, and to the poet himself:

Possessions have I that are solely mine,
Something within which yet is shared by none,
Not even the nearest to me and most dear,
Something which power and effort may impart,
I would impart it, I would spread it wide,
Immortal in the world which is to come (686–91).

He then turns back briefly to his childhood, to recall his delight in
danger, courage and violence; this is the child who one day
stumbled on the paradisal vale, now the mature man who knows it is
not a pastoral Arcadia, but who knows where its value lies. And just
as Milton rejected the older epic values in favour of 'patience and
heroic martydom/Unsung', so Wordsworth hears the voice of
Reason supporting Nature: 'Be mild and cleave to gentle things,/
Thy glory and thy happiness be there' (735–6). For this peace, which
corresponds to the peaceful vale, Wordsworth says farewell to the
'Warrior's schemes' (745), and to his hope 'to fill/The Heroic
trumpet with the Muse's breath' (749–50). Like Milton, he has
other things to sing of, 'The simple produce of a common
day'.

The poet's relationship to the community, his connecting link
with other men, is through a common love of nature. It is this which
also enables the poet to discern the paradise in ordinary life, and to
turn from ordinary man to prophet in the process. Throughout the
first 750 lines of 'Home at Grasmere' the poet is qualifying,
reasoning, understanding; at the end, in the section printed in
Wordsworth's lifetime as the *Prospectus* to *The Excursion*, he emerges
(as the winter turns to spring) as prophet. For most of the poem,
however, the liminal position in which the poet finds himself –
arriving, yet not fully arrived – is responsible for the complex,

mature vision which is aware of the actual as well as the ideal. The poem is a celebration of Grasmere as paradise, yet it also, as we have seen, contains an awareness of the possibility of evil. The poet is the same person who came across the vale as a child (he is careful to tell us) but he now has an awareness of complexities and difficulties; even when remembering his childhood experience, he uses words like 'Mortal separation' which suggest an adult interpretation of a childhood moment:

> What happy fortune were it here to live!
> And, if a thought of dying, if a thought
> Of mortal separation, could intrude
> With paradise before him, here to die (11–15)!

The thought of dying certainly does intrude into 'Home at Grasmere', notably in the cases of the two swans and the shepherd; and throughout the poem there is an unusual mixture of a rational view of Grasmere and a sense that it embodies some kind of mythic paradise. It is as though the poet is half in the mythic mode of perception, and half still in the profane and historical mode; only at the end does he emerge from this liminal state.

This is partly in accordance with the poet's function within the poem. Kenneth Johnston, in his subtle reading,[2] suggests that if *The Prelude* is predominantly a prophetic book, *The Recluse* aims at being a priestly book, celebrating what is known already, the continual return to the central relationship between man and nature. To this may be added Weber's distinction between the prophet and the priest, in which the priest lays claim to authority by virtue of his service in a sacred tradition, while the prophet's claim is based on personal revelation and charisma. Until the end, 'Home at Grasmere' is essentially unconcerned with charisma: it is tentative and celebratory. The child, we are told explicitly, is 'No Prophet', and the adult is fallible and uncertain. As early as the second line, we are given something very different from the precise timing of *The Prelude* – 'what the Adventurer's age/Hath now escaped his memory' – and throughout the poem there are doubts and uncertainties, and the kind of questions which would only occur to an adult. In order to return to Grasmere, for instance, the adult has to take responsible decisions which involve choices; and that his final choice is made after much thought and against some pressure, is indicated by a confusing series of questions:

> And was the cost so great? and could it seem
> An act of courage, and the thing itself
> A conquest? who must bear the blame? sage Man
> Thy prudence, thy experience – thy desires,
> Thy apprehensions – blush thou for them all (60–4).

Behind these questions is a mature awareness of what is involved in taking such a decision: it takes courage, and self-sacrifice. That this is so is a consequence of man's prudence and fear, which man in his wisdom – a wisdom which the poet sees as doubtful – has developed. This suggests that there should have been no doubt that he was taking the right decision; yet, as so often in the poetry of this period, Wordsworth can see two sides to the question. He embraces the new life with joy, and yet admits that there have been great benefits from the other life, the *vita activa* of the outside world:

> Yes, the realities of life so cold,
> So cowardly, so ready to betray,
> So stinted in the measure of their grace
> As we pronounce them, doing them much wrong,
> Have been to me more bountiful than hope,
> Less timid than desire – but that is passed (65–70).

This recognition is nevertheless succeeded by the claim that 'On Nature's invitation do I come,/By Reason sanctioned'; and it is not so much answered as pushed aside by the contemplation of life with Dorothy in Grasmere:

> Can the choice mislead,
> That made the calmest, fairest spot of earth,
> With all its unappropriated good,
> My own; and not mine only, for with me
> Entrenched, say rather peacefully embowered,
> Under yon Orchard, in yon humble Cot,
> A younger Orphan of a Home extinct,
> The only Daughter of my Parents, dwells (72–9).

The reference to the extinct home and the dead parents is important: it underlines the element of re-establishing, re-creating a home at Grasmere, a substitute for the home that was lost. If Grasmere is a paradise, it is a paradise which in part has been

discovered, but in part regained, and which is all the more valued
for its having been lost:

> – What Being, therefore, since the birth of Man
> Had ever more abundant cause to speak
> Thanks, and if favours of the heavenly Muse
> Make him more thankful, then to call on verse
> To aid him, and in Song resound his joy.
> The boon is absolute; surpassing grace
> To me hath been vouchsafed; among the bowers
> Of blissful Eden this was neither given,
> Nor could be given, possession of the good
> Which had been sighed for, ancient thought fulfilled
> And dear Imaginations realized
> Up to their highest measure, yea and more (98–109).

There is thus an intricate pattern of paradise and its opposite, the
world in which the poet discovers loss but also blessing in his own
kind of fortunate fall. The echo of Milton is clear throughout:
Adam, outside Eden, understands something of the purposes of
God, and the archangel counsels him to add to this knowledge faith,
virtue, patience, temperance, and love, 'By name to come call'd
Charitie, the soul/Of all the rest . . . ' (*Paradise Lost*, xii. 584–5).
Wordsworth, like Adam, is standing with one foot in Eden (Adam is
just leaving, Wordsworth just entering). He is fully conscious of the
accidents and difficulties of living, yet also of the possibilities of
perfection in such a place. For the vale has its own un-nameable
qualities:

> 'Tis, but I cannot name it, 'tis the sense
> Of majesty, and beauty, and repose,
> A blended holiness of earth and sky,
> Something that makes this individual Spot,
> This small Abiding-place of many Men,
> A termination, and a last retreat,
> A Centre, come from whereso'er you will,
> A Whole without dependence or defect,
> Made for itself; and happy in itself,
> Perfect Contentment, Unity entire (142–51).

The accumulative style, always pushing forwards ('Tis . . . 'tis),

which is so noticeable throughout 'Home at Grasmere' is here used
to approach the place with the right kind of tentative assertion. The
sentence itself begins hesitantly, and then becomes more assured as
the religious language takes over, emerging finally with the
triumphant 'Perfect Contentment, Unity entire'. It is clear that
Grasmere, although not a perfect society, has the characteristics for
the poet of what we have come to recognize as sacred space: it is a
centre, a whole , a place of contentment and unity. The next section,
which describes the journey taken to arrive there, emphasizes these
qualities: it was a difficult journey to a centre, a termination and
retreat. The poet has reached home, and in 'Home at Grasmere'
Wordsworth is using home in the spiritual as well as the geographical or physical sense; Grasmere is a abiding place of the spirit, an
end of the journey. It is where the poet reconstitutes his home, the
home that he and Dorothy lost as children, but also the home that he
has been seeking to rediscover spiritually. *Four Quartets*, which
touches 'Home at Grasmere' at several places, is concerned with the
same process:

> Home is where on starts from. As we grow older
> The world becomes stranger, the pattern more complicated
> Of dead and living ('East Coker', v).

Wordsworth, after experiencing the complexities of the world
beyond Grasmere, is returning to it as to a centre, an end:

> We shall not cease from exploration
> And the end of all our exploring
> Will be to arrive where we started
> And know the place for the first time.
> Through the unknown, remembered gate
> When the last of earth left to discover
> Is that which was the beginning ('Little Gidding', v);

Eliot, like Wordsworth, is concerned with place, with the journey to
arrive and what the journey signifies; in Wordsworth's case there is a
comfortless journey across north Yorkshire ('Stern was the face of
Nature') which emphasizes the dangerous passage, the narrow way
from the ordinary world to the ideal one. And when he and Dorothy
arrive at Grasmere, they do not come 'to kneel/Where prayer has

been valid', but to set up home, to become a part of a community and share its relationship to the external world.

This satisfies a set of needs: to restore the lost home of childhood, to participate in a meaningful relationship with nature, to become part of life in such a place. Yet just as Wordsworth recognizes that the community is not perfect, so he also sees the residence in Grasmere as not permanent. It is a retreat, a centre, and a sacred space, but there are other demands which must be met: the coming 'home', both physically and in spirit, has to be seen as a welcome pause in the journey of life:

> What, if I floated down a pleasant Stream
> And now am landed, and the motion gone,
> Shall I reprove myself? Ah no, the Stream
> Is flowing, and will never cease to flow,
> And I shall float upon that Stream again (292–6).

The coming home to Grasmere thus becomes something like the periodic return to a sacred space of *Homo religiosus*. It makes a vital and enlivening return to the ideal, to the primordial sacred time; but the remainder, the ordinary profane human time-bound existence, must not be forgotten, and the beauty of Grasmere also involves a forgetfulness:

> By such forgetfulness the Soul becomes,
> Words cannot say, how beautiful; then hail,
> Hail to the visible Presence, hail to thee,
> Delightful Valley, habitation fair (297–300)!

The forgetfulness here involves the idea, suggested in the previous paragraph, that the people of Grasmere have 'an overflowing love'; it is a beautiful idea, and one that is consonant with the idea of Grasmere as sacred place, but it is also seen as ignoring other claims. So Wordsworth hails this beauty as elevating, but also deceiving:

> hail to thee,
> Delightful Valley, habitation fair!
> And to whatever else of outward form
> Can give us inward help, can purify,
> And elevate, and harmonise, and soothe,
> And steal away, and for a while deceive

And lap in pleasing rest, and bear us on
Without desire in full complacency,
Contemplating perfection absolute
And entertained as in a placid sleep (299–308).

The effect here is complex, but clear in its implications: the beauty
which elevates also ignores, and if Grasmere is 'home' the poet also
acknowledges the primary claims of the other world outside. The
absolute perfection is the perfection of a dream.

'Home at Grasmere' is a poem, therefore, that operates on two
levels. It is powerfully and vividly aware of possible perfection, of
Grasmere as a perfect centre and whole, and of the community as an
ideal society; yet it is also profoundly and humanly cognizant of the
actual circumstances which exist there and elsewhere. Yet although
the ideal is categorized as part of a dream, it is throughout portrayed
with more vividness than the actual. The poet dwells on the
conception of Grasmere as paradise, celebrates it, describes it
lovingly:

– How vast the compass of this theatre,
Yet nothing to be seen but lovely pomp
And silent majesty; the birch-tree woods
Are hung with thousand thousand diamond drops
Of melted hoar-frost, every tiny knot
In the bare twigs, each little budding-place
Cased with its several bead, what myriads there
Upon one tree, while all the distant grove
That rises to the summit of the steep
Shows like a mountain built of silver light (560–9).

Miraculously, here, the minute effect of the beads of melted frost
extends over the whole hillside, so that it is all transformed; indeed,
transformation and illusion are effects which the poet celebrates:

See yonder the same pageant, and again
Behold the universal imagery
Inverted, all its sun-bright features touched
As with the varnish, and the gloss of dreams;
Dreamlike the blending also of the whole
Harmonious landscape; all along the shore
The boundary lost, the line invisible

That parts the image from reality;
And the clear hills, as high as they ascend
Heavenward, so piercing deep the lake below (570–9).

This is illusory, dream-like, yet it is also there, a perceivable natural effect; and 'Home at Grasmere' is a poem which deals, again and again, with the dream, the illusion, becoming actual. The shepherd's widow, for example, is someone who has a strong relationship to her surroundings, and especially to the covert which she and her husband had planted for the sheep. Yet in spite of this, the poet remains firmly cognizant of the world which he is leaving. If he is 'at home' at Grasmere, in this place which can correspond to his dream world, he also knows that this is not the whole truth: that there is ill-neighbourhood, strife and wrong, here as elsewhere. It is thus a poem which is about a personal view: in that view the unhappiness of the outside world exists, but (as Kenneth Johnston points out) the poem continually turns inward upon itself – to Grasmere, embraced by the mountains, to the poet's home, within the village and embraced by it. It is, quite simply, a dream come true, though a dream which does not invalidate the rest of experience.

II

The poem may be 'reclusive', in Johnston's phrase, but its awareness of a wider world is reflected in its acknowledgment that such a privileged existence has its obligations. 'Something', says the poet firmly, 'must be done':

I must not walk in unreproved delight
These narrow bounds, and think of nothing more,
No duty that looks further, and no care (665–8).

Once again the matter is seen in geographical terms, with the vale of Grasmere as the enclosed narrow bounds, and the world of duty outside. Wordsworth sees a poet's duty as extending to others, and not as involving the development of his own mind and sensibilities to the exclusion of others. He is to send out from Grasmere, that is from his own centre, his own individual vision of what that centre is:

Possessions have I that are solely mine,
Something within which yet is shared by none,
Not even the nearest to me and most dear,
Something which power and effort may impart,
I would impart it, I would spread it wide,
Immortal in the world which is to come (686–91).

It is this assertion that the poet himself has unique possessions, not
shared even by his sister (who earlier in the poem was so important to
his sense of being 'at home'), which prepares the reader for the
transformation of the ordinary man into the prophet. With this goes
the setting out of the subject, firstly in a negative way, and then
positively. The poet surveys his early love of danger, savagery and
conflict, and, like Milton, he turns from these to less turbulent
matters. Nature says

                 Be mild and cleave to gentle things,
Thy glory and thy happiness be there.
Nor fear, though thou confide in me, a want
Of aspirations that *have* been, of foes
To wrestle with, and victory to complete,
Bounds to be leapt, darkness to be explored (735–40).

Like Milton, Wordsworth claims that his subject-matter is more
than adequate as a substitute for the old heroic virtues; that, indeed,
it contains its own heroism. And with this he moves into the most
Miltonic of all his poems (except perhaps the first book of *The
Prelude*), the passage beginning 'On Man, on Nature, and on
Human Life' which was printed as the *Prospectus* of *The Excursion*.

Because it was taken out of 'Home at Grasmere' and printed
separately, the *Prospectus* section has customarily been considered as
a powerful statement in its own right, notably by M. H. Abrams,
who places it firmly in the tradition of apocalyptic literature.[3] It
gains further significance, I suggest, if it is seen as the conclusion to
the poem which has explored the poet's entry into his true 'home',
and his application of this to the external world, the outer world
beyond Grasmere. As the complex exploration of home and
beyond, dream and reality, internal and external comes to an end,
the poet turns inwards, settling into a contemplation of his home,
and what it involves for him. In retirement, he finds himself: not

losing his awareness of humanity and its problems, but rather recognizing them as an inevitable part of the process of living. So he is able to muse in solitude, 'On Man, on Nature, and on Human Life'; this includes delight and sadness, good and evil, with the good soothing the mind, but the evil elevating it. Yet as with the pedlar, these necessarily mixed patterns are seen with equanimity, as 'Fair trains of imagery',

> Accompanied by feelings of delight
> Pure, or with no unpleasing sadness mixed;
> And I am conscious of affecting thoughts
> And dear remembrances, whose presence soothes
> Or elevates the Mind, intent to weigh
> The good and evil of our mortal state.

Since the poet has achieved his own stability, since he feels 'at home', he is able to undertake this extensive view. The subjects proposed continue to demonstrate the relationship between the grand survey and the single mind at peace with itself:

> Of Truth, of Grandeur, Beauty, Love, and Hope,
> And melancholy Fear subdued by Faith;
> Of blessed consolations in distress;
> Of moral strength, and intellectual Power;
> Of joy in widest commonalty spread;
> Of the individual Mind that keeps her own
> Inviolate retirement, subject there
> To Conscience only, and the law supreme
> Of that Intelligence which governs all –
> I sing: – 'fit audience let me find though few!'

Even before the quotation, the pattern of good coming out of evil is reflective of *Paradise Lost*; as Edwin Muir was later to write

> What had Eden ever to say
> Of hope and faith and pity and love
> Until was buried all its day
> And memory found its treasure trove ('One Foot in Eden')?

and Wordsworth's combination of an understanding of the mixed fortunes of man with the inviolate mind of man echoes Adam's final

understanding of the purposes of God in Milton's epic. If Adam
adds deeds to his knowledge, the archangel assures him,

> then wilt thou not be loath
> To leave this Paradise, but shalt possess
> A paradise within thee, happier far (xii. 585–7).

'A paradise within thee' is perhaps the truest equivalent of
Wordsworth's sense of being 'at home' at Grasmere. He knows that
Grasmere is not a perfect society, but it is for him 'Home', a centre;
and having this stability, he can contemplate both beauty and
suffering. Both are found within the mind of man, and it is in this
contemplation that Wordsworth claims to enter a world which is
beyond the reach of most men – indeed, beyond his reach without
help from a higher power:

> Paradise, and groves
> Elysian, Fortunate Fields – like those of old
> Sought in the Atlantic Main – why should they be
> A history only of departed things,
> Or a mere fiction of what never was?
> For the discerning intellect of Man,
> When wedded to this goodly universe
> In love and holy passion, shall find these
> A simple produce of the common day.

Once again we have the confrontation of the ideal and the actual,
but to the mind at home which Wordsworth has been exploring
throughout the poem this is a consummation and not a
confrontation: the ideal is made actual, and becomes in his
exquisitely simple line 'the simple produce of a common day'. Since
the poet, as we have seen, has a duty to do something, it is clear that
Wordsworth sees that duty as anticipating a golden age when all
men will feel this, and paradise will be restored. So he intends to sing
alone, but in peace, 'the spousal verse/Of this great consummation'.
He is, indeed, fulfilling what he saw (in the 1802 letter to John
Wilson) as the poet's function: 'He ought to travel before men
occasionally as well as at their sides.'[4] If the poet is before men, then
beauty goes before the poet, leading him on like Moses in the
wilderness:

– Beauty – a living Presence of the earth,
Surpassing the most fair ideal Forms
Which craft of delicate Spirits hath composed
From earth's materials – waits upon my steps;
Pitches her tents before me as I move,
An hourly neighbour.

          Urania, I shall need
Thy guidance, or a greater Muse, if such
Descend to earth or dwell in highest heaven!
For I must tread on shadowy ground, must sink
Deep – and, aloft ascending, breathe in worlds
To which the heaven of heavens is but a veil.

At this point the whole process of 'Home at Grasmere' begins to become clear. From the child who first stumbles upon the valley and thinks it paradise, we have seen the arrival of the poet and his sister who know that it cannot, externally, be paradise, for nowhere on this earth is free from the vices of man – ill-neighbourhood, strife and wrong. Yet the poet knows that Grasmere corresponds to something deep within himself, and that to be at home in it represents a paradise within himself, happier than any external paradise. Such a discovery, and its exploration, is truly awe-inspiring: that paradise is not in the external world, but in the marriage between the external world and the mind:

          Not Chaos, not
The darkest pit of lowest Erebus,
Nor aught of blinder vacancy, scooped out
By help of dreams – can breed such fear and awe
As fall upon us often when we look
Into our Minds, into the Mind of Man –
My haunt, and the main region of my song.

The Miltonic pattern of rhetoric – 'not . . . not' – is responsible for the impressive effect of elevation; yet Wordsworth brilliantly returns to earth (literally) with his next question, which asserts that paradise is not some historical phenomenon, but is existing in the here and now. The poet has his own equivalent of the wilderness: as well as singing of the beauty of the world and the marriage of man and nature, he has also the prospect that he may often

                    travel near the tribes
And fellowships of men, and see ill sights
Of madding passions mutually inflamed;
Must hear Humanity in fields and groves
Pipe solitary anguish; or must hang
Brooding above the fierce confederate storm
Of sorrow, barricadoed evermore
Within the walls of cities –

and, both for his treatment of beauty and his exposure of suffering, he prays, finally, for the descent of the prophetic spirit. If 'Home at Grasmere' began with the child – 'No Prophet was he' – it ends with the adult, sure of his role and convinced of his subject. He is now ready for the descent of the prophetic spirit; he has 'found himself', in the stability of home.

III

The 'Home' of 'Home at Grasmere' is thus a vital place, a place for living with Dorothy (and John, and other friends), and a place in the mind where the external world corresponds to the internal mind. From its security the poet can look out to the world beyond, with its complexities of joy and pain. Not surprisingly, perhaps, the idea of home plays an important part in a number of the poems written in the years 1800–2. In 'Michael', for instance, the shepherd and his wife live in frugal simplicity. Their life is one of 'eager industry', their food pottage, skimmed milk, oat-cakes and home-made cottage cheese. Outside, the place for Michael, as for the shepherds in 'Home at Grasmere', 'swarms with sensation':

And grossly that man errs, who should suppose
That the green valleys, and the streams and rocks,
Were things indifferent to the Shepherd's thoughts.
Fields, where with cheerful spirits he had breathed
The common air; hills, which with vigorous step
He had so often climbed; . . .
                              had laid
Strong hold on his affections, were to him
A pleasurable feeling of blind love,
The pleasure which there is in life itself (62–7, 74–7).

Yet this simple life, this beautiful valley, are not immune from trouble: financial difficulties reach out and destroy the simple family pattern even here. The family is united, and the community gives them support, with the neighbours coming out to wish Luke well when he leaves and having pity for Michael after his son's fall. But Michael's desolation, at the end, is complete, and his cottage has been destroyed. 'Michael' is in some ways a mirror-image of 'Home at Grasmere': instead of someone arriving and building a home, the main pattern is of someone leaving and destroying a home.

Wordsworth makes it clear that he is not just building a home but rebuilding it. He is recreating the home which he and Dorothy had lost, and looking forward to an integration into a community after years of wandering. Many of the lyric poems of 1802, similarly, look back across the wandering years to the stability of the poet's infancy; in them, as Jared R. Curtis has pointed out, 'the poet slips back in time, seeks roots in the past wherever they can be found'.[5] In 'To a Butterfly' (the first of the two poems with that title) the unrevised text, 'Much reading do I find in thee;/Thou Bible of my infancy!' connects, as Curtis points out, present to past 'by means of the Butterfly, who, like the divinely given Bible, not only renders the past meaningful to the present but promises a meaningful future as well'.[6] In the poem Dorothy is seen as a small child, a gentle creature who would never hurt the butterfly, and the butterfly itself brings to the poet's heart 'A solemn image' – 'My Father's family'. Another poem of the spring of 1802, transcribed by Coleridge in the same letter as 'To a Butterfly', is 'The Sparrow's Nest', which again returns to the simple delights of childhood and emphasizes the joys of infancy. When the poet sees the sparrow's nest with its five blue eggs,

> I started seeming to espy
> The home and little bed
> The sparrow's dwelling which hard by
> My Father's house in wet or dry
> My Sister Dorothy and I
> Together visited (p. 197).

The birds of the air have nests, and the children have a home with its little bed. Similarly the lark, in 'To a Skylark' (p. 216) is a flying and rejoicing bird, but

> Thou hast a nest which thou lov'st best;
> And though little troubled with sloth,
> Drunken Lark! thou wouldst be loth
> To be such a traveller as I.

The poet envies the lark not only its joyful singing, but also the stable base to which it returns. Meanwhile, 'I on earth will go plodding on/By myself chearfully till the day is done' (p. 217). Here the poet takes up the role of the traveller again; more frequently he is the figure who has a home, and who looks with curiosity and compassion, and even with awe, on those who have lost home and family. In 'Beggars' (Curtis p. 156) the woman is tall as a man, brown-faced,

> Fit person was she for a queen
> To head those Ancient Amazonian files
> Or ruling Banditt's wife among the Grecian Isles

and the sailor's mother has a natural dignity:

> – Majestic seem'd she as a mountain storm;
> A Roman Matron's gait – like feature & like form

> The ancient spirit is not dead;
> Old times thought I, are breathing there;

other figures are pathetic, like the emigrant mother or Alice Fell. Indeed, 'Alice Fell' appears less sentimental if the child is seen as one of the orphans for whom Wordsworth feels a particular tenderness (a few years later the tragic deaths of George and Sarah Green aroused his most active philanthropy on behalf of their young family). The capacity for continuing endurance in children, the deprived and aged, is a continuing source of wonder and amazement to the poet: it is one of the foundations of 'Michael', and of 'Resolution and Independence'. Side by side with this, however, is a contrary movement, in which the stability of home is enriched and enlivened by some stimulus from outside, or by change. Passing things, or changing weather, bring life to the home or bower – the butterfly, the cuckoo, the green linnet, the rainbow. The most striking example of this is the glowworm in 'Among all lovely things my Love had been', which is brought from outside to enrich the

loved one's experience. The poet, who is 'riding on a stormy night,/
Not far from her Abode', brings his Emma the glow-worm which he
spies. Here the home, as in 'Home at Grasmere', is beloved because
of Dorothy ('The incident of this Poem took place about 7 years ago
between Dorothy and me').[7] The pattern is thus one of stability and
love, qualities which are associated with Dorothy, given joy and life
and energy by the travelling poet and his discoveries. One such
energetic figure in the lyric poems of 1802 is the tinker, the merry
figure who mends the kettles and pans,

> And when it is done away he is gone
> And in his scarlet coat
> With a merry note
> He sings the sun to bed
> And without making a pother
> Finds some place or other
> For his own careless head (p. 178).

The tinker represents something else which, even at this time of
establishing a home, appeals to Wordsworth – the lack of
responsibility, the simple careless life 'with work or none'. This is
associated in the poet's mind, as 'Resolution and Independence'
makes clear, with his own life and with the craft of poet; yet the
reality is more complex, and requires not only the freedom and
stimulus of the traveller but also the happiness of a secure domestic
life.

12 Reintegration

The figure of the merry tinker is one of the many wanderers in Wordsworth's poetry. His carelessness about a home, or even a place to sleep, makes a strong contrast with the poet of 'Home at Grasmere', who is rejoicing in the fact of having arrived at a place where he feels at home. The contrast between the tinker and the poet is an interesting one: Wordsworth seems to see a virtue in the wandering life, as well as having an emotional attachment to the stability of home. 'Home at Grasmere' celebrates a settlement, a fixing of the self in one place, a specific example of the marriage of the mind and the external world. Yet from this security the mind is able to contemplate other experiences: the careless gaiety of the homeless, or their fortitude in independence, or the sense that those who do not have a home on earth are sometimes those whose true 'home' is a spiritual one elsewhere. A choice of where to live has to be made, and thought has to be taken for the morrow by some people. Wordsworth puts himself into this category in one of his most non-prophetic poems, 'Resolution and Independence'; here he adopts the role of the ordinary, worrying man, the man without much courage and insight, who derives hope and instruction from a man who has both. The leech gatherer is a liminal figure, who is nevertheless fully human. 'I saw a Man', writes the poet; 'Such seemed this Man',

> not all alive nor dead,
> Nor all asleep – in his extreme old age:
> His body was bent double, feet and head
> Coming together in life's pilgrimage;

The poet and the old man are both engaged on the same pilgrimage; and 'pilgrimage' is one of the words which, in this poem, tend to reverberate with reference to the human condition. In this context the old man's strange wandering life suggests that his true home is not on this earth, though he is fully human: he seemed

Like one whom I had met with in a dream;
Or like a man from some far region sent,
To give me human strength, by apt admonishment.

The poet seems, by contrast, concerned with the here-and-now,
with himself and his future; although he describes himself as a
'traveller then upon the moor', he seems to have a home, in which
he listened to the rain in the night and the roaring of the wind. His
worries are familiar ones about the provision for the future. The
leech gatherer, on the other hand, is unusual and unfamiliar:

As a huge stone is sometimes seen to lie
Couched on the bald top of an eminence
Wonder to all who do the same espy,
By what means it could thither come, and whence;
So that it seems a thing endued with sense:
Like a sea-beast crawled forth, that on a shelf
Of rock or sand reposeth, there to sun itself;

The awkwardness of the metre finely reinforces this. 'Couched on
the top of an eminence' would be dactylic, but 'Couched on the *bald
top*' throws a spondee (echoing 'huge stone') into the pattern. The
leech gatherer, too, sticks out as an unfamiliar and unexpected
element in the landscape, like a stone or a sea-beast, or like a stone
which itself seems a sea-beast. Throughout, the human blends with
the other-worldly – the old man propping himself 'limbs, body, and
pale face' on his staff, yet also being 'Motionless as a cloud', 'That
heareth not the loud winds when they call;/And moveth all
together, if it move at all'. The biblical rhythm ('Consider the lilies
of the field, how they grow') and the archaic 'heareth' and
'moveth', together with the subjunctive 'if it move', all help to
remove the leech gatherer from the world of every-day activity,
from the poet worrying about the prospects for his old age. When
the poet first questions the leech gatherer, 'a flash of mild surprise/
Broke from the sable orbs of his yet-vivid eyes'. Here the 'flash'
connects with the Miltonic 'sable orbs' and 'yet-vivid' to give an
impression of the exotic; yet it is immediately followed by a line
which is simple yet full of effort, like an old man's breathing – 'His
words came feebly, from a feeble chest'. The old man is an example
of spirit triumphing over bodily weakness: and one of the poem's
great achievements is that his serenity appears both human and

other-worldly. At one point he seems like a figure in a dream: but when the poet awakens to his former thoughts and fears, the old man is still there. His answers to the poet's questions, delivered with a smile of tolerance, are the same on each occasion – that he is a travelling man, with no home, who gathers leeches and whose trade is becoming more difficult than it was.

The admirable resolution of the leech gatherer, and his independence of mind and spirit, indicate a strength beyond that of the poet in his role as ordinary anxious man. The non-prophetic function of the poet here is repeated in the 'Immortality Ode', a poem which is closely connected to 'Resolution and Independence' (one theory is that the latter poem was the 'timely utterance' referred to in stanza III of the Ode). In the Ode, as Lionel Trilling has said, Wordsworth is looking at man 'on a double way':

> seeing man both in his ideal nature and in his earthly activity. The two views do not so much contradict as supplement each other. If in stanzas v–vIII Wordsworth tells us that we live by decrease, in stanzas IX–XI he tells us of the everlasting connection of the diminished person with his own ideal personality. The child hands on to the hampered adult the imperial nature, the 'primal sympathy/Which having been must ever be', the mind fitted to the universe, the universe to the mind. The sympathy is not so pure and intense in maturity as in childhood, but only because another relation grows up beside the relation of man to Nature – the relation of man to his fellows in the moral world of difficulty and pain.[1]

The leech gatherer and the poet supplement each other in 'Resolution and Independence', in the same way that the child and the adult are complementary in the 'Immortality Ode', though in the Ode the poet-figure is more assured and confident. Both poet figures, while conscious of their own limitations, find something 'upon which to rejoice' when coming to terms with what Trilling calls 'the moral world of difficulty and pain'.

One difference between the poems is that while 'Resolution and Independence' looks forward to the future with all its unpredictable qualities, the 'Immortality Ode' looks back at the past. In the exploration of the remembered past, the first section of the poem (stanzas I to IV) is so thrilling that it has tended to unbalance the structure as a whole, to make the second part appear to consist of complaint and consolation: complaint that the child actually provokes the years 'to bring the inevitable yoke', consolation

> that in our embers
> Is something that doth live,
> That nature yet remembers
> What was so fugitive!

However consolatory this might be, it still seems a poor substitute for the celestial light, for 'The glory and the freshness of a dream'. And although the first verses admit that the vision has disappeared, the recreation of it is so vivid that it is easy to see why critics have seen the poem as a resigned farewell. If the fire is now embers, and there is joy that in them *something* still lives, this is a sad anti-climax from the original glory. If it is, as Trilling says, a welcome to new powers, it is a welcome which is deeply tinged with sadness and regret. The poet is still desperate to partake of the joy of the spring morning – 'Shout round me, let me hear thy shouts, thou Happy Shepherd-boy!' – and he is consciously aware of an ability still to feel something – 'I feel – I feel it all', 'I hear, I hear, with joy I hear!' Yet if 'Heaven lies about us in our infancy', there can be no doubt that the man is firmly excluded from the paradise which the child knew. Seen in this light, the earth is not a mother, but a foster-mother; the sense of autochthony which is found elsewhere in Wordsworth's poetry is replaced by a neo-Platonic awareness of a reality elsewhere, of the child having another home. Thus we have the view of life as a sleep and a forgetting, gradual but inexorable, of the great courts of heaven:

> Not in entire forgetfulness,
> And not in utter nakedness,
> But trailing clouds of glory do we come
> From God, who is our home:
> Heaven lies about us in our infancy!

The poet sees the child becoming gradually accustomed to the world, beholding the transition with a kind of tenderness and wonder. The child, whose home is heaven, bends all his energies towards making earth his adoptive home:

> Thou little Child, yet glorious in the might
> Of heaven-born freedom on thy being's height,

Why with such earnest pains dost thou provoke
The years to bring the inevitable yoke,
Thus blindly with thy blessedness at strife?

The child is possessed of extraordinary powers, of which he is only
dimly aware. The 'Immortality Ode', like Keats's 'Ode on a
Grecian Urn', teases us out of thought by presenting a state in which
the child has these powers unaware, while the adult is fully aware of
them but cannot repossess them. The situation is sharply focused by
the sheer closeness of the child, who is so naturally bending his
attention to things of earth: 'A wedding or a festival,/A mourning or
a funeral'; And although the child has heaven shining about him, he
is not remote like a prophet: he may be still in possession of the vision
and freedom of his true home, but the child is one who can be
watched at play, walked with, talked to (like Wordsworth's French
daughter on Calais Sands).

For the adult, who is so close to the childhood vision but
irreversibly beyond it, the consolations are two-fold. The first is that
there is still some memory of what was, some recollection of the
moments of childhood which remains. The second is that adult life
brings a mature understanding and sympathy:

> We will grieve not, rather find
> Strength in what remains behind;
> In the primal sympathy
> Which having been must ever be;
> In the soothing thoughts that spring
> Out of human suffering;
> In the faith that looks through death,
> In years that bring the philosophic mind.

And although the glory may have departed, the poet is at pains to
establish that he lives now in a material world of beauty which
exercises a more constant hold on his affections. As in *The Prelude*, he
has fallen from paradise only to find a more mature love and
understanding:

> And O, ye Fountains, Meadows, Hills, and Groves,
> Forebode not any severing of our loves!
> Yet in my heart of hearts I feel your might;
> I only have relinquished one delight

To live beneath your more habitual sway.
I love the Brooks which down their channels fret,
Even more than when I tripped lightly as they;
The innocent brightness of a new-born Day
        Is lovely yet;

In reconciling himself to living beneath a more habitual sway of
material objects, the poet is not only bidding farewell to the ecstasies
of childhood and youth, but he is affirming his faith in the mature
appreciation of the earth and natural beauty. It is a recurring theme
in Wordsworth: it appears in 'Tintern Abbey', in *Peter Bell*, where
the poet returns from his imaginative journey 'back to Earth, the
dear green Earth' –

Long have I loved what I behold,
The night that calms, the day that cheers;
The common growth of mother-earth
Suffices me – her tears, her mirth,
Her humblest mirth and tears (131–5).

– and, above all, it occurs in *The Excursion*, which is Wordsworth's
most extensive discussion of the value of simple human stability and
domestic happiness, seen against a background of human tragedy,
political upheaval, and morality.

II

The Excursion begins with a ruined cottage, and the story of a family
whose fragile and unprotected happiness is destroyed by the
accidents of sickness, unemployment, economic recession and war.
It ends with a family in prosperity: the Pastor's house is connected to
the church by a path, 'as by a beautiful yet solemn train' (VIII. 457),
and it is old and well featured, surrounded by gardens of gay flowers
and sober trees. The family is introduced one by one: the radiant
girl, 'light as the silver fawn' (VIII. 493), the mother, and the two
boys who rush in, 'confusion checking their delight' (VIII. 546). The
picture is one of charm and energy, the boisterous and lively boys,
and the fawn-like girl, complemented by the mother, 'To that
complexion brought which prudence trusts in/And wisdom
loves'(VIII. 505–6). These are the fortunate ones, living healthy,

unostentatious, secure, and well-intentioned lives. They represent
an ideal to which the poem is moving from the beginning: a life of
happiness on earth and reverence for God. Such an existence marks
a brief, transient and fragile recovery of paradise, as the pastor
declares. Contemplating the remains of a stone circle, and musing
on the primitive rites of human sacrifice, he exclaims:

> From such, how changed
> The existing worship; and with those compared,
> The worshippers how innocent and blest!
> So wide the difference, a willing mind
> Might almost think, at this affecting hour,
> That paradise, the lost abode of man,
> Was raised again: and to a happy few,
> In its original beauty, here restored (ix. 712–19).

The pastor treads on the edge of complacency, but he is attempting
to establish what is for Wordsworth an important ideal, the
recreation of paradise in the simple pleasure of an English country
day. Book ix of *The Excursion*, in which the description of the family
and friends picnicking on the island and climbing the hillside is
found, is a sustained enquiry into the ideal society, in beautiful
surroundings, seen under the eye of God. From the hillside, the
church tower is central:

> In majesty presiding over fields
> And habitations seemingly preserved
> From all intrusion of the restless world
> By rocks impassable and mountains huge (ix. 576–9).

Within this valley the celebration of nature, society, and God, is
appropriately divided between the poet himself, who describes the
scene, the Wanderer, who speaks of education and a better society,
and the Pastor, who gives thanks to God. Only the Solitary introduces a different note, as he contemplates the dying ashes of the fire:

> Behold an emblem here
> Of one day's pleasure, and all mortal joys!
> And, in this unpremeditated slight
> Of that which is no longer needed, see
> The common course of human gratitude (ix. 554–8)!

His point is never answered. Instead, rather as in a piece of music, its discordant note is replaced by the sound of all the other instruments. As the poet blandly says: 'This plaintive note disturbed not the repose/Of the still evening'(559–60), and the celebration is resumed. Even the Solitary himself is affected by the atmosphere of the Pastor and his family, for we learn that he 'resumed the manners of his happier days' (VIII. 527). And although he goes home to his cottage at the end of the day, he promises to return to share the pleasures of another summer day. Wordsworth's final note to *The Excursion* indicates that he had intended to make the Solitary revisit Scotland, where he could have witnessed

> some religious ceremony – a sacrament, say, in the open fields, or a preaching among the mountains – which, by recalling to his mind the days of his early Childhood, when he had been present on such occasions in company with his Parents and nearest kindred, might have dissolved his heart into tenderness, and so done more towards restoring the Christian faith in which he had been educated, and, with that, contentedness and even cheerfulness of mind, than all that the Wanderer and Pastor, by their several effusions and addresses, had been able to effect (*PW*. v. 474–5).

The process of healing here is pre-psychoanalytical, involving the setting up of a childhood situation and overcoming the inhibitions which have arisen as a result of the Solitary's suffering and disillusion. Within *The Excursion*, however, the Solitary is able to function as a voice for many of the uncomfortable realities which exist outside the paradise of Book IX. He does so with such effectiveness that he makes the harmony of the Pastor and the Wanderer seem to be the result of their own predetermined insistence on seeing the world with an optimistic eye. Yet, as Wordsworth makes clear, neither the Pastor nor the Wanderer is ignorant of the world and its miseries: it is the way in which they contemplate them which makes the difference.

III

The Solitary's history is first told to the poet by the Wanderer: how he was a military chaplain, married, then lost his wife and children;

how he became an enthusiast for the French revolution, became
disillusioned, and retired to a lonely cottage in the hills. This leaves
no room for mistake when the Solitary first appears. As the poet and
the Wanderer come upon him, he is soothing a bereaved child; yet
we have been told that in general he

> wastes the sad remainder of his hours,
> Steeped in a self-indulging spleen, that wants not
> Its own voluptuousness; – on this resolved,
> With this content, that he will live and die
> Forgotten, – at safe distance from 'a world
> Not moving to his mind' (II. 310–15).

His reading of *Candide* is of a piece with this, for Candide and his
friends have, in common with the Solitary, a solution to their problems
which involves retirement from the world. Wordsworth's objection
to Voltaire may not be (as J. S. Lyon has suggested)[2] that he treats
serious subjects too lightly, but that he leaves Candide in a situation
which is cut off from the instability and unhappiness of the majority
of human beings. After the story of Margaret, and the description of
the Wanderer and his sympathy for her, the Solitary appears in
direct contrast. Like the Wanderer, he exists on the edge of society,
but his is a liminality that is uncreative and self-indulgent. It is part
of Wordsworth's pattern that he should not appear to be utterly
remote and misanthropic; indeed, he has an attractive natural
kindness, which is shown in the consolation of the mourning child,
his courteous reception of the visitors, and his going out to search for
the old man who is lost in the storm. Such moments of proper care
for others look forward to the possibility of reintegration which is
hinted at in Books VIII and IX. At this stage of the poem, his bitterness
and disillusion make the spectacular beauty of nature both
wonderful and disturbing for him:

> Right in the midst, where interspace appeared
> Of open court, an object like a throne
> Under a shining canopy of state
> Stood fixed; and fixed resemblances were seen
> To implements of ordinary use,
> But vast in size, in substance glorified;
> Such as by Hebrew Prophets were beheld
> In vision – forms uncouth of mightiest power

For admiration and mysterious awe.
This little Vale, a dwelling-place of Man,
Lay low beneath my feet; 'twas visible –
I saw not, but I felt that it was there.
That which I *saw* was the revealed abode
Of Spirits in beatitude: my heart
Swelled in my breast. – 'I have been dead,' I cried,
'And now I live! Oh! wherefore do I live?'
And with that pang I prayed to be no more (II. 861–77)!

The vision, and its description, suggests a capacity to see but not to feel. The Solitary can see a spectacle like that of Ezekiel or Isaiah, and he even sees the vale as transformed from a habitation of man into a place of blessed spirits; but in spite of this he is not prophetic – the sight is 'such *as* by Hebrew Prophets were beheld' – and he draws back from prophecy into self-questioning. There is a clear contrast here between the character of the Wanderer, whose role is prophetic and charismatic, and the Solitary; and between the Solitary and the Pastor, whose reaction to the sunset in Book IX is one of gratitude to the Supreme Power. In their different ways, the Wanderer and the Pastor represent a creative response to natural beauty: the former in a way which allows him to become involved with human suffering, as in the case of Margaret and her family, the latter as shepherd of his flock and as orthodox mediator between man and God.

The Solitary stands apart, by his own decision, from both prophet and priest. In Book III, for instance, the nook of ground with its strange rock formations allows him to indulge a perverse antiquarian humour, and encourages him in his moodiness:

But if the spirit be oppressed by sense
Of instability, revolt, decay,
And change, and emptiness, these freaks of Nature
And her blind helper Chance, do *then* suffice
To quicken, and to aggravate – to feed
Pity and scorn, and melancholy pride (137–42).

Not surprisingly, he echoes Spenser's Despayre:

Night is than day more acceptable; sleep
Doth, in my estimate of good, appear

A better state than waking; death than sleep:
Feelingly sweet is stillness after storm,
Though under covert of the wormy ground (277–81)!

and his autobiography, which follows, shows how he came to be
disillusioned and desperate through bereavement, political disappointment over the French revolution, and the failure of the New
World to match up to his expectations of primitive goodness.

The Wanderer's reply is in direct descent from *Paradise Lost*, for it
recommends a belief in a supreme power 'Whose everlasting
purposes embrace/All accidents, converting them to good' (IV. 16–
17). Acquiescence in the Divine will means that 'The darts of
anguish *fix* not' (18); the italicized *fix* is important, because it asserts,
not that suffering and misery can be avoided, but that they need not
become permanent and dominating. The Solitary has become
obsessed by his unhappy condition; the Wanderer recommends the
Pauline triad of abiding virtues, a living

                    by faith,
     Faith absolute in God, including hope,
     And the defence that lies in boundless love
     Of his perfections (IV. 21–4);

The long Book IV of which this is a beginning is entitled
'Despondency Corrected'. Its orthodox foundations are Old Testament rather than New Testament, celebrating a Being 'of infinite
benevolence and power' (14–15), who is beyond the touch of time
and circumstance, who is the source of all beauty, and who is
present in the world through the working of conscience:

          conscience reverenced and obeyed,
     As God's most intimate presence in the soul,
     And his most perfect image in the world (IV. 225–7).

Into this scheme are accommodated a number of Wordsworth's
most cherished apprehensions: the power of infancy to remain in
contact with the supreme power; the joy which comes from the
contemplation of bountiful nature; the patterns of fall and
restoration; and above all, perhaps, the goodness, wisdom and
tenderness which result from the love of nature and lead to the love
of man. The failure of the French revolution is seen as the triumph of

the well-organized bad over the 'vacillating, inconsistent good'. The Wanderer suggests two consolations: a hope that things will be different in the future, and a trust in individual integrity, in which

> the wise
> Have still the keeping of their proper peace;
> Are guardians of their own tranquillity (IV. 320–2).

Such an Epicurean tranquillity is enhanced by the contemplation of the natural laws of the external world, where are reflected so many of the emotions of man, and where man can find comfort in the lives of small creatures, in healthy exercise of body and mind, and in the condition of religious simplicity. For primitive man, the wanderer makes clear, was naturally religious: all early civilizations had their God, or gods. For them, nature was endowed with 'a spiritual presence' (IV. 927):

> Beyond their own poor natures and above
> They looked; were humbly thankful for the good
> Which the warm sun solicited, and earth
> Bestowed; were gladsome, – and their moral sense
> They fortified with reverence for the Gods;
> And they had hopes that overstepped the Grave (IV. 935–40).

The whole of this section is an extended expression of the 'natural piety' of which Wordsworth writes in 'My heart leaps up'. Its opposite is a divisive and unimaginative reason, 'Viewing all objects unremittingly/In disconnection dead and spiritless' (IV. 961–2); and the fundamental strength of Book IV of *The Excursion* is that it associates the power of feeling with a benevolent natural religion, so that to have a religious sense is to be linked with nature and joined with other human beings in a community of spiritual interest. The Wanderer is suggesting a life of love and harmony with nature which is also one of re-integration.

Book IV is Wordsworth's most sustained demonstration of the love of nature leading to the love of man. It is for this reason that the Wanderer's long discourse finishes not on a sublime note, with nature as awesome, but with nature as the inspiration of human love. The Wanderer asserts, in a beautifully-shaped line, that he who communes with nature in the correct spirit will find 'A holy tenderness pervade his frame' (1220); this will lead to the blessings of philanthropy, to the beneficent employment of science, and to the natural promotion 'of order and of good':

> Whate'er we see,
> Or feel, shall tend to quicken and refine
> The humblest functions of corporeal sense;
> Shall fix, in calmer seats of moral strength,
> Earthly desires; and raise, to loftier heights
> Of divine love, our intellectual soul (IV. 1270–5).

If this is grand theory, the books which follow (V–VII) are practical demonstrations of the workings of human lives. As the Wanderer says to the Pastor: 'Give us, for our abstractions, solid facts;/For our disputes, plain pictures' (V. 637–8). He hopes that the Pastor, by giving information about the lives of those whose graves lie nearby, will be able to counter the Solitary's sense of human life as either mindless toil or fruitless speculation. His aim is that through the Pastor's examples they will all be led ' *To prize the breath we share with human kind;/And look upon the dust of man with awe*' (V. 656–7). The structure of the Pastor's reply seems at first sight odd. After a brief description of the wedded pair who live, childless, in an austere solitude (an account which is supplemented by the Wanderer), he moves to a series of general observations. He argues that it is not just the heart of man, but also his practice of religion, that fosters and preserves the benevolent impulses of mankind. From this he turns, in the opening of Book VI, to an address to the State and Church of England, establishing the idea of England as a community of social love infused with religious zeal. It is a bold conception, in which Wordsworth is extending and broadening his idea of community to include an ideal of national life. It is an ideal which is obviously far removed from the actual circumstances of life, as revealed by the social conditions under which Margaret and her family suffer in the ruined cottage; and yet the ideal emerges at this point in *The Excursion* to become a central feature of the poem. It holds up to the view an ideal of Britain as a nation where the king sits upon a throne

> whose deep foundations lie
> In veneration and the people's love;
> Whose steps are equity, whose seat is law (VI. 3–5).

and where the church stands as a centre 'Of pious sentiment diffused afar,/And human charity, and social love,' (28–9). There is, we may suspect, an implied contrast with France, where the re- volutionary disasters had helped to destroy the happiness of the Solitary: the English scene of domestic tranquillity and beautiful landscape with which the poem concludes may be an embodiment of the values which Wordsworth wishes to assert. To the same end, the final version of Book IX is of a changed Britain, a country of the future benevolently colonizing an empire of happiness and prosperity. The expansion of Britain into a great imperial power, and its beneficent influence, are the subjects of the Wanderer's last speech:

> Change wide, and deep, and silently performed,
> This Land shall witness; and as days roll on,
> Earth's universal frame shall feel the effect;
> Even till the smallest habitable rock,
> Beaten by lonely billows, hear the songs
> Of humanised society; and bloom
> With civil arts, that shall breathe forth their fragrance,
> A grateful tribute to all-ruling Heaven
> From culture, unexclusively bestowed
> On Albion's noble Race in freedom born,
> Except these mighty issues: from the pains
> And faithful care of unambitious schools
> Instructing simple childhood's ready ear:
> Thence look for these magnificent results (IX. 384–97)!

The four main participants in *The Excursion* all have a part to play in the exploration of this great public theme. The poet records and observes, supplementing the Wanderer's prophetic vision: the Pastor has his priestly role, in which he is able to extol and represent a stable religious life as central to national happiness; the Solitary, while continually challenging the assumptions and the optimism of the others, indicates the distance that has to be travelled and the obstacles that have to be overcome. For *The Excursion* abounds in tragic figures, and there is no doubt that Wordsworth's conception of the ideal is balanced by a clear-eyed appreciation of the actual. In addition to the obvious failure of society to ameliorate the sufferings of Margaret and her children in Book I, the Solitary has his own disillusion with the contemporary political scene as a testimony that all is not well: his last speech, in Book VIII, comprehensively outlines

the deprivation of children in England. The poorest are begging,
while others are condemned to lives of toil and ignorance.

In these ways the form of *The Excursion* is designed to express the
complex mixture of neglect, failure, hope and happiness which are
found in a nation's life. The general situation is found in the
speeches of the major figures; and in addition, the figures whose lives
are described by the Pastor make up a part of the great web of
English life. The unrequited lover (VI. 118–211), the miner (212–
54), the Prodigal (275–375), the Jacobite and the Hanoverian
(413–521), the uncharitable woman (675–777), Ellen and her child
(787–1052), Wilfred Armathwaite (1080–114), and the young
mother (1115–91) are obscure, subject to mortality, and representative of the fluctuations of human fortune. They are specific
examples of the changes and chances of this fleeting world,
individuals whose lives and deaths are a part of the national life
which is referred to by the major characters of the poem. This is, as
Geoffrey Hartman has suggested, the poet of *Lyrical Ballads*
changing into a pseudo-narrative mode.[3] Hartman also emphasizes
what he sees as the poem's refusal to blink the awkward issues:
'Nowhere does Wordsworth acknowledge more explicitly the
difficulty in reforming human nature.'[4] Yet against that difficulty,
Wordsworth sets the possibility of a well-spent life, of a family life
which can be seen as an example of responsible living within the
community. As so often in Wordsworth's poetry, the final book
concludes with a movement homewards, and the Pastor's home,
and his family life, stand as a microcosm of the national life of which
the Wanderer speaks. It is a home from which it is an easy step to the
lake, and a boat trip to the island, followed by the walk up the hill to
see the sunset. It is the Pastor who gives expression to the emotions
which are felt by the onlookers, except perhaps by the Solitary (who
is silent, after his 'plaintive note' at IX. 550–8, and whose farewell
speech at the end suggests a happier frame of mind). The Pastor's
speech integrates many elements of the poem: it begins with
adoration and thanks to the Creator for the beauty of the created
world, and goes on to pray for a world converted to Christianity and
perfected in grace. The process of converting the world to
Christianity is, like so much else in *The Excursion*, described in a way
that is both discursive and emblematic: it is the bringing of good out
of evil, in which the Pastor relates the great cosmic processes of
change in religious belief to the time and place of the poem's action.
From the description of the way in which Christianity superseded

the ancient religions of sacrifice and barbarity, the Pastor brings his
discourse to an end by describing a fusion between religion and
place, a landscape of paradise:

> – A few rude monuments of mountain-stone
> Survive; all else is swept away. – How bright
> The appearances of things! From such, how changed
> The existing worship; and with those compared,
> The worshippers how innocent and blest!
> So wide the difference, a willing mind
> Might almost think, at this affecting hour,
> That paradise, the lost abode of man,
> Was raised again: and to a happy few,
> In its original beauty, here restored (IX. 710–19).

He gives thanks to God on behalf of his parishioners,

> Conscious of that abundant favour showered
> On you, the children of my humble care,
> And this dear land, our country (738–40),

and finally sees the landscape itself as actively aware of his worship
and religious thought:

> These barren rocks, your stern inheritance;
> These fertile fields, that recompense your pains;
> The shadowy vale, the sunny mountain-top;
> Woods waving in the wind their lofty heads,
> Or hushed; the roaring waters, and the still –
> They see the offering of my lifted hands,
> They hear my lips present their sacrifice,
> They know if I be silent, morn or even:
> For, though in whispers speaking, the full heart
> Will find a vent; and thought is praise to him,
> Audible praise, to thee, omniscient Mind,
> From whom all gifts descend, all blessings flow (743–54)!

The landscape is a carefully balanced set of opposites – barren and
fertile, shadow and sunshine, woods moving and silent, waters
roaring and still. The doubling effect gives a final impassioned effect
to the Pastor's speech, in the same way as it does to Wordsworth's in

'Tintern Abbey': it is a compressed farewell to the landscape which has been so omnipresent in *The Excursion*, and within which the human lives of the poem are being played out. To that same landscape, as the Pastor's *exempla* indicate, they will return when they die and are buried in the 'churchyard among the mountains'.

IV

Although Wordsworth ends the poem with a suggestion of future labours which will tell of renovation and healing, *The Excursion* moves splendidly towards a conclusion which is sufficient unto itself. Its religious orthodoxy has perhaps tended to disguise the very skilful way in which the various structural elements of the poem are fused at the end. The Solitary's plaintive note is drowned by the accumulated sound of the other instruments, proclaiming the possibility of a right relationship between man, nature and God, of a restored paradise: in spite of human despair over bereavement, the failure of political change, and the wreckage of family life, Wordsworth continues to assert the possibility of good. It is based upon the Pastor rather than the Wanderer, because the Pastor is associated, by virtue of his office and function, with 'the faith that looks through death'.

The presence in the poem of the dead who lie in the churchyard is a reminder that life is changeable, uncertain and short; and since suffering comes to some, such as Margaret and her children, and the Solitary, it must be recognized as a necessary risk of being human. Yet Wordsworth also needed to proclaim that human life can take another course: that it can be led simply and in humility, surrounded by the beneficent influences of nature, and in a right relationship with man and God. The Pastor, who concludes the poem, is an example of such a life: he is fully integrated within the community, fully conscious of the natural beauty around him, and has an ideal family life. *The Excursion*, like *The Prelude* and 'Home at Grasmere', is concerned with the stability of home, and the place of man within the community; it proposes the reintegration of a figure such as the Solitary, who has cut himself off from other men in an uncreative liminality, a state which is directly contrasted with the liminality of the Wanderer. Such a reintegration may seem too simple a conclusion to the problems posed by *The Excursion*; but it remains the only creative possibility, and the alternative is solitude and despair.

The Excursion makes a fitting conclusion to this study, because it includes the three major preoccupations which I have tried to discern in Wordsworth's poetry: the importance of community, the awareness of natural religion, and the longing for stability and the regained paradise of home. The synthesis of these in *The Excursion* is presented, not as a solution to the problems of man, but as an ideal. Given the fullness and complexity with which Wordsworth presents both local and national problems in *The Excursion*, a solution seems impossible: all the poet can do is to point to alternatives in man's response to the web of human happiness and misfortune. What the poet can do is to testify, and this is what *The Excursion* does so well: with all the authority of the Wanderer, and with all the example of the Pastor, Wordsworth sets forth what he has learned. He has learned through his own experience to value a natural religious sense of wonder and reverence, which leads him towards a life based on the community, on religion, and on the tenderness of family affection. The alternative is isolation and cynicism; and if these oppositions point towards a conventional and orthodox Christianity, such an orthodoxy develops naturally from the experience of the early years.

What this book has tried to demonstrate is the power of those early religious apprehensions, the weight of coherence and authority which comes from Wordsworth's individual experience of simple yet profound patterns of belief; it has tried to assert the importance for his poetry of fundamental, even primitive, ideas of the sacred, the assumption of the prophetic role, and, above all, the relationship which exists between man and man, and man and God, bound together in a natural love within the mind of man,

In beauty exalted, as it is itself
Of quality and fabric more divine.

Notes and References

INTRODUCTION

1. *The George Eliot Letters*, ed. Gordon S. Haight (New Haven and London, 1954–5) III. 382; quoted in Robert H. Dunham, '*Silas Marner* and the Wordsworthian Child', *Studies in English Literature*, XVI (1966) pp. 645–59. I am indebted to this article for pointing out the significant connections between Wordsworth and George Eliot which I have used here.
2. *Biographia Literaria*, ed. J. Shawcross (Oxford, 1907) II. 6.
3. *The George Eliot Letters*, III. 382.
4. Wallace Jackson, 'Wordsworth and his predecessors: Private Sensations and Public Tones', *Criticism*, XVII (1975) pp. 41–58.
5. S. T. Coleridge, *Lay Sermons*, ed. R. J. White (London, 1972) p. 30.
6. *Defending Ancient Springs* (London, 1967) p. 107.
7. Quoted by Helen Darbishire, *The Poet Wordsworth* (Oxford, 1950) p. 49.
8. 'The Sparrow's Nest', printed in Jared R. Curtis, *Wordsworth's Experiments with Tradition* (Ithaca and London, 1971) p. 197.
9. *The Complete Works of Percy Bysshe Shelley*, ed. R. Ingpen and W. E. Peck (London, 1965) VII. 112.
10. *Lay Sermons*, ed. White, pp. 28–9.
11. 'Interview with Peter Redgrove', by Jed Rasula and Mike Erwin, *Hudson Review* XXVIII (1975) pp. 377–401.
12. E. W. Heaton, *The Old Testament Prophets* (Harmondsworth, 1958) p. 130.
13. Barbara Gates, '*The Prelude* and the Development of Wordsworth's Historical Imagination', *Etudes Anglaises*, XXX (1977) pp. 169–78.
14. Heaton, op. cit., pp. 95–6.
15. Ibid., p. 96.
16. W. J. T. Mitchell, 'Style and Epistemology: Blake and the Movement toward Abstraction in Romantic Art', *Studies in Romanticism*, 16 (1977) p. 146.
17. See John Alban Finch, 'Wordsworth's Two-Handed Engine', *Bicentenary Wordsworth Studies*, ed. J. Wordsworth (Ithaca and London, 1970) pp. 1–13.
18. Philip Wheelwright, *The Burning Fountain* (Bloomington and London, 1966) pp. 18–19.
19. Ibid., p. 272.
20. Mircea Eliade, *The Sacred and the Profane* (New York, 1959) p. 14.
21. *Lyrical Ballads*, ed. by R. L. Brett and A. R. Jones (London, 1963) p. 252.

CHAPTER 1: CHILDHOOD

1. Lower case numbers ('i') refer to the two-part *Prelude*, now printed in *The*

Prelude, 1798–99, ed. Stephen Parrish (Ithaca and Hassocks, 1977). Small capitals ('I') refer to the 1805 text.

2. C. Lévi-Strauss, *The Savage Mind* (London, 1966) p. 11.
3. C. Lévi-Strauss, *Totemism*, trans. Rodney Needham, introd. by Roger C. Poole (Harmondsworth, 1969) p. 40.
4. *The Savage Mind*, p. 18.
5. Ibid., p. 16.
6. *Totemism*, p. 173.
7. Quoted in ibid., p. 173.
8. For Rousseau as a forerunner of structural anthropology, see *Totemism*, pp. 172–5; for his connections with Wordsworth, see Newton P. Stallknecht, *Strange Seas of Thought*, Bloomington, 1968, pp. 273–5.
9. William Boyd, *The Educational Theory of Jean-Jacques Rousseau*, 1911, reprinted New York, 1963, p. 76.
10. Rousseau, *Oeuvres Complètes* (Pléiade Paris, 1964) III. 155.
11. *Totemism*, p. 174.
12. Léon Emery, 'Rousseau and the Foundations of Human Regeneration', *Yale French Studies* XXVIII (Fall–Winter, 1961–2) pp. 3–12.
13. 'The Wild Man's Return: The Enclosed Vision of Rousseau's *Discours*' in *The Wild Man Within*, ed. by Edward Dudley and Maximillian E. Novak (Pittsburgh, 1972) p. 243.
14. *Oeuvres Complètes*, III. 164.
15. *The Task*, I. 672–3.
16. *Émile (Oeuvres Complètes*, Paris, 1969) IV. 483–4. All references are to this volume of the Pléiade edition.
17. Ibid., p. 301.
18. Ibid., p. 302.
19. Ibid., p. 312.
20. Ibid., p. 415.
21. Ibid., p. 382.
22. Ibid., p. 319.
23. *Totemism*, p. 133.
24. Ibid., p. 39.
25. *Between Man and Man*, trans. R. Gregor Smith (London, 1947) p. 101.
26. *I and Thou*, trans. R. Gregor Smith (Edinburgh, 1937) p. 5.
27. Ibid., p. 7.
28. Ibid., p. 66.
29. Ibid., p. 18.
30. Ibid., p. 37.
31. Ibid., p. 25.
32. Ibid., pp. 25–6.
33. Ibid., p. 26.
34. The phrase used by Patricia M. Ball as the title for her book on the self in Romantic poetry.
35. *Henry Crabb Robinson on Books and their Writers*, ed. Edith J. Morley (London, 1938) i. 330.
36. *Biographia Literaria*, ed. Shawcross, I. 202.
37. *I and Thou*, p. 75.
38. Ibid., p. 22.

CHAPTER 2: COMMUNITY

1. See Arnold van Gennep, *The Rites of Passage*, trans. Monika B. Vizedom and Gabrielle L. Caffee (London, 1960).
2. Victor W. Turner, *The Ritual Process* (Harmondsworth, 1974) p. 82.
3. *Between Man and Man*, p. 51.
4. *The Ritual Process*, p. 114.
5. See *Home at Grasmere*, ed. Beth Darlington (Ithaca and Hassocks, 1977) pp. 8–10.
6. Line numbers are from the 1793 text.
7. Geoffrey H. Hartman, *Wordsworth's Poetry, 1787–1814* (New Haven and London, 1964) p. 92.
8. Edward Shils, 'The Theory of Mass Society', in *The Concept of Community*, ed. by David W. Minar and Scott Greer (Chicago, 1969) p. 299.
9. For an interesting study of Wordsworth in relation to modern society and urban living, see J. P. Ward, 'Wordsworth and the Sociological Idea', *Critical Quarterly*, xvi (1974) pp. 331–55.

CHAPTER 3: MAN IN SOCIETY – THE POETRY OF REFORM

1. *PW*, I. 330.
2. Mary Moorman, *William Wordsworth, The Early Years, 1770–1803* (Oxford, 1957) p. 236.
3. Ibid., p. 238.
4. *The Ritual Process*, pp. 80–1.
5. Ibid., p. 81.
6. Ibid., p. 115.
7. *PW*, I. 308.
8. Ibid., 94–5.
9. Stephen Gill (ed.), *The Salisbury Plain Poems of William Wordsworth* (Ithaca and Hassocks, 1975). Texts of each version are taken from this edition.
10. *The Salisbury Plain Poems*, p. 310.
11. *The Journals of Dorothy Wordsworth*, ed. E. de Selincourt (London, 1941) i. 40. I am indebted to Dr Charles Holmes, of Penrith, for this example.
12. *Prose Works*, i. 79.

CHAPTER 4: MAN IN SOCIETY – CREATIVE AND UNCREATIVE SEPARATION

1. Jonathan Wordsworth, *The Music of Humanity* (London, 1969) pp. 150–1. The text of *The Ruined Cottage* used here is that established by Jonathan Wordsworth and printed in this book.
2. Ibid., p. 5.
3. *The Music of Humanity*, p. 216.

4. Max Weber, *The Theory of Social and Economic Organization*, trans. A. R. Henderson and T. Parsons, revised edition (London, 1947) p. 329.
5. Max Weber, 'The Sociology of Charismatic Authority', reprinted in *Max Weber on Charisma and Institution Building*, ed. S. N. Eisenstadt (Chicago and London, 1968) p. 21.
6. Ibid.
7. Eisenstadt, op. cit., p. 51.
8. *Edinburgh Review*, XXIV (November 1814); reprinted in part in John O. Hayden (ed.), *Romantic Bards and British Reviewers* (London, 1971) pp. 39–52 (p. 52).
9. The pedlar's character may be illuminated by contrasting it with the figure in 'Lines left upon a Seat in a Yew-tree', written in April and May 1797, whose solitude is static and sterile.

CHAPTER 5: *LYRICAL BALLADS*: PREFACE AND PREPARATION

1. Max Weber, *The Sociology of Religion*, trans. E. Fischoff (London, 1965) p. 46.
2. Ibid., pp. 47–8.
3. Ibid., p. 53.
4. *EL*, p. 355.
5. *Lyrical Ballads*, ed. by R. L. Brett and A. R. Jones (London, 1963) pp. 238–9.
6. Ibid., pp. 249–50.
7. Ibid., p. 250.
8. Ibid.
9. Mircea Eliade, 'Symbolisms of Ascension and "Waking Dreams"', in *Myths, Dreams and Mysteries* (London, 1960; Fontana, 1968) p. 120.
10. Ibid., p. 252.
11. Ibid.
12. Ibid., p. 253.
13. Ibid.
14. Ibid., p. 255.
15. *Oeuvres Complètes*, III. 165.
16. *Lyrical Ballads*, p. 256.
17. Ibid., pp. 243–4.
18. Ibid., pp. 241–2.
19. Ibid., p. 243.
20. *Between Man and Man*, p. 5.
21. Ibid., p. 6.
22. Ibid., p. 9.
23. Ibid., p. 8.
24. Ibid., p. 9.
25. Ibid.
26. Ibid., p. 10.
27. *Lyrical Ballads*, p. 251.
28. Ibid., p. 253.
29. *Between Man and Man*, pp. 32–3.
30. Ibid., p. 20.
31. Ibid.

32. *Lyrical Ballads*, pp. 253–4.
33. Ibid., p. 239.
34. Ibid.
35. *Between Man and Man*, p. 20.
36. Ibid., pp. 22–3.
37. *Lyrical Ballads*, pp. 264–5.

CHAPTER 6: *LYRICAL BALLADS*: DIALOGUE AND SUFFERING

1. I take Mark Reed's dating here, which places 'The Convict' before 'The Old Cumberland Beggar' (*Chronology*, pp. 26–7).
2. *Biographia Literaria*, ed. J. Shawcross, II. 6.
3. *PW*, IV. 445.
4. Ibid., IV. 446.
5. Ibid., IV. 448.
6. 'Sense-Experience and Mystical Experience among Primitives', in *Myths, Dreams and Mysteries*, pp. 84–5.
7. See, for instance, the criticisms of John Jones (*The Egotistical Sublime*, p. 63) and Mary Jacobus (*Tradition and Experiment in Lyrical Ballads*, pp. 180–1).
8. *PW*, II. 478.
9. *EL*, pp. 357–8.
10. 'The Idiot Boy', in *Bicentenary Wordsworth Studies*, ed. by Jonathan Wordsworth (1970) p. 247.
11. *El*, p. 357.
12. *PW*, II. 478.
13. *Wordsworth's Poetry 1787–1814*, p. 151.
14. *PW*, II. 512.
15. Thomas L. Ashton has made a neat contrast between this and the Wordsworth who climbed Snowdon in '*The Thorn*: Wordsworth's Insensitive Plant', *Huntington Library Quarterly*, XXXV (1971–2), pp. 171–87.
16. *Lyrical Ballads*, p. 276.
17. Printed in *Dramas, Fields and Metaphors* (Ithaca and London, 1974).
18. Ibid., p. 233.
19. Ibid., p. 234.
20. *Lyrical Ballads*, pp. 241–2.
21. *Dramas, Fields and Metaphors*, p. 268.
22. *Monthly Review* (June 1799); quoted by Mary Jacobus, op. cit., p. 237.
23. *Dramas, Fields and Metaphors*, p. 241.
24. Ibid.
25. *Lyrical Ballads*, p. 239.

CHAPTER 7: CHILDHOOD (II)

1. See Herman Baumann, quoted by Mircea Eliade, 'Nostalgia for Paradise in

the Primitive Traditions', in *Myths, Dreams and Mysteries*, p. 57.

2. *The Sacred and the Profane*, pp. 118–19.
3. *I and Thou*, p. 20.
4. Ibid.
5. *The Sacred and the Profane*, pp. 88–9.
6. Ibid., p. 89.
7. *William Wordsworth, The Early Years*, p. 110.
8. Eliade, *The Sacred and the Profane*, p. 28.
9. Ibid.
10. Ibid., p. 64.
11. E. B. Greenwood, 'Poetry and Paradise', *Essays in Criticism*, XVII (1967), pp. 6–25.
12. Review of Crabbe's *Poems*, *Edinburgh Review* (April 1808).
13. *Wordsworth, a re-interpretation*, p. 21.
14. *EL*, p. 39.

CHAPTER 8: *LYRICAL BALLADS*: TIME, PLACE AND NATURE

1. A. C. Bradley, *Oxford Lectures on Poetry* (London, 1909) p. 102n.
2. Ibid., p. 102.
3. *The Early Life of William Wordsworth*, p. 465.
4. *The Sacred and the Profane*, p. 75.
5. Ibid., p. 73.
6. Ibid., pp. 77–8.
7. Ibid., p. 89.
8. Ibid., p. 80.
9. Sydney G. Dimond, *The Psychology of the Methodist Revival* (London, 1926) p. 173.
10. William James, *The Varieties of Religious Experience* (London, 1902) p. 248.
11. *The Sacred and the Profane*, p. 26.
12. Ibid., p. 81.
13. *The Sacred and the Profane*, pp. 116–17.
14. Ibid., p. 12.
15. Ibid., p. 203.
16. *The Sacred and the Profane*, pp. 91–2.
17. Ibid., pp. 68–9.
18. *Between Man and Man*, p. 13.
19. Emile Durkheim, *The Elementary Forms of the Religious Life*, trans. J. W. Swain (London, 1915) p. 240.
20. Ibid., p. 249.
21. Ibid., pp. 50 ff.
22. *PW*, II. 517: The Duke heard Wordsworth read the poem in 1848, fifty years after the event: 'It was not till after the reading was over that we found out that the old paralytic and *doited* woman we had seen in the morning was the sister to whom T. A. was addressed . . ..'

CHAPTER 9: THE LUCY POEMS

1. *PW*, II. 472, 506. I have followed the convention which takes the Lucy poems to be 'Strange fits of passion have I known', 'She dwelt among the untrodden ways', 'I travelled among unknown men', 'Three years she grew in sun and shower', and 'A slumber did my spirit seal'.
2. Thomas de Quincey, *Recollections of the Lakes and the Lake Poets*, ed. David Wright (Harmondsworth, 1970) p. 188.
3. Hugh Sykes Davies, in 'Another New Poem by Wordsworth' (*Essays in Criticism*, XV (1965) pp. 135–61) questions the validity of the grouping together of the Lucy poems, suggesting that it was a nineteenth-century idea. Other critics have argued that the poems should be taken together; recent ones include James Taaffe, in 'Poet and Lover in Wordsworth's "Lucy" Poems' (*Modern Language Review*, LXI (1966), pp. 175–9), and Spencer Hall, in 'Wordsworth's "Lucy" Poems: Context and Meaning' (*Studies in Romanticism*, X (1971) pp. 159–75).
4. *Wordsworth, a Re-interpretation*, pp. 31–5.
5. *Myths, Dreams and Mysteries*, p. 166.
6. *Wordsworth's Poetry, 1787–1814*, p. 162.

CHAPTER 10: THE GROWTH OF TENDERNESS

1. *Oeuvres Complètes*, I. 168.
2. Christopher Ricks, *Keats and Embarrassment* (Oxford, 1974) p. 13.
3. 'Wordsworth's Card Games', *The Wordsworth Circle*, VI (1975) pp. 299–302.
4. Wordsworth may have been influenced by Coleridge in this. See *The Collected Letters of Samuel Taylor Coleridge*, ed. E. L. Griggs (Oxford, 1956–71) I. 354: 'From my early reading of Faery Tales, & Genii &c &c – my mind had been habituated *to the Vast*.'
5. Wordsworth's reaction to this death may be compared with Clare's fainting fits, 'the cause of which, I always imagined, came from seeing – when I was younger – a man named Thomas Drake, after he had fell off a load of hay and broke his neck. The ghastly paleness of death struck such a terror on me that I could not forget it for years, and my dreams was constantly wanderings in churchyards, digging graves, seeing spirits in charnel houses, &c., &c.' (*Sketches in the Life of John Clare, written by Himself*, ed. Edmund Blunden (London, 1931) p. 70.
6. *Prose Works*, ii. 13. All references are to this edition.
7. *The Sacred and the Profane*, pp. 116–17.

CHAPTER 11: THE STABILITY OF HOME

1. *EL*, p. 115.
2. '"Home at Grasmere": Reclusive Song', *Studies in Romanticism* XIV (1975) pp. 1–28.

3. See M. H. Abrams, *Natural Supernaturalism* (New York, 1971).
4. *EL*, p. 355.
5. *Wordsworth's Experiments with Tradition*, p. 50.
6. Ibid., p. 44.
7. Ibid., p. 171.

CHAPTER 12: REINTEGRATION

1. Lionel Trilling, *The Liberal Imagination* (London, 1951) pp. 150–1.
2. See J. S. Lyon, *The Excursion* (New Haven, 1950) pp. 75–6: 'This description of *Candide* has perplexed many, but Wordsworth's real objection to Voltaire must have been that Voltaire treats subjects humorously which are really serious and should never be treated with levity.'
3. *Wordsworth's Poetry, 1787–1814*, p. 320.
4. Ibid., p. 320.

Bibliography

1 PRIMARY TEXTS

The Poetical Works of William Wordsworth, ed. E. de Selincourt (Oxford, 1940–5).
The Salisbury Plain Poems of William Wordsworth, ed. Stephen Gill, The Cornell Wordsworth, vol. 1 (Ithaca and Hassocks, 1975).
The Prelude, 1798–1799, by William Wordsworth, ed. Stephen Parrish, The Cornell Wordsworth, vol. 2 (Ithaca and Hassocks, 1977).
Home at Grasmere, Part First, Book First of the Recluse, by William Wordsworth, ed. Beth Darlington, The Cornell Wordsworth, vol. 3 (Ithaca and Hassocks, 1977).
The Prelude, ed. E. de Selincourt, revised Helen Darbishire (Oxford, 1959).
The Letters of William and Dorothy Wordsworth, I, The Early Years, ed. E. de Selincourt, revised Chester L. Shaver (Oxford, 1967).
The Prose Works of William Wordsworth, ed. W. J. B. Owen and J. W. Smyser (Oxford, 1974).
The Journals of Dorothy Wordsworth, ed. E. de Selincourt (London, 1941).

2 BOOKS

Abrams, M. H., *Natural Supernaturalism* (New York, 1971).
Bateson, F. W., *Wordsworth: a Re-interpretation*, 2nd edn (London, 1956).
Boyd, William, *The Educational Theory of Jean-Jacques Rousseau* (1911), (New York, 1963).
Bradley, A. C., *Oxford Lectures on Poetry* (London, 1909).
Buber, Martin, *Between Man and Man*, trans. R. Gregor Smith (London, 1947).
——, *I and Thou*, trans. R. Gregor Smith (Edinburgh, 1937).
Coleridge, S.T., *Biographia Literaria*, ed. J. Shawcross (Oxford, 1907).
——, *Lay Sermons*, ed. R. J. White (London, 1972).
Curtis, Jared R., *Wordsworth's Experiments with Tradition* (Ithaca and London, 1971).
Danby, J. F., *The Simple Wordsworth* (London, 1960).
Darbishire, Helen, *The Poet Wordsworth* (Oxford, 1950).
Dimond, Sydney G., *The Psychology of the Methodist Revival* (London, 1926).
Dudley, E., and Novak, M. E. (eds) *The Wild Man Within* (Pittsburgh, 1972).
Durkheim, Emile, *The Elementary Forms of the Religious Life*, trans. J. W. Swain (London, 1915).
Eliade, Mircea, *The Sacred and the Profane*, trans. W. R. Trask (New York, 1959).
——, *Myths, Dreams and Mysteries* (London, 1960) (Fontana, 1968).
Gennep, Arnold van, *The Rites of Passage*, trans. Monika B. Vizedom and Gabrielle L. Caffee (London, 1960).

Haight, Gordon S. (ed.), *The George Eliot Letters* (New Haven and London, 1954–5).

Hartman, Geoffrey, *The Unmediated Vision* (New Haven and London, 1954).

——, *Wordsworth's Poetry, 1787–1814* (New Haven and London, 1964).

Heaton, E. W., *The Old Testament Prophets* (Harmondsworth, 1958).

Jacobus, Mary, *Tradition and Experiment in Wordsworth's Lyrical Ballads, 1798* (Oxford, 1976).

James, William, *The Varieties of Religious Experience* (London, 1902).

Jones, John, *The Egotistical Sublime* (London, 1954).

Legouis, Emile, *The Early Life of William Wordsworth*, trans. J. W. Matthews (London, 1897).

Lévi-Strauss, Claude, *The Savage Mind* (London, 1966).

——, *Totemism*, trans. R. Needham (Harmondsworth, 1969).

Lindenberger, Herbert, *On Wordsworth's Prelude* (Princeton, 1963).

Lyon, J. S., *The Excursion* (New Haven, 1950).

Minar, David W. and Greer, Scott (eds), *The Concept of Community* (Chicago, 1969).

Moorman, Mary, *William Wordsworth, The Early Years, 1770–1803* (Oxford, 1957).

——, *William Wordsworth, The Later Years, 1803–1850* (Oxford, 1965).

Morley, Edith J. (ed.), *Henry Crabb Robinson on Books and their Writers* (London, 1938).

Parrish, Stephen M., *The Art of the Lyrical Ballads* (London, 1973).

Raine, Kathleen, *Defending Ancient Springs* (London, 1967).

Ricks, Christopher, *Keats and Embarrassment* (Oxford, 1974).

Salvesen, C., *The Landscape of Memory* (London, 1965).

Selincourt, E. de, *Oxford Lectures on Poetry* (Oxford, 1934).

Sheats, Paul D., *The Making of Wordsworth's Poetry, 1785–1798* (London, 1973).

Stallknecht, Newton P., *Strange Seas of Thought* (Bloomington and London, 1968).

Turner, Victor W., *The Ritual Process* (Harmondsworth, 1974).

——, *Dramas, Fields and Metaphors* (Ithaca and London, 1974).

Weber, Max, *The Sociology of Religion*, trans. E. Fischoff (London, 1965).

——, *The Theory of Social and Economic Organization*, trans. A. R. Henderson and T. Parsons, rev. edn. (London, 1947).

——, *Max Weber on Charisma and Institution Building*, ed. S. N. Eisenstadt (Chicago and London, 1968).

Wheelwright, Philip, *The Burning Fountain* (Bloomingtom and London, 1968).

Wordsworth, Jonathan (ed.), *Bicentenary Wordsworth Studies* (Ithaca and London, 1970).

——, *The Music of Humanity* (London, 1969).

Index